# Career Choice
## The Guide to Careers and Courses in Ireland

# Career Choice
*The Guide to Careers and Courses in Ireland*

## Anne Byrne

THE COLLINS PRESS

Published by The Collins Press, West Link Park, Doughcloyne, Wilton, Cork
1998

© 1998 Anne Byrne

All rights reserved. No part of this publication may be reproduced or transmitted in any form or by any means electronic, mechanical, photocopying, recording or otherwise, without written permission of the publishers, or else under the terms of any licence permitting limited copying issued by The Irish Writers' Centre, 19 Parnell Square, Dublin 1.

British Library Cataloguing in Publication data.

Printed in Ireland by Sci Print, Shannon

Typesetting by Red Barn Publishing, Skeagh, Skibbereen, Co. Cork

Jacket design by Cathy Dineen

ISBN: 1-898256-56-X

# Contents

## Part One: Practical Advice

| | |
|---|---:|
| Introduction | 1 |
| Reasons for continuing your studies | 5 |
| Securing that third-level place | 9 |
| The central applications systems | 15 |
| Art and design application procedures | 28 |
| Mature students | 34 |
| Money matters | 39 |
| Common queries | 46 |
| Post Leaving Certificate courses | 52 |
| Add-on degrees | 58 |
| Arts degrees | 63 |
| Business studies | 70 |
| Engineering | 80 |
| Science | 84 |
| Paramedical options | 92 |
| Teagasc courses | 101 |
| FÁS apprenticeships | 107 |
| CERT courses | 116 |
| The Defence forces | 126 |

## Part Two: Careers

| | |
|---|---|
| Nurse | 137 |
| Doctor | 144 |
| Social worker | 152 |
| Radiographer | 160 |
| Medical laboratory sciences | 167 |
| Dietician | 175 |
| Food science | 182 |
| Law | 190 |
| Hairdresser | 199 |
| Construction trades | 206 |
| Actuary | 213 |
| Electronic engineer | 220 |
| Careers in film | 230 |
| Garda | 238 |
| Amenity horticulture | 245 |
| Marketing with languages | 253 |
| Polymer engineering | 260 |
| Estate agent | 266 |
| Secondary teacher | 273 |
| Primary teacher | 281 |
| Veterinary medicine | 286 |
| Software engineer | 291 |
| Accountant | 303 |
| Graphic designer | 309 |
| Sport science at UL | 317 |
| Agricultural science at UCD | 321 |

The education world is littered with abbreviations and specialised phrases. The following are some of the more common examples which appear in this book.

Ab-initio: This is used to refer to the "ordinary" degree courses as opposed to add-on degrees which are completed by post-diploma students.

AQA: All Qualified Applicants. Used in relation to cut-off points for third-level places where all qualified applicants were offered a place

BESS: Business Economics and Social Studies

CAO: Central Applications Office. Handles applications for undergraduate courses in third-level colleges in the Republic

CERT: The State tourism training body

CIF: Construction Industry Federation

DCU: Dublin City University

DIT: Dublin Institute of Technology

ESF: European Social Fund – pays the fees for many of the courses in the Institutes of Technology

H. Dip: Higher Diploma in Education, the main method of qualifying as a second-level teacher. This is a post-graduate qualification

HEA Higher Education Authority

IT: Institute of Technology (formerly the regional technical colleges)

Ladder system: the means by which students progress from certificate to diploma to degree

LCA: Leaving Certificate Applied – a radically new form of the Leaving Certificate where students complete a number of modules

LCV Leaving Certificate Vocational: a Leaving Certificate with subjects which are grouped vocationally and additional link modules (see below)

Link modules: modules completed by Leaving Certificate Vocational students in addition to their traditional subjects

LEA: Local Education Authority (refers to the United Kingdom)

LSB: College Private third-level college offering a range of fee-paying third-level courses

PLC: Post Leaving Certificate course, usually one year in duration

Post-graduate: refers to courses or qualifications attained after students have completed a primary degree

NCAD: National College of Art and Design, Dublin

NCVA: National Council for Vocational Awards. Most PLC students do an NCVA level 2 award

NCEA: National Council for Educational Awards. Validates courses and awards qualifications in the non-university third-level sector

NCI: National College of Ireland (formerly known as the National College of Industrial Relations or NCIR)

NUI: National University of Ireland

NUIG: National University of Ireland Galway (formerly known as University College Galway or UCG)

NUI: Maynooth National University of Ireland Maynooth (formerly known as St Patrick's College, Maynooth or Maynooth University)

RCSI: Royal College of Surgeons, offers fee-paying courses

Restricted-application courses: Courses within the CAO system for which you must apply by 1 February and which have an additional assessment component in addition to the Leaving Cert.

TCD: Trinity College Dublin

UCAS University and College Admissions Service, the central applications body for undergraduate courses in Britain and Northern Ireland

UCC: University College Cork

UCD: University College Dublin

UL: University of Limerick

Undergraduate: refers to any course which leads to a certificate, degree or diploma

USI: Union of Students of Ireland

UU: Ulster University

WIT: Waterford Institute of Technology

# Part One

# Practical Advice

## *Introduction*

Out of doors, in an office, on a building site, in a hospital theatre, in a classroom, down a mine or in a bank, in Ireland or abroad, your career choice will determine where you will spend much of your adult life.

Most students, who have participated in Transition Year or the Leaving Certificate Applied are at an advantage in that they will have gained some work experience. Even if you only spent two weeks filing photos in a newspaper office, you know a lot more now . . . what time people start work at, how they operate, the type of stress they may be under. Work shadowing, where you follow a person around as they do their daily job, or work experience, where you participate, is invaluable.

If you have already decided on a particular career, you should try and make sure that the work experience you get is relevant. You may think you want to be a medical laboratory scientist until you find yourself in a laboratory faced with 100 urine samples to be analysed for microbiological growth. On the other hand, one peek down the microscope at those tiny bacteria, and you may be hooked for life.

Outdoor life may seem very attractive if the only time you visit the country is in summer. Try wading through thick mud to tend a sick sheep, with your fingers frozen, your hair dripping wet and dusk falling.

# Career choice

Television soaps may have given you a romanticised notion of what a particular job entails. When an accident victim is brought into casualty, an entire team surround him in seconds in *ER*. Instructions are shouted out, drips are put in, surgery is imminent. In real life, it could be just you and one other person coping in an overcrowded, out-of-date casualty department. And remember that, sadly, most doctors bear little resemblance to George Clooney.

So, research your future career. Find out about pay, work conditions, and possible career paths. Spend some time with your guidance counsellor and in the school library. Think about your hobbies and interests. What are your favourite subjects at school? Do you like theory or the practical side of things?

Just over half of the students who sit their Leaving Certificate go directly into third-level education. This includes institutes of technology, teacher training colleges, and private colleges as well as universities. Some third-level courses are specialised right from the start. These are called direct-entry programmes. If you know what you want to do, then direct-entry means you can start studying your area of choice in first year.

However, if you are undecided, a common-entry or omnibus programme (both names are used) might suit you better. Going into a programme such as science, arts, engineering or business gives you a little time to sample various subjects and to make up your mind about which area you want to specialise in later.

Outside of third-level, the next biggest sector is the Post Leaving Certificate sector which takes in about 16,000 first years. These are largely one year courses which prepare students directly for employment. However, PLCs can also serve as a route into third-level.

## Introduction

Then there are apprenticeships – with the booming economy it is expected that about 5,000 students will begin FÁS apprenticeships this year. Most apprenticeships last four years and apprentices are paid while they train.

CERT, the State tourism body training body, offered 2,500 places in 1997, outside the CAO system. Teagasc, which trains people for careers in agriculture and horticulture, took in almost 1,000 students. This year, there are about 1,200 nurse training positions available. The defence forces and the Gardai recruit periodically. Bord Iascaigh Mhara trains people for careers at sea and in aquaculture.

So, if you do not have the points for third-level or are not interested in the more academic options, there are still plenty of career options out there.

Girls and boys still tend to decide their careers in a gender-biased fashion with girls opting for 'caring' professions such as nursing and boys going for engineering and the 'harder' sciences. There is no reason for us to continue thinking in these old gender stereotypes. Take a little time to consider non-traditional careers and courses.

Do you really need further education or training after the Leaving Certificate? With a booming economy, school-leavers can find work but it is usually low-paid and progression is difficult. All of the current research shows that the better qualified a person is, the more chance he or she will have of securing employment. And the level of qualification usually equates with the salary. So the more qualified you are, the more likely it is that you will be better paid.

Yes, it is a lot of work but choosing a course or career is as important as concentrating on your English, Irish or maths. Put in the time, and talk to your guidance counsellor.

This book includes chapters on the CAO, the Irish central application system for third-level courses and UCAS, the

## Career choice

British central applications system. Fees and grants, the Post Leaving Certificate sector, FÁS, CERT, Teagasc and the Defence Forces are also included. Many of these chapters are based on articles which appeared in 'Education and Living' in *The Irish Times*.

There are general chapters on arts, business, science, engineering, art and design application procedures and add-on degrees. These are based on the College Choice series which appeared in *The Irish Times*.

The second half of the book contains a series of career focuses and 'Me and My Job' pieces which appeared in the Education and Living supplement of *The Irish Times*. Catherine Foley interviewed individuals about the ups and downs of their jobs and I would like to thank her for allowing me to include these vignettes, which provide a real insight into the world of work.

Thanks to everyone in 'E and L' who was concerned with the articles which have been reproduced here.

Thanks also to *The Irish Times* photography department which supplied the accompanying photographs.

Anne Byrne is Careers and Guidance correspondent with *The Irish Times*. Catherine Foley is an 'Education and Living' writer for *The Irish Times*.

Whilst every effort has been made to ensure that the information given in this book is accurate and up to date, the publishers and authors do not accept responsibility for any errors or omissions. Students should consult their guidance counsellor or the relevant college or training institution before they apply for a course.

# Reasons for continuing your studies

## THE CELTIC TIGER DOES WHAT TIGERS DO BEST FOR GRADUATES

Graduate unemployment has fallen to 3.6 per cent, the lowest in 15 years. The Celtic tiger is roaring for those leaving third-level with certificates, diplomas, degrees and postgraduate qualifications. The latest graduate survey carried out by the Higher Education Authority shows that the proportion of graduates entering employment directly after graduation has risen to 54 per cent. The survey of 1996 graduates was carried out in April 1997 and published in January 1998.

Emigration is dropping, with more students finding work at home. And the percentage who opted for further study or training stands at 39 per cent, a decrease of one per cent on 1995 graduate levels.

Of course, the situation varies, depending on the level of the award. As might be expected, the proportion of students with certificates and diplomas going on to further study is higher than for primary degree graduates. At certificate level, almost one-third of graduates entered the labour market directly while 63 per cent went on to further study. At diploma level, 47 per cent of graduates began work directly after leaving college while 45 per cent continued their studies.

Only 3.3 per cent of certificate holders and 4.8 per cent of diploma holders were seeking work, after completing their studies. These figures emphasise the value of certificates and diplomas in the labour market.

The substantial proportion of students going on to further study demonstrate the extent to which the so-called ladder of opportunity from certificate to diploma to degree is working. This is particularly relevant in the light of the 2,000 fewer students starting certificate/diploma courses in 1997 compared to 1996. Statistics from the Central Applications Office show that more than 50,000 certificate/diploma offers were made in 1997 but only 15,658 students took up their offers. The substantial drop in students opting for certificates and diplomas is worrying in light of the skills shortages in high-tech areas.

Why are students spurning certs and diplomas? The reasons are not known but may well include academic snobbery as well as a genuine ignorance of the value of these qualifications and the fact that they can act as a stepping stone to the much-sought-after degree. More jobs for school-leavers may also be a factor – a recent ESRI report showed that 44 per cent of school-leavers were in employment within a year after they had left school, the highest proportion since 1990.

However, starting salaries increase with the level of qualification. Some 11 per cent of certificate holders employed in Ireland were earning less than £5,000 a year. A majority of certificate holders – almost 60 per cent – earned between £5,000 and £11,000 per annum while 25 per cent earned above this level. A few students (0.8 per cent) did very well, beginning work at £19,000 plus.

At diploma level, just 5.5 per cent of graduates earned up to £5,000 per annum while 38 per cent fell into the category between £5,000 and £11,000. Forty-seven per cent achieved

# Reasons for continuing your studies

salaries above this level with 4.4 per cent earning £19,000 plus.

At degree level, as few as 4.2 per cent of graduates working at home were in receipt of salaries up to £5,000 per annum. Some 24 per cent were in the range £5,000 to £11,000, while half of the primary degree graduates earned £11,000 plus. The proportion earning £19,000 plus was slightly lower than diploma holders at 3.4 per cent. However, 17.5 per cent of those leaving college with higher degrees fell into this category, showing the rewards possible for those who stay longer in higher education.

Some 55 per cent of primary degree holders were in employment soon after graduation, compared with 81 per cent of higher-degree holders.

Of course, these overall figures represent graduates of all faculties – arts, commerce, business, law, engineering, computing. Salaries are highest where skills shortages are greatest. For instance, careers officers say that salaries for software and engineering graduates are usually in the region of £15,000 to £17,000 or even higher.

The skills shortages in computing, electronics and applied languages have led to the creation of more third-level places. Under the Government Skills Shortages Initiative, it is planned to increase the numbers on software degrees by 1,000. The target for technicians is 750 additional places.

Unemployment rates vary across faculties. The highest proportion of primary degree graduates seeking employment was in the food science and technology faculties (7.3 per cent), followed by arts and social science graduates at 4.4 per cent. Next came architecture, followed by engineering and science. Law and agriculture had the lowest proportion of students seeking employment at 2.1 per cent.

## Career choice

At diploma level, the proportion seeking employment was highest in arts, social science and humanities at 7.7 per cent, followed by commerce and business studies at 4.7 per cent, science at 4.6 per cent and engineering at 3.3 per cent.

The bad news for students from outside the Pale is that the eastern region of the country provided most employment. Some 62 per cent of primary degree holders and 70 per cent of higher degree holders were employed in the east. This pattern was repeated at certificate and diploma level with the prospects of employment in their own region greatest for those in the east (86 per cent) and poorest in the midlands (38 per cent). The majority of cert/diploma and degree level graduates who went overseas found work in Britain.

## *Securing that third-level place*

Each year, students worry about the difficulties of securing a college place, as demand continually outstrips supply. Last year, there was roughly one place for every two applicants.

This year, the Department of Education estimates that 62,000 school-based students will sit the Leaving Certificate. An additional 3,000 to 4,000 external candidates can also be expected. This is similar to the 1997 figures (the CAO received 62,600 applications in 1997) and, while the number of college places may increase slightly, roughly the same ratio – one place for every two applicants – can be expected.

Of course, generalisations are of little value. There were a number of courses which experienced difficulty in filling their quota of students in 1997. These courses advertised vacant places. At the same time, there were 21 courses where demand far exceeded supply and points soared to 525 or beyond.

Just to get it in perspective, the 'points' that everyone talks about are the cut-off level for a particular course. In effect, they are the points of the last student who secured a place on the course. So, a cut-off of 350 means that the last student who accepted a place had 350 points. His or her fellow students all have points equal to or above 350. It is possible that some students have 500 plus.

## Career choice

Points are set by the demand for a course – the number and quality of the applicants (as measured in points) versus the number of places. The points levels have absolutely nothing to do with the quality of the course.

A look at the 1997 CAO statistics will give some idea of the competition for the various disciplines. The chances of securing a place ranged from one-in-two for science/applied science degrees to a daunting one-in-30 for health care certificates and diplomas.

The ratio of first-preference applicants to the number of available places is an indication of the relative difficulty of securing a place as you would expect that all applicants would accept their first-preference if they are made an offer.

Students applying for degrees in business/administration had roughly a three-to-one chance of securing a place, compared with those looking for veterinary medicine where the odds went up to ten-to-one. There were only 64 veterinary medicine places available compared with 3,535 in business/administration.

At certificate/diploma level, there were ten applicants for every arts/social science place while there were 2.6 applicants for every engineering/technology place.

Medical, paramedical, dentistry, veterinary medicine and pharmacy are perennial favourites with school-leavers. The 'caring' professions in particular attract droves of girls with high points. Law is also a favourite with school-leavers year in, year out.

The more traditional professions continue to exercise a strong fascination for young people. But students who are willing to look beyond these professions to less traditional courses can increase their chances of securing a college place. In fact, it is virtually possible to guarantee yourself a third-level place. After you have listed your top nine choices in genuine order of preference (the course you want most should head the list, regardless of the 1997 points), you could choose a 'banker' course – something you are fairly confident you can achieve. For instance, in 1997 some certificates took students with the basic five passes in the Leaving Cert. The advantage of doing this is that when it comes to early autumn, you may not want to repeat the Leaving Cert and this could provide you with an alternative.

When you are perusing the college prospectuses in the search for courses and colleges, you should spend a little time studying the common-entry options. The advantage of opting for a general science or arts or business or engineering course is that you can sample various subjects before specialising. Of course, if you already know what you want to do, a direct-entry programme means that you can get to work in that particular discipline immediately.

The good news is that, next January, you will be asked to choose from the widest ever menu of third-level courses available in the history of the State. January is a time of opportunity for students. It should be an optimistic month, as they look forward to life after school.

Instead of taking hope from this and researching interesting new options such as mechatronics, forest management or heritage studies, many students spend their time worrying about points levels and juggling course choices accordingly.

The hype and tension that surround college entry and the so-called Points Race is just that. Take a look at the figures. As well as looking at the number of places, you should look at the number of offers made. Last year, more than 77,000 offers of college places were made through the Central Admissions Office. That is 7,000 more than the previous year. And this year, we can expect even more offers to be made.

## Career choice

However, what happened last summer (1997) after the offers were made was truly startling. In all, 32,674 students took up their offers and are now mid-way through their first year of study. Compare that with the previous year, when 34,311 students accepted college places. In other words, about 1,600 fewer students accepted college places through the CAO. So, even though the number of college offers was increased, the number of students who actually began college is down.

What happened? At degree level, 17,016 students took up college places, an increase of more than 300 on the previous year. At cert/diploma level, there was a dramatic drop in acceptances with 15,658 students beginning certificates and diplomas compared to 17,644 the year before. So, this is where the big drop in college acceptances occurred as students spurned certificate and diploma courses. The 'degree or nothing' syndrome is becoming even more pronounced.

And, as the CAO offers were being made to individual students, the CAO was also advertising courses with vacant places which were open to everyone. In all, by the time the three main rounds of CAO offers were made, there were 42 courses advertising vacant places.

Yes, these were mainly certificates and diplomas in the institutes of technology. No, medicine, veterinary and dentistry were not included. But courses such as mechanical engineering, applied chemistry, polymer engineering and business studies were on the list.

Undoubtedly, the most sought-after qualification is the degree. However, many students miss the point. Certificates and diplomas are often the first rung on a much-trodden ladder to a degree. (Certificates and diplomas are also valid qualifications in their own right).

The number of add-on degrees available in the institutes of technology increases each year. But, you will not find them

## Securing a third-level place

by reading the CAO handbook. You must trawl through the college prospectuses.

Of course, this will not interest students who do not really care about the course content or the prospects it offers. They want to go to a university, not an institute of technology. They would never be able to face their friends if they had to admit to packing a bag and heading to college in the midlands. If snobbery is the guiding reason for your course choice, naturally you are wise to avoid the certificate/diploma list on the CAO form. However, if you have the maturity to consider all third-level options, then both lists deserve equal attention.

Geography is also a compounding factor when it comes to college choice. Home is the cheapest place to spend your college years. With one-quarter of the Republic's population living in the Dublin area, competition for college places is steepest there.

Students with their sights set on third-level should read the college prospectuses. Find out about the subjects on offer each year of the courses. Enquire about future prospects. Go to college open days and see the campus for yourself. Meet the staff and ask those burning questions.

The CAO handbook should be the definitive guide to third-level application but it is printed early in the year and colleges add and cancel courses. If you do not keep up with the changes, it is possible you could squander one of your choices or miss the very course for you.

Just to add to the confusion, a number of third-level colleges have recently changed their names. The regional technical colleges have been renamed as institutes of technology. Dun Laoghaire College of Art and Design has become the Dun Laoghaire Institute of Art, Design and Technology.

In the university sector, UCG has become NUI Galway and NUI Maynooth is now the official title for St Patrick's

College, Maynooth. The pontifical university at Maynooth, which offers a degree in theology and arts, retains the title St Patrick's College.

# *The Central Application System*

There are two main central applications bodies that you need to consider. The Central Applications Office (CAO) allocates places on most undergraduate courses in the Republic while the University and College Admissions Service (UCAS) allocates places in colleges in Britain and Northern Ireland. The two systems are quite different in their application procedures, closing dates and system of college offers.

## THE CAO SYSTEM

More than 35,000 third-level college places will be allocated through the Central Applications Office this year. The CAO handbook lists courses on offer.

Filling out the CAO form is one of the most important tasks facing students each January. The choices you list on your CAO form will determine your future college course.

The form itself is simple but you should first read the detailed instructions in the CAO handbook. These guide you through the process step by step. It is a good idea to photocopy the form before you put pen to paper. This way, you can make your mistakes in comfort without fear of the re-submission penalty which the CAO levies on forms it must return because of mistakes.

Most school-leavers will only have to deal with the first two pages of the CAO form. The first page asks for your name,

## Career choice

address, date of birth, country of birth, nationality, second-level school, Leaving Cert and matriculation details. It may seem ridiculously straightforward but, each year, the CAO reports that it must return hundreds of forms for re-submission because of errors on page one. The commonest error is filling out the day's date rather than your date of birth. So, take a little time. Nerves can cause silly mistakes. Get a friend, parent or guidance counsellor to double-check the details.

Page two contains two lists: one for certificates and diplomas and the other for degrees. There are ten choices on each list so you can list a total of 20 courses. If you are serious about going to third-level, you will not rely on the CAO handbook as your sole source of information. At the very least, read the college prospectuses. Talk to your guidance counsellor and, if possible, bring some of the literature home so that you can study it in peace and your parents can also read it.

When you are looking at the college brochures, read the subject choices offered in each year of the course. Almost every year, one or two students end up in the Dublin Institute of Technology's applied science degree, hoping to specialise in applied biology. The catch – that degree does not include biology. Take a little time now and save yourself embarrassment, and a lost year, later.

Courses fall into two main categories: common-entry and direct-entry. The common-entry courses allow you to choose a broad area such as science or engineering and then to specialise later. For instance, if you are know you want to become an engineer but are not sure which branch (mechanical, civil, electronic, computer . . .) will best suit you, then a common-entry programme makes sense. There is one possible disadvantage in that some courses have limited numbers of places in the various specialisms so you may have to compete for a place in second or third year. Read the college prospectus to find out. If you know exactly what you want, then a direct-entry programme should suit you.

The CAO asks for your choice of courses in order of preference. This simply means put the course you like most at the top of the list and work your way down. The course in second place on your list should be your second choice. As already mentioned, there are two lists. These lists operate independently of each other and deserve equal attention. Many students leave the certificate/diploma list blank, listing only degrees. This means that they are ignoring perfectly good courses which may well have lower points requirements and the option of follow-on degrees later. Sadly, the reason many young people ignore the certificates and diplomas is simply snobbery. Don't cut yourself off from a career choice because your school friends may not be impressed. It's your life and your career.

Above all, do not list courses in order according to the cut-off points in 1997. Points levels vary each year. You do not know what you will achieve in the Leaving Certificate. Many students decide to guess-timate points for courses as well as their own possible scores and come up with a list of courses based on these guess-timates.

Be aware how the CAO operates. Once the Leaving Certificate is over, the computer programme first checks whether you have the points and the required subjects for your first preference course – the course at the top of your list. If you qualify for an offer of a place, all of your lower preferences are wiped out. The courses listed below your first preference simply cease to exist. This should not worry you. Getting your first preference should be a time for rejoicing.

But, every year, without fail, we get one or two students on *The Irish Times* helpline, crying because they got their first preference course but what they really wanted was one or two places below it on the list. They did better than they expected in the Leaving Cert or the points went down. Don't be one of those people – put your dream choice at the top of the list.

If you don't qualify for your first preference, the computer moves on to your second choice and checks whether you fulfil the requirements and so on down the list.

If the points requirement drops, during the college offers season, you will be reconsidered for the higher choices whether you have accepted or rejected an offer. The rule is that *you can move upwards in your list of choices but never downwards*. So, if you are offered your first preference, you cannot decide to opt for a lower choice – no matter what. This is why it is so important to list your courses in genuine order of preference.

The certificate/diploma and degree lists operate independently. So, you may get two offers but, of course, you can only accept one.

When filling out your list of choices, you should ensure that you fulfil any subject and grade requirements. For instance, most engineering courses require a C in higher-level maths. There is no point in listing these courses if you are not taking higher-level maths – you are simply wasting a choice.

Many students study the previous year's points levels in order to choose a banker course – something they would study rather than repeat the Leaving Certificate. It makes sense to choose something for the bottom of your list which had very low points requirements in the previous year. This should afford you a choice of studying this course or repeating. Each year, fewer students are opting to repeat. When it comes to autumn, you may not feel like starting school all over again so try and spread your choices wisely.

# The Central Application System

Try to fill out all 20 choices – it doesn't cost any extra and you can always reject them later if you don't want them. Your perspective may change in the autumn if you are faced with no college offer when you had the points to secure a place on a good number of courses but you didn't list them.

Before you post your form to the CAO, take a photocopy and put it away safely for future reference. And don't forget to get your certificate of posting (on the back page of the CAO/CAS book) stamped.

## Restricted application courses:

Courses where assessment other than Leaving Certificate points apply fall into a special category known as restricted application courses. These courses are in the areas of architecture, art, design, drama, film/TV, furniture, graphics, marine engineering, music, nautical science, photography, radio/broadcasting and primary teacher training in the Church of Ireland college.

The important point to remember is that applications must be with the CAO by 1 February. Late applications will NOT be considered for restricted application courses.

## Application dates:

EU applicants (ordinary fee): closing date is 1 February 1999
Non-EU applicants (ordinary fee): closing date is 15 December 1998
Late applications (EU and non-EU applicants): closing date is 1 May 1999

## The CAO can be contacted at:

Tower House, Eglinton Street, Galway
Telephone: 091 563318 and 091 563269; Fax: 091 562344
Monday to Friday 9.30 to 13.00 and 14.00 to 17.15.

*Free fees scheme:*
Not all courses listed in the CAO handbook qualify for the free fees scheme. For instance, there are fees payable to the Royal College of Surgeons and to the private commercial colleges. You should check the college prospectus to ensure that the course you are interested in does qualify for the free fees scheme. Standard rate tax relief may be allowable against fees in certain approved colleges.

*Non-standard applicants:*
Special category applicants fall into a number of groups – students who have sat alternative exams to the Leaving Certificate, such as A-levels, Senior Cert or the Baccalaureat; mature students; students with NCVA level 2 or PLC qualifications; people with previous third-level or trade or craft qualifications.

Applicants with health problems which require special facilities at college – for instance, students with a physical disability or sight or hearing problems – also fall into a special category.

All special category students must fill out pages three and four of the CAO form. You must submit photocopies of pages three and four to the CAO also – one photocopy for each college to which you are applying. You must also supply certificates for all qualifications you have mentioned on page 3, with the exception of this year's A levels (Northern Ireland boards only). Photocopies are also required – again one for each college is necessary.

The certificates should show dates, subjects and results. They should NOT be originals; they should be certified photocopies.

# The Central Application System

*Change of mind facility:*
It is possible to change your mind when it comes to course choices right up until 1 July. This means that the Leaving Cert will be out of the way. Course choices can be changed, with no additional fee, as often as you like, up until 5.15 p.m on 1 July.

Once you submit a change-of-mind form, your previous course choices are cancelled. The degree and certificate/diploma lists are considered to be completely separate from each other for this purpose. You may not introduce any new restricted application courses.

*Offers and acceptances:*
The Department of Education supplies the Leaving Certificate results to the CAO in August. The examination authority in the North of Ireland supplies the A level results directly also.

In early August, a small number of offers may be made to students who are not waiting for this year's examination results. This is known as round zero.

The main round of offers takes place shortly after the Leaving Certificate results become available. This is known as round one and usually takes place late in August. Students may receive one offer from either list, two offers or no offer. In all cases, students will be notified.

The cut-off points for round one are published in the national newspapers. These points are simply a function of supply and demand, not an indication of the quality of the course. The smaller the number of places and the larger the demand, the higher the points.

But, this is not the end of the business. Students must now accept or reject their offers. A second round of offers takes place, usually in early September. Here, any vacant places are re-offered. A third round of offers will also take place.

Further rounds will continue up until late in October. However, there are usually very few places left after the first three rounds. Any courses with vacant places will advertise in the newspaper and these are open to students who have already applied to the CAO as well as students who have not applied.

*Calculating your points:*

In most cases, places are offered through the CAO on the basis of points. For instance, if there are 20 places, the 20 applicants with the highest points levels will be offered a place. The exception is the restricted application courses where an interview, portfolio assessment, music test, drawing test or other assessment will also be taken into account.

*Points scheme:*

| Leaving Certificate grade | Higher paper | Ordinary paper |
|:-:|:-:|:-:|
| A1 | 100 | 60 |
| B2 | 90 | 50 |
| B1 | 85 | 45 |
| B2 | 80 | 40 |
| B3 | 75 | 35 |
| C1 | 70 | 30 |
| C2 | 65 | 25 |
| C3 | 60 | 20 |
| D1 | 55 | 15 |
| D2 | 50 | 10 |
| D3 | 45 | 5 |

University of Limerick awards additional bonus points for higher-level maths in all courses and DIT awards a bonus for higher-level maths and a number of science subjects for electrical/electronic engineering.

*Leaving Certificate Vocational Programme link modules:*
Certain institutions award points for results in the LCVP link modules in place of a sixth subject.
    Distinction    70 points
    Merit    50 points
    Pass    30 points

*Deferrals:*
Almost all colleges will consider a request to defer taking up an offer for a year. Taking a year out is an increasingly popular

option – allowing students time to accumulate some money to finance their college years or to travel or mature.

If you wish to defer a place, you must contact the college directly. If the college confirms that it operates deferred entry into the course in question:

You should NOT accept the offer in the manner shown in the offer notice and do NOT make any payment. Instead, write immediately to the admissions office of the college in question, setting out the reasons why you are requesting a deferral. Mark 'deferred entry' on the envelope.

*Points for new courses:*
It is impossible to predict points levels for new courses. Points are simply a function of supply and demand so it is you, the students, who set the cut-off levels.

## UCAS

Each year, about 10,000 Irish students apply to colleges in Britain and Northern Ireland through the Universities and College Admissions Service (UCAS).

Application forms must be filled in and returned before 15 December. Applications which include Oxford or Cambridge must reach UCAS considerably early – 15 October. Different dates may also apply in the case of art and design courses (see below).

Your school guidance counsellor will have copies of the form as well as the UCAS handbook – a huge book listing thousands of courses. If you are no longer in education, you can get a form from UCAS Applications Requests, Cheltenham, Glos GL50 3SF, England.

Filling out the form demands some time and thought as it differs from the Irish CAO form in a number of ways. As you work your way through, keep the detailed instructions at hand

## The Central Application System

at all times. Again, it would be a good idea to photocopy the form and to make your mistakes in comfort before filling in the real thing.

The first section of the form asks for personal details and a correspondence address. For students in boarding schools, now is the time to make up your mind whether you want all correspondence to go to the school or your home. Further personal details required include age on 30 September, 1999, and date of birth.

The next question asks who will pay your fees? And they are not looking for the obvious 'mammy and daddy' type reply. UCAS is asking if you are an EU applicant and whether you will qualify for your fees to be paid by the local education authority in the area of which ever college you choose. For most Irish applicants, the LEA will pay the fees. However, a means test now applies.

The third section asks students to list the colleges and courses for which they are applying. Colleges should be listed in the order in which they appear in the UCAS handbook as opposed to the CAO system where you are asked to list your choices in order of preference. Students may select a total of six courses. You should use a separate line for each course, even if they are in the same college.

The mix of courses you select will influence the college admissions tutor reading your form, so choose a number of related courses rather than six totally different courses. This section also asks you for point of entry, which for school-leavers is year one. If you are hoping to defer a place for a year, tick the appropriate box for the relevant course.

If you have previously applied to any of the colleges you are listing, you must give the college code and your most recent application number. Some British colleges will not consider repeat Leaving Certificate students for certain courses with high entry requirements such as medicine.

Sections four, five and six are straightforward. Section seven asks students to fill out examinations completed. You should give full details of your Junior Certificate results as it is the only State exam you have completed. Under qualifications pending, list the subjects you are sitting in the Leaving Certificate.

Students are asked to list special needs in section eight. Remember colleges in Britain and Northern Ireland will go out of their way to accommodate students with special needs so be specific.

Details of employment to date are requested in section nine. Guidance counsellors advise students to fill out formal employment only. Babysitting may be lucrative but it does not count for the purposes of this form.

The next section, which asks you for a PERSONAL STATEMENT is probably the MOST IMPORTANT part of your application. It is your chance to sell yourself. Places are allocated by admissions tutors who take more than your examination results into account.

Think out your strategy and write it out in draft form. Don't commit anything to the actual form until you have discussed it with your parents and your guidance counsellor. UCAS lists a number of headings you should cover and you should make sure that you get to grips with these. But a little originality is sure to impress a college tutor faced with an enormous bundle of forms with little to differentiate them.

When you have signed the declaration that the information you have given is correct, it's time to hand the form over to your school principal or guidance counsellor who will complete the final section which asks for a reference. Give them plenty of time to think about it.

# The Central Application System

UCAS produces a number of useful leaflets including *The Parent's Guide to Higher Education, How to apply to Universities and Colleges in the UK for entry to third-level Education* and *Instructions for Completion of the Application Form*. There is also a UCAS qualifications guide for Irish applicants which lists minimum Leaving Cert requirements for various courses.

### AND, FINALLY, ART AND DESIGN

Art and design courses fall into two application routes, imaginatively named Route A and Route B. The origins of the distinction are historical rather than logical. Both routes are of equal status.

Students applying through Route A must have their applications in by 15 December (the ordinary UCAS closing date). The exception is Ruskin School of Fine Art, Oxford, where the earlier date of 15 October applies. Applicants may make up to six choices through Route A and these should be listed in section 3 of the application form in UCAS handbook.

Applications through Route B should be made between 1 January and 24 March. Up to four choices may be made, and, again, these should be listed in section 3 of the application form in UCAS handbook order.

Just to add to the confusion, you may apply through both Route A and Route B. A total of six colleges/courses may be selected but with a maximum of four in Route B. The advantage of using Route B is that it allows you a little more time to build up your portfolio.

## *Art and design application procedures*

Artistically inclined students need to be nimble on their feet as the annual portfolio marathon (sorry, art and design application process) gets underway.

Each year, we hear of exhausted parents and their offspring who have travelled the length and breadth of the country, ferrying that precious bundle, the portfolio.

And, of course, it's not that simple. Transport or long-distance running skills alone will not secure you a place. You must be able to navigate through the maze of drawing tests, portfolio assessments, interviews and projects.

Each college has its own way of assessing which students are most suitable for their courses. This seems reasonable until you consider the implications for the individual student, who is likely to be applying to more than one college. He or she could conceivably have to prepare a portfolio, do a drawing test, and a project, and prepare for an interview(s), while studying for the Leaving Certificate. Closing dates must be juggled and portfolios retrieved for the next application.

The following is an attempt to unravel the mysteries of applying for art and design courses in the various colleges.

# Art and design application procedures

## NCAD

The National College of Art and Design offers three courses to school-leavers, two of which are in the CAO system.

The first-year core programme, which is the common first year for NCAD's four-year degree courses in fine art, craft design, fashion design, textile design, visual communications and the joint courses in history of art with either fine art or any of the four design options, is not in the CAO system.

Applications for first-year core must be made directly to the college and the minimum academic standard is two higher-level grade C3s in the Leaving Certificate and four D3s on ordinary-level papers including a language (Irish, English or continental). There is no Leaving Certificate points system. Places are allocated on the basis of a portfolio.

There is no need to deliver portfolios personally but many students, understandably, want to make sure that they reach the college in pristine condition. To give NCAD its due, portfolios are assessed with great efficiency and are usually available for collection two weeks later.

Applicants to NCAD's BA in art and design education must apply through the CAO, with a closing date of 1 February. Mature students should apply directly to the college. All applicants to the course will be offered an interview. They will be sent a brief for a drawing test before the interview. Applicants must bring the completed test and a portfolio of work with them to the interview. The minimum academic requirements are the same as for first-year core and, again, a Leaving Cert points system is not used.

NCAD's third offering, the BDes in industrial design is offered jointly by the University of Limerick and NCAD. Students spend first year at UL and the subsequent three years at NCAD. The course appears under UL in the CAO handbook.

*Career choice*

Places are allocated on the basis of a portfolio and interview. A minimum of two grade C3s at higher level and four D3s at ordinary level is needed and there are specific maths/science/engineering requirements, as there is some engineering content in the course.

As with the BA in art and design education, mature applicants should contact the college directly.

NCAD is included in the free fees scheme and students are also eligible to apply for Higher Education Authority grants and Vocational Education Committee scholarships.

## INSTITUTES OF TECHNOLOGY

All of the following colleges are in the central applications system and almost all are listed by the CAO as restricted-application courses. No late applications (after 1 February closing date) will be accepted for any of the restricted courses. And the change-of-mind form may not be used to introduce any new restricted application course.

DIT: There are six art and design courses offered by the Dublin Institute of Technology. Students must submit a portfolio to DIT Mountjoy Square, Dublin. Usually, about half of those who submit a portfolio are called for interview. Last year (1997), more than 1,000 students applied and about 500 were called to interview.

A maximum of 600 points is awarded for portfolio and interview. These points are then added to the Leaving Cert points to allocate places. Candidates are scored separately for each course for which they apply.

Three of the courses, which were four-year advanced diplomas, are now four-year DIT degrees. So, there may be increased demand for these courses this year – design (envi-

## Art and design application procedures

ronmental/spatial), design (visual communications) and fine art.

ATHLONE INSTITUTE OF TECHNOLOGY: participates in the CAO project assessment system. If an applicant passes the project, he or she is asked to attend a portfolio assessment and information session at the college. The idea of the information session is to meet staff to discuss the candidate's suitability for the course. There are points awarded for the portfolio and these are added to Leaving Cert points to allocate places.

CARLOW INSTITUTE OF TECHNOLOGY: does not require a project or portfolio for its industrial design course. Places are awarded on the basis of Leaving Cert points alone. It is not a restricted application course so late applications will be accepted by the CAO.

CORK AND LIMERICK INSTITUTES OF TECHNOLOGY: operate within the CAO admissions process for the project section with the project scored on a pass/fail basis. Those who are successful in the project are called for a portfolio assessment/interview. A maximum of 600 points is available for the portfolio/interview, which are then added to normal Leaving Cert points.

Cork and Limerick ITs usually operate a combined portfolio assessment/interview so some students applying for both colleges need attend only one interview. Both colleges offer similar courses – national diplomas followed by add-on degrees.

DUN LAOGHAIRE INSTITUTE OF ART, DESIGN AND TECHNOLOGY (formerly Dun Laoghaire College of Art and Design): In March, applicants are asked, in writing, to submit a portfolio which is assessed on a pass/fail basis. Each year, after 1 February, the CAO closing date, a number of students come to the admissions office in the college clutching portfolios. Please wait until you are asked to submit it. The college hires a hall in Dun Laoghaire which is convenient to the DART and buses and that is where the portfolios are assessed in March – not in the college itself.

If your portfolio passes the initial assessment, you will be called to an interview/portfolio assessment which carries a maximum of 600 points (the portfolio can be further developed between the initial assessment and the interview). These are then added to the Leaving Cert points to allocate places.

GALWAY MAYO INSTITUTE OF TECHNOLOGY: operates within the CAO project system but, here, the project is scored and this score is added to the normal Leaving Cert points to allocate places.

LETTERKENNY INSTITUTE OF TECHNOLOGY: applicants for graphic design and industrial design courses have the option of attending a portfolio/assessment. This was mandatory in the past. Students with a strong portfolio, who decide to go this route, will have their portfolio/assessment marked out of 600 points and their score added to their Leaving Cert points. Students who opt to be assessed on the basis of the Leaving Cert alone will have their points doubled for the purposes of ranking.

SLIGO INSTITUTE OF TECHNOLOGY: Applicants for the national diploma in fine art must submit a portfolio in April. This is scored out of 600 and these points are then added to Leaving Cert points to allocate places.

# Art and design application procedures

Students also have the OPTION of submitting portfolios in December – this seems to confuse some students who think they have to have their portfolio with the college before Christmas. It is simply an additional optional facility which allows students to obtain their portfolio scores early. This allows students to change their course option if they do badly or, on the advice of the college, to put in some additional work and re-submit their portfolio in April.

WATERFORD INSTITUTE OF TECHNOLOGY: A project is no longer required for entry to the national diploma in art. Students must have a minimum of an ordinary-level B3 or a higher-level C3 in art in the Leaving Certificate. Mature students and students who do not satisfy the Leaving Certificate art requirement will be required to satisfy the college as to their suitability for the course. This is not a restricted application course.

# *Mature students*

Mature college applicants are becoming more numerous and more vociferous. Colleges will become more dependent on these mature applicants in the future. However, many of these applicants are unhappy with the way in which they are treated by the colleges. Applicants outnumber places. Application procedures are cumbersome and students may have been turned down for a place but are unsure why. Whatever you think about the points system, at least you know why you did or did not get a place.

The main problem for colleges is ensuring that applicants will be able to cope with the course. A variety of methods are used from essays to tests to interviews to reviewing the application form. Many colleges simply state that they deal with applications on an individual basis. This is not particularly helpful for would-be students who are trying to maximise their chances of getting that coveted college place.

Mature students invest a lot of time and effort in preparing their applications and they want to be reassured that they are getting a fair deal.

APPLYING TO COLLEGE AS A MATURE STUDENT:
You are deemed mature by most colleges if you are at least 23 years of age on 1 January of the year of entry or re-entry to college. Mature applicants should turn to page eight of the

## Mature students

CAO handbook which lists closing dates and application procedures.

Direct application: A number of colleges require direct applications: All Hallows Colleges; American College; Coláiste Mhuire, Marino; Dublin City University; Froebel College of Education (2 April); LSB College; Mary Immaculate College of Education; Milltown Institute; National College of Art and Design; National College of Industrial Relations; St Patrick's College, Drumcondra; Portobello College; Royal College of Surgeons in Ireland and University of Limerick.

Applying by two: St Catherine's College and Trinity College require mature applicants to apply directly to the college and also to apply through the CAO.

Applications through the CAO: Institutions not mentioned in either category above require students to apply through the CAO only.

All of this means that mature applicants must sit down and wrestle with a variety of closing dates. It has been argued that mature students target only one college or course. However, as the number of mature applicants now far outnumbers available places, applicants must consider a number of options. Surely, it would be more sensible if the 1 February closing date applied to both mature students and school-leavers.

Mature students applying through the CAO should be aware that it is the colleges who allocate places, not the CAO which has a purely administrative purpose.

### THE CAO FORM

Mature applicants must fill out all four pages of the CAO form. Pages one and two are straightforward. Page one asks students for basic information while page two is where applicants list their course choices.

Mature applicants should tick box seven on page three. If you have completed qualifications which are listed in any other boxes on this page, you should tick these boxes also.

Mature applicants are asked to write a short curriculum vitae on page four covering education, work experience, achievements, interests and motivation. If you ticked any other boxes, further details should also be given here. You may attach one additional page if you need more space. Remember, the college admissions officer or faculty member is trying to satisfy him or herself as to your suitability for the course.

Professor Nollaig Mac Congáil of NUI Galway notes that mature students fall into two groups – those who have matriculated and those who have not. The latter category is by far the largest, he says. 'It is very important for these people to spend as much time as possible selling themselves in the information they supply on the CAO form,' he adds.

When going through the forms, he is looking for some indication that they are focused people, that they are informed as to what a degree is, and that their aspirations are realistic. NUI Galway uses the CAO forms as a screening procedure to select people for interview. The college usually calls three times as many applicants as there are places. Many of these will fail to turn up to interview, he adds.

At interview, they get a flavour of the college and find out about the reality of full-time third-level education. Mac Congáil says that going to college is a major upheaval, emotionally, economically, culturally and personally for mature students. Students may begin courses and drop out for reasons other than the obvious academic ones. The college is in the process of appointing an officer to deal with mature students.

## Mature students

Back to the form: It's not enough to simply fill out all four pages including your opus on page four. You must send one photocopy of pages three and four for each college to which to you are applying. In addition, you must send certified photocopies of each qualification you mention on page three.

### RESERVED PLACES

The Department of Education and Science produces an information guide for mature students who wish to enter full-time courses. This is an indispensable booklet which lists all of the colleges and details the proportion of places that have been set aside for mature students. It also gives information on the selection procedures that are used in each college.

For instance, Dublin City University reserves five to ten per cent of places in all faculties for mature students. The selection procedure involves an interview and, possibly, an aptitude test. The faculties of arts, philosophy, Celtic Studies and science in NUI Maynooth set aside 10 per cent of places for mature applicants. The college requires a curriculum vitae and two references.

In Univeristy College Cork, each faculty differs with about 80 places set aside on the BA programme, 40 on the Bachelor of social science and three each on the BA (music) and BMusic. There are assessment tests and, for the music degrees, a special entrance test. In University College Dublin, the situation also varies by faculty, with no engineering places reserved for mature applicants but there are 14 social science places set aside.

Again, in the NUI Galway, each faculty has its own policy at present but the college's strategic plan sets a target quota of 10 per cent in all faculties (similar to the college's arts faculty quota at present where 70 of the 700 places are reserved for mature students).

## Career choice

In Trinity College Dublin, about 10 per cent of places are set aside for mature students in arts, BESS, engineering and systems science, health sciences, science and arts (two subject moderatorship). And in Univerity Limerick, places are awarded on merit in all faculties with no set quotas.

Mature students interested in arts degrees should not forget St Patrick's College, Drumcondra, where 20 per cent of places are reserved for mature students, and Mary Immaculate College, Limerick, where 20 to 25 places on humanities courses are set aside for mature students.

QUOTAS IN THE INSTITUTES OF TECHNOLOGY:
No fixed quota: Athlone IT, Carlow IT, Dundalk IT, Dun Laoghaire IT, Letterkenny IT, Limerick IT, Tralee IT, Waterford IT, Dublin IT

Cork IT: Reserves places up to five per cent of places for special category applicants, including mature students.

Galway/Mayo and Tallaght ITs: up to 10 per cent of places are reserved.

Sligo IT: one place reserved per 20 students per course.

Copies of the guide (which is updated annually) are available, free of charge, from the Curriculum Development Unit, Sundrive Road, Dublin 12. Tel: (01) 453 5487

## *Money matters*

One of the major worries facing anyone going to college is money, or the lack of it. Despite the free fees initiative, going to college is still an expensive undertaking.

A student living at home will spend almost £5,000 during the academic year, according to figures prepared by the Union of Students in Ireland. Dublin City University, which also prepares figures on the cost of going to college, estimates the cost at a slightly lower £4,000. Students must also pay at least £250 or more to cover exams, administration and capitation.

The free fees initiative applies to eligible students who are first-time undergraduates and who are EU nationals. You must also have been resident in an EU country for at least three of the five years before you begin college.

Courses approved for the free fees initiative are full-time undergraduate courses, other than ESF-funded courses in the institutes of technology. (Tuition fees on ESF-funded courses are paid by the European Social Fund.) Courses must be a minimum of two years in duration to qualify for the free fees initiative.

In practice, this means that first-time students will not have to pay fees for the majority of the courses listed in the CAO handbook. Notable exceptions are courses offered by the private commercial third-level colleges, courses offered by the Royal College of Surgeons, modular part-time arts courses

## Career choice

in UCD, and foundation-level courses in Dublin Institute of Technology. There has been some confusion in the past about Mater Dei and the National College of Industrial Relations – full-time undergraduate courses in these colleges do qualify for the free fees initiative.

Free fees are not payable for students who are repeating a year, having failed their end-of-year exams or as a result of changing course. There may be an exception made for students who have to repeat a year due to serious certified illness. Slightly different rules apply to ESF-funded courses where students may change their minds in first year, do a substantially different ESF-funded course, and still retain their free fees entitlement.

Means-tested maintenance grants are available but, as you can see from the tables below, they do not meet the real cost of going to college. In general, if a course qualifies for the free fees initiative or is ESF-funded, then students were eligible to apply for maintenance grants. There are two exceptions – the Royal College of Surgeons and Mount St Mary's Montessori in Dundrum. Students who are awarded a 'full' grant in these colleges will have their fees paid up to a maximum limit set by the Department.

You must send your grant application in to the local authority before you know if you have a college place – otherwise there may be delays in payment. A full list of local authorities is included in the Department of Education's annual publication, *'Third Level Student Support'*. Write to the Higher Education Grants Section, Department of Education, Tullamore. Tel: (0506) 21363 or (01) 873 4700

If you run into financial trouble during your time in college, there are a number of places you can try for help. Most colleges operate student assistance funds which can provide some financial assistance to students. Counselling services are also there to help. The student officer in your local bank will provide advice and help in negotiating a loan. Talk to your student's union – they have years of experience.

THE COST OF COLLEGE:

*Monthly cost for a student living away from home (1997/98)*

| Estimated cost | DCU (£) | USI (£) |
| --- | --- | --- |
| Rent | 152 | 160 |
| Light/heat/telephone | 29 | 100 |
| Food | 140 | 128 |
| Travel | 39 | 20 |
| Books etc | 30 | 33 |
| Clothes, laundry, medical | 22 | 60 |
| Social life, other travel | 72 | 95 |
| Total | 484 | 596 |
| Annual total (8 months) | 3,872 | 4,768 |
| Non-tuition fee | 250 | 250 |
| Final total | 4,122 | 5,018 |

*Monthly cost for a student living at home (1997/98)*

| Estimated cost | DCU (£) | USI (£) |
|---|---|---|
| Cost to family of food, accom. | 62 | 64 |
| Food in college | 45 | 100 |
| Travel | 39 | 40 |
| Books etc | 29 | 33 |
| Clothes, laundry, medical | 22 | 60 |
| Social life, other travel | 72 | 80 |
| Total | 269 | 377 |
| Annual total (8 months) | 2,152 | 3,016 |
| Non-tuition fee | 250 | 250 |
| Final total | 2,400 | 4,020 |

USI calculates its figures based on a nine-month year. The figures were adjusted to compare with DCU's. USI estimates that a student living away from home will spend £5,614 over a nine-month academic year while a student living at home will spend £3,643

## GRANT LEVELS 1998–98

| Dependent children | Full maint. | Part maint. |
|---|---|---|
|  | payable to income of | |
| Fewer than four | £18,308 | £19,525 |
| Four to seven | £20,139 | £21,357 |
| Eight or more | £21,971 | £23,189 |

The above limits are increased by £2,060 where two or more children (or the candidate's parents) are attending full-time third-level education. And the limits are further increased by £2,060 for each subsequent child in full-time third-level education.

| Maintenance grants 1998–99 | Away from home | At home |
|---|---|---|
| Full maintenance | £1,652 | £660 |
| Part maintenance | £826 | £330 |

## FEES AND BRITISH UNIVERSITIES

From the start of the 1998–99 academic year, everyone beginning full-time undergraduate higher education in the UK will have to pay up to £1,000 a year towards their tuition fees. Irish nationals studying in the UK may qualify for help from the UK authorities if they satisfy certain conditions. If your income is below Stg£17,000 a year, you may not have to pay anything towards your tuition costs. However, if your income is the equivalent of Stg£35,000 a year, you will probably not qualify for assistance. For people with incomes in between these two figures (and who satisfy the various conditions) help is available on a sliding scale.

In order to apply for financial support towards their fees, Irish students should apply, as previously, to the appropriate UK Local Education Authority (LEA). This is usually the authority in the area in which the college is situated. Application forms will be issued from the LEA to the student. The Department of Education and Employment will assess the applicant's financial resources and calculate what fee support, if any, should be made by the LEA. The LEAs will continue to be the initial and final point of contact for the EU as they are now, according to the British Council.

*Career choice*

The British Department for Education and Employment has produced two leaflets: *Investing in the future: Help with tuition fees for EU students* and *Financial support for students*. These are available from: The British Council, Newmount House, 22/24 Lower Mount Street, Dublin 2. Tel: (01) 676 4088

Maintenance grants are paid by the Irish Government to eligible students attending approved undergraduate courses in Britain and other EU member states. These courses must be full-time undergraduate courses of not less than two years duration in a university or third-level institution which is maintained or assisted by recurrent grants from public funds in another EU member State with the exception of the following:

1. Courses in medicine, dentistry, veterinary medicine and teacher training courses including those leading to the award of Bachelor of Education
2. Courses in colleges of further and higher education (other than those which are at higher national diploma level or higher)
3. Courses provided in a college which are offered in private commercial third level colleges in the State, and which are validated by the college
4. Courses in colleges akin to private commercial colleges in Ireland

## PRIVATE COLLEGES AND TAX RELIEF

The 1995 Finance Act provides for tax relief, at the standard rate of tax, for tuition fees (maximum £2,500) paid in respect of students attending approved courses in approved private third-level colleges.

These courses must be of a minimum two-year duration and must satisfy the standards set down by the Minister for

Education. A list of approved courses in approved colleges is available from the Revenue Commissioners.

### PART-TIME COURSES AND TAX RELIEF

Tax relief at the standard rate is also available on tuition fees for approved part-time third-level courses. Again, apply to the Revenue Commissioners for a list of approved courses.

### SPECIAL FUND FOR STUDENTS WITH DISABILITIES

A special fund was set up in 1994. This fund is administered centrally by the Department of Education and is specifically designed to help students with physical disability who wish to attend third-level colleges. Applications are invited each September/October.

# *Common queries*

Each year, *The Irish Times* helpline, which is staffed by guidance counsellors, is inundated with queries. Some of these turn up year after year. Here are some of the commonest queries . . . along with the answers.

*Are all courses listed in the CAO handbook covered by the free fees initiative?*
Most courses listed in the CAO handbook are covered but not all.

For instance, private third-level colleges are now offering courses through the CAO. Full fees are payable for courses offered by these colleges. However, standard-rate tax relief may be claimed. Students in these colleges are not eligible to apply for maintenance grants.

Students embarking on medicine in the Royal College of Surgeons in Ireland must also pay fees but, of the 40 first-year places reserved for EU students, there are scholarships available for 10 students. These scholarships include total remission of the fees and £1,000 per student.

There are three course codes listed in the CAO handbook. RC001 is for students who will accept a place in medicine in the RCSI without a scholarship. RC002 is for students who are hoping to get a scholarship through the college's entrance exam while RC003 is for students who are hoping to secure a scholarship through their Leaving Cert results. Students can use all three course codes. However, this means using up three of their ten degree choices.

There is now no restriction on the number of times students can sit the entrance exam or the Leaving Cert in hopes of gaining a scholarship, says the RCSI's admissions officer.

UCD's modular arts degrees are part-time courses, so full fees are payable but tax relief at the standard rate may be claimed.

Fees are also payable for Dublin Institute of Technology's preliminary engineering and music foundation courses. The Department of Education does not recognise these courses as fulfilling the criteria for third-level courses so full fees must be paid.

*What happens to my free fees if I fail my exams and have to repeat a year?*
Students who have to repeat a year, for reasons other than certified illness, are liable to pay full fees for their repeat year.

*Will I have to pay fees next year if I drop out in first year and begin again next year?*
Students who drop out of an undergraduate course (other than a course funded by the European Social Fund) before the halfway mark, 31 January, has passed, need only pay half-fees for a subsequent first year.

However, if the 31 January deadline has passed, you will be liable for full fees for your next first year. Students on ESF-funded courses may drop out during first year and re-apply for a substantially different ESF-funded course without affecting their free fees entitlement.

If you decide to leave your course midway through the year, you should notify your college.

# Career choice

*I have completed a certificate – will I have to pay fees for a diploma?*
The free fees initiative applies for eligible students progressing up the ladder from certificate to diploma to degree. This process may take four or five years: a two-year cert, followed by a one-year diploma, followed by a one or two-year degree. For the purposes of the free fees initiative, it doesn't matter if the process takes four or five years.

*I have sent in a CAO form but now I want to change my mind – what do I do?*
Every CAO applicant will receive an application record and change-of-mind form in May. You may change your mind about your choice of courses as often as you like up until 5.15 p.m. on 1 July. This means students will have completed the Leaving Certificate and have a little time to re-consider before the final closing date. There is no fee charged for changes of mind.

*Is it true that applicants from the Gaeltacht get preference for teacher-training places?*
An irate Dublin mother wanted to know why her son – who is doing higher-level Irish and who wants to be a primary teacher – is not being rewarded for his efforts. Why should his interest in and skills in Irish be ignored because he doesn't live in the Gaeltacht? she asks.

A glance at the 1997s points shows that general applicants for teacher training in St Patrick's College, Drumcondra, required 470* (* means random selection applied) to secure a place while the cut-off level for Gaeltacht applicants was 440. Similarly, there was a 40 point difference between places awarded to Gaeltacht applicants and general applicants in Mary Immaculate College, Limerick. Gaeltacht applicants for

Coláiste Mhuire, Marino, and Froebel College of Education, Dublin, needed 25 and 40 points fewer respectively to secure a place.

The Department of Education and Science points out that, for more than 30 years, Government policy in support of the Irish language has included provision of up to 10 per cent of places in the colleges of education to be reserved for Gaeltacht applicants. Each college is required to reserve up to 10 per cent of its annual intake for Gaeltacht applicants and to ensure that the places are filled in the CAO offers procedure.

Gaeltacht applicants compete separately from other applicants for these places, and, given the small number of such applicants, this may mean that the points required are lower. However, the Department's statement adds that not all Gaeltacht applicants necessarily have lower points than other applicants.

*Can I add points over two Leaving Certs?*
No, points can not be accumulated over a number of Leaving Certs. They will be calculated on the basis of one sitting only. But, you can accumulate subject requirements over two or more Leaving Certs. For instance, if you needed a higher-level B in maths to secure a place on UCD's engineering course, you need only achieve this in one sitting of the Leaving Cert. Or if you need Irish for the NUI colleges, once you have passed it, that is sufficient. You don't need to do it again.

If you are repeating the Leaving, remember to fill out the appropriate box or boxes on page one of the CAO form. The CAO reports that this is quite a common omission and, if it is not picked up by students in the May statement, they will not get credit for a previous year's exam.

# Career choice

*How do the bonus points for maths work?*
Bonus points for higher-level Leaving Cert maths are awarded by the University of Limerick. Bonuses are as follows: 40 points for an A1, 35 for an A2, 30 for a B1, 25 for a B2, 20 for a B3, 15 for a C1, 10 for a C2 and five for a C3. These are added to the points for the particular grade you obtained. The DIT also awards points for maths and a number of science subjects in the case of the electrical/electronic engineering.

*How can I qualify for an exemption from the Irish requirement of NUI?*
You can claim an exemption if you were born outside Ireland (32 counties); if you received your primary education up to age of 11 years outside the Republic; if you resided outside Ireland (32 counties) for at least three years immediately before you become eligible for matriculation or if you received your post-primary education outside the Republic for the three years immediately preceding matriculation.

In addition, you may compensate for a grade E on a higher-level Irish paper or any other subject if you have three other grade C3s on higher-level papers or at least one grade B3 and one grade C3 at higher-level or the equivalent grade at the matriculation or on the joint results of both examinations.

*What will the points be like for new courses?*
The simple answer is – nobody knows.

Some people are still under the impression that points are decided arbitrarily by the colleges. In fact, points are set by the students. The number and quality of applicants (as measured in points) and the number of places, determine the points level. The cut-off points are simply the points achieved by the last student who was offered a place on the course. In other words, everyone else in the class will have similar or higher points.

In general, the fewer the places and the higher the demand, the higher the points are likely to be.

# Post Leaving Certificate courses

WHERE CAN YOU GO WITH A PLC QUALIFICATION?
The primary aim of Post Leaving Certificate courses is to prepare students for direct entry into the jobs market. However, a proportion of students use PLCs as a stepping stone to third-level. Other courses act as preparation, or pre-training, for areas as diverse as apprenticeships, nursing and third-level art and design courses.

Last year, there were 18,720 students enrolled in the Post-Leaving Cert sector. Most PLC courses are one year in duration with students completing a National Council for Vocational Awards (NCVA) level two qualification (NCVA level 2).

Some 37,000 level 2 awards have been made since 1994. These awards span art, craft and design; business and administration; science, technology and natural resources; services, leisure and tourism; communications, performing arts and general studies.

Last year, there was a significant increase in the numbers achieving certificates in computer-aided design, craft, business studies, horticulture, horsemanship, electronic technology, performing arts and print journalism.

Almost 4,000 students received NCVA level 2 awards in 1997, with a further 8,500 getting records of achievement. Students must complete eight modules satisfactorily to attain a certificate. More than 1,800 candidates achieved nine or ten modules while 34 candidates achieved 13 modules or more.

The modules must include five vocational modules (including mandatory and elective modules), two general studies (one of which must be communications) and one preparation for work or work experience module. A record of achievement is awarded to students who reach the required standard in one or more modules but who do not achieve the eight required for a certificate.

The list of new modules that became available late in 1997 gives some indication of the huge variety of PLC courses on offer: animal anatomy and physiology, animal grooming, appreciation of art/craft/design, animal welfare, Gaeilge for pre-school services, music industry services, nutrition, hotel and catering modules, tourism modules, printmaking, sound engineering, úsáid Gaeilge le paistí óga.

There are no tuition fees for PLCs and students applying for PLC courses, beginning from autumn 1998, will be eligible to apply for maintenance grants (these are means tested).

One of the main strengths of the PLC sector is its ability to respond rapidly to the changing needs of the labour market. For instance, the teleservices industry employs about 3,500 people at present. It is predicted that this will rise to 10,000 within three years. Call centres engaged in the teleservices business provide marketing and support services for international companies.

These services range from hotel reservations to airline flight bookings, car rental, information technology, software and hardware support.

All of these call centres need people who are computer-literate and who possess good communication skills. Some of the companies require fluency in one or more European languages (other than English).

As more companies locate here, a shortage of skilled people is predicted. The Government responded in 1997 by making a new Post-Leaving Certificate course in international teleservices available in 20 colleges around the State. Ballyfermot Senior College in Dublin pioneered the programme in 1996. A target of 750 places was set and 690 were filled despite the late advertisement of these courses in 1997.

This year, expect lots of interest in these innovative courses, which virtually guarantee employment. Students need a minimum of grade B in ordinary-level Leaving Cert English and one continental language or an equivalent qualification.

The course includes up to six months' placement in a European country. Students receive £100 a week living expenses while they are in Europe. They also have 75 per cent of their air fares refunded (maximum £300 for airfare and £1,700 for living expenses).

The PLC colleges offering this course have been given a substantial investment for new equipment.

## Applying for PLC courses

There is no centralised application system for PLC courses. You must apply directly to each college, and places are usually allocated on the basis of an interview. Popular courses tend to fill early and some colleges hold interviews in May.

In the past, many students regarded these courses as a fallback if they did not get the CAO offer they wanted – however, this is no longer the case.

Students applying for PLC courses must ask themselves why they are embarking on a particular course. If they are hoping for employment directly after the course, they should check how graduates of that course have fared in the marketplace. If they want to use the PLC qualification as a backdoor into third-level education, it is very important to check the PLC course's linkage with third-level courses.

## LEAVING CERTIFICATE APPLIED

Students taking the new Leaving Certificate Applied programme are not eligible to apply directly for third-level places through the CAO. So, Post-Leaving Certificate courses are of increased importance as students can progress via a PLC to a variety of national certs and diplomas. And, if they do sufficiently well in their exams, they can continue to degree level.

Last year, 752 students sat the LCA and it is estimated that about 2,000 students will complete the programme this year.

## PLC COURSES AS A ROUTE TO THIRD-LEVEL

Almost all school-leavers compete for third-level places on the basis of Leaving Cert points. However, there are other routes to third-level education.

One of the newer options is to progress via the Post-Leaving Certificate (PLC) sector. The main aim of PLC courses is to prepare students directly for employment but a pilot project also links PLC courses with a variety of third-level certificates and diplomas. Each year since 1995, more than 1,000 places have been set aside for students with NCVA level 2 qualifications.

Dr Dermot Douglas, the registrar of Tallaght IT, explains that the advantage of going this route is that it allows you time to find out whether you are suited to a particular discipline. In the meantime, you pick up a useful qualification.

Students who do not get sufficient points in the Leaving Cert can use this route to get to college if they perform sufficiently well at PLC level.

The institutes of technology, other than Dublin Institute of Technology, assess students solely on the basis of their

NCVA qualification. The DIT requires students to possess the minimum Leaving Cert requirements for the particular course. This seems a rather counter-productive approach as it may undermine their achievement at PLC level.

If you intend using this route to third level, you must check that the particular PLC you are interested in links in directly with a third-level course. The NCVA publishes a list of PLC courses along with the corresponding third-level courses (the NCVA can be contacted at 01 853 1910). Some college prospectuses list these courses also. For instance, Tallaght IT has a list of linking PLCs at the back of its prospectus.

Particular modules may be specified as a requirement. For instance, students need to take a mathematical methods module in their NCVA level 2 qualification if they want to study engineering at Tallaght IT. Dr Douglas explains that, without this module, students would not be able to cope with first year.

NCVA students apply through the CAO in the normal way and their results are automatically forwarded to the CAO. You must achieve a full level 2 certificate in order to be considered for admission to third level. Places are awarded on the basis of students' performance – three points for a distinction (80–100 per cent), two for a merit (65–80 per cent) and one for a pass (50–65 per cent).

The DIT calculates a grade point average – total points divided by eight and a minimum grade point average of 2.2 is required. The other colleges simply rank students on the basis of their total scores. There is a slight variation in treatment here, in that some colleges' total points for eight modules only while others allow students to add up points for eight plus modules.

## Post Leaving Certificate courses

NCVA candidates are not competing with Leaving Cert students, as about 1,000 places are reserved for them, but they may have to compete with each other. In fact, not all of these places are taken up and competition only occurs in high-demand courses. Dr Douglas suggests that students maximise their chances by following their choice of courses around the State. It is more difficult to get places in urban colleges, as higher population density means more competition.

In general, if the cut-off points are high for a course – meaning that the course is in demand with school-leavers – there will also be increased demand from NCVA holders.

Dr Douglas says that NCVA students have an advantage in first year as they will already have some background in their chosen area; however, they are competing on an equal footing from second year. 'By and large, these people enter on a focused choice so they tend to progress well,' he says.

## *Add-on degrees*

THINK CERT, DIPLOMA, IF YOU WANT A DEGREE
What, you say? Why look at the certs and diplomas if I want a degree?

That's where the greatest chance of getting a college place lies. And certificates can lead to diplomas to degrees. And certs and diplomas are valid qualifications in their own right. I should know – I have one of each.

The number of add-on degrees has expanded hugely in the past few years. The usual route is via a two-year certificate to a one-year diploma to a one- or two-year add-on degree. Students must achieve certain grades in their exams to progress directly. However, a year's work experience and a pass diploma is equally acceptable.

Here's how it works. Take students who successfully complete a two-year certificate in civil engineering and then achieve a merit in a one-year diploma in any institute of technology. They are now eligible to apply to Sligo Institute of Technology which offers a two-year add-on BEng in civil engineering. The first graduates of this course finished in June 1997 and were conferred in November 1997.

Of the 25 students who graduated, three are now engaged in master's programmes and the remaining 22 are all employed

## Add-on degrees

as civil engineers, according to Mr Jim Hanly, head of the department of civil engineering and construction studies.

The BEng (civil) in Sligo IT is the first recognised civil engineering degree course in the history of the State as the equivalent courses in the traditional university sector were recognised under British administration, says Mr Hanly.

Students climbing the ladder from certificate to diploma to degree are eligible for free fees (the usual conditions apply re repeating, etc) and are also eligible to apply for maintenance grants, whether it takes four or five years to get to degree.

Using the cert/diploma route to a degree may take a little longer but the degrees are the same as ab-initio degrees.

The following is a list of add-on degrees compiled earlier this year. New courses are constantly being added so, by the time you graduate, you can expect lots of additions to the list. The current list gives you some indication of the variety of add-on routes available. These are all full-time add-on options – a number of colleges also offer add-on degrees in a part-time mode.

ATHLONE IT: Bachelor of Business Studies; BA in accounting and finance; BBS in tourism and hospitality management; BA in applied social studies in social care; BDes in multimedia studies; BEng (polymer engineering); BEng (software engineering); BSc in applied chemistry; BSc in toxicology.

The college has a transfer arrangement with Camborne School of Mines, Cornwall, and the University of Portsmouth, for graduates of the diploma in mineral engineering.

CARLOW IT: BSc in industrial biology; BSc is software engineering; Btech in product technology; BBS in services marketing.

There are formal transfer arrangements between Carlow IT and Essex University, England, for the BSc in physical optoelectronics and the BSc in environmental and industrial chemistry

CORK IT: BA degrees in fine arts and applied social studies; BSc in biomedical science offered in conjunction with UCC; BSc in analytical chemistry with quality assurance; BSc in applied physics and instrumentation; BEng in structural engineering; BDes in ceramics.

DUNDALK IT: It is possible to advance from any of the college's four business studies certificates through a diploma to a one-year add-on bachelor of business studies. The college also offers a BSc in commercial computing; BSc in building surveying; BSc in food science; BSc in product design engineering.

DUN LAOGHAIRE IT: It has four add-on degrees: BDes in interactive media; BA in film/video studies; BDes in film/video design and BDes in production design. Applicants who hold a national diploma in design/communications or art (or equivalent) are eligible to apply for these courses.

GALWAY MAYO IT: BBS programme which incorporates a bridging module as an integral part of the course; BSc in furniture technology; BEng in digital and software systems engineering; BSc in software development; BSc in computing in business applications. There are also transfer opportunities into the BTech in manufacturing technology and the BA in hotel and catering management.

# Add-on degrees

LETTERKENNY IT: Students who have completed any one of a number of business-related diplomas and certs can apply for a degree in business studies. An add-on degree option in applied computing is now on offer.

LIMERICK IT: Add-on degrees in fine art (painting, printmaking and sculpture) and design (graphics, fashion and ceramics) are available to holders of an appropriate diploma in art and/or design. An add-on post-graduate diploma for art and design teachers is also available. An add-on BSc in information systems is available to holders of an appropriate national diploma. There are also transfer opportunities into the college's BSc in chartered surveying courses (quantity surveying, valuation surveying, building engineering and management).

SLIGO IT: Offers ten add-on degree options. There are three options in the Bachelor of Business Studies – finance, marketing and management; BSc in computing; BA in fine art; BA in social care; BEng in civil engineering; BSc in quality assurance (open to graduates of computing, science and engineering diplomas); BEng in product development and design (open to graduates of any engineering diploma); BSc in environmental chemistry; BSc in occupational health and safety. There is also a transfer facility into the college's ab-initio degree in environmental science and technology.

TALLAGHT IT: BBS with marketing and languages with options in French, Spanish and German; two other business degrees with options in accounting and management; BSc in computing (information technology); BEng manufacturing engineering; BEng electronic engineering; BSc in applied chemistry; BSc in bioanalytical science.

*Career choice*

TRALEE IT: BBS in business studies in marketing or accountancy; BA in information systems management; BSc in computing; BSc in health and leisure studies; BSc in construction management and facilities management; BSc in analytical science with product/process development. There is a transfer arrangement with the University of Limerick for students who pass the advanced certificate in business studies.

WATERFORD IT: BA degree in the following options – business and financial studies; recreation and leisure; applied social studies in social care; legal and business studies; applied languages. There are BSc degrees in chemistry and quality management, commercial software development and applied biology with quality management. The Btech in computer-aided manufacture is a follow-on to a diploma in manufacturing technology. A new add-on BA in financial services is also on offer.

DUBLIN IT: Most of DIT's degrees are ab-initio, which means that you go directly into the degree programme. But, there is the possibility of transferring from the various diplomas offered by the DIT into these degree programmes. Usually, a student will need a merit of distinction in a relevant programme and they will transfer into year three of a degree. It is possible to transfer from diploma programmes in other colleges into degrees in DIT but DIT's own students will get preference (exception – biomedical sciences).

NATIONAL COLLEGE OF IRELAND: Students who gain a merit or distinction in the college's national certificate in business studies may be considered for a place in the second year of the BA in accounting and human resource management. They may also apply as transfer students to other third-level institutes.

## Arts degrees

What use is an arts degree? This is one of the most frequently asked questions of the college applications season as parents try to steer their children towards more obviously career-orientated courses.

'Why can't she do computing and get a good job at the end of four years?' is a common refrain as parents begin to count the cost of college education. Another frequent remark is that the points for arts are relatively low so it can't be any good.

If you look at the 1997 points table you will see that cut-off points for arts in one large college were 380* (random selection applied) while commerce in the same college registered 430*. However, 361 commerce offers were made and far more arts offers. Points for the $361^{st}$ place in the arts list were 470. So, if there had only been 361 arts places, the cut-off would have been 470.

What does that say to you? Is arts then more useful than commerce? In fact, points tell you nothing about the relative value of a particular course. The cut-off points are simply a function of supply (the number of first-year places) and demand (the number and quality of applicants – as measured in points).

The cut-off level is simply the points achieved by the last person offered a place on the course. As the arts statistics show, everyone else on the course has equal or higher points to the last person who was made an offer – in some cases, substantially higher.

### THE VALUE OF ARTS

Loretta Jennings, careers officer at NUI Maynooth, says parents are often concerned about the subjects their sons and daughters want to study in their arts degree. They want to get the right mix so that a range of jobs is open to the students. But about 40 per cent of employers are looking for graduates of any discipline, she says; they are looking for a trained mind.

Students are far better off doing well in something that they enjoy and coming out as a well-rounded graduate, says Ms Jennings. They can go into areas as diverse as accounting, law, journalism and research, and not necessarily via a conversion course.

A number of students take a modern language because they are good at it and may have spent some time abroad but they don't realise that they will be studying the literature at college, she cautions. These students might find that applied language courses would suit them better, advises Ms Jennings.

Peter Keane, careers officer at NUI Galway, says arts graduates must be prepared to do a top-up vocational qualification. Of course, some arts subjects are more vocationally-orientated than others. Professor Nollaig MacCongail, dean of the college's arts faculty, notes that there are 21 disciplines available in the faculty, including a number of non-traditional subjects like information technology, legal science and social sciences through arts.

Seamus McEvoy, UCC's careers officer, suggests that students who do not have a very clear idea of what they want to do can keep their options open by opting for a general science, business or arts programme. 'What is important is how academically successful they are, whether they can take the responsibility, whether they have any work experience.'

He also mentions the value of a top-up qualification. UCC's most recent graduate survey found that people with higher degrees started on higher salaries. If you invest an extra year, you may come out with £3,000 to £4,000 more in your starting salary.

Arts in UCC, UCD, NUI Galway and NUI Maynooth is offered as a common-entry option on the CAO form, with students choosing their subjects later. In contrast, students opting for TCD's two-subject moderatorship (TR001) apply for places to study particular subjects. Points for two-subject moderatorships in 1997 ranged from 535* for psychology to 305 for Russian and biblical and theological studies. TCD also offers a range of single-honour subjects.

Often, when students think of arts, they focus on the traditional universities. There are a number of other options on offer, so students should study the CAO handbook carefully.

Three colleges better known for their teacher training courses also offer arts options. St Patrick's College, Drumcondra has a three-year BA with first-year options in English, Gaeilge, human development, history, maths, French, geography, bioscience, music and religious studies. Students take three subjects in first year and two in second and third year. Bioscience is a first-year subject only. This degree is linked with DCU.

Mary Immaculate College, Limerick, has a four-year liberal arts programme, which includes English, French, Gaeilge, history, Irish heritage studies, media and communication studies, music, philosophy and religious studies. Students take four subjects in first year and two for the remainder of the programme. Irish heritage studies is a first-year subject only. This degree is awarded by the University of Limerick.

This year, St Angela's College, Sligo, in partnership with NUI Galway, has introduced an arts degree in economics and social studies.

DCU, UL, the institutes of technology and the private colleges offer a variety of certificates, diplomas and degrees encompassing the arts. These programmes include languages, music, language and cultural studies, heritage studies, social studies and folk theatre studies.

## FATE OF 1996 GRADUATES

Slightly more than one-third of 1996 arts and social science graduates (the two categories are grouped together by the Higher Education Authority) were in full-time employment when they were surveyed by the HEA in April 1997.

A further 4.9 per cent were in part-time employment. The single biggest sector of employment for arts and social science graduates in Ireland was insurance, financial, business and commercial computer services.

Unsurprisingly, a substantial proportion (25.5 per cent) of graduates were engaged in further research of academic study, while 7.8 per cent were in teacher-training. Other vocational and training options accounted for 17.5 per cent of the graduates.

The proportion of arts and social science graduate seeking employment fell slightly from five per cent in 1995 to 4.4 per cent in 1996. This compares with an overall graduate unemployment rate of 3.6 per cent. The emigration rate for arts graduates fell from 14.6 per cent in 1995 to 13.0 per cent for 1996 graduates.

## AS GAEILGE

There are eight full-time third-level courses offered through the CAO which are delivered through the medium of Irish. There are also some third-level courses which allow students to study Irish as a subject within a degree programme and others which provide sections of the course through Irish.

The first graduates of DCU's new BSc in airgeadas, ríomhaireacht agus fiontraíocht (finance, computing and enterprise) finished their studies this summer. Good employment prospects are expected by the college.

Galway IT offers a teastas náisiúnta sa staidéar gnó (national certificate in business studies) and Letterkenny IT has a teasta náisiúnta sna córais eolais oifige (national certificate in office information systems). There is an all-Irish bachelor of education on offer in Coláiste Mhuire, Marino, Dublin, which takes in 50 students each year.

## NUI GALWAY

Certain subjects are offered through Irish within the arts, commerce and science degrees. Arts students can take history, geography, economics, maths and French, and, of course, Irish, through Irish. Commerce in NUI Galway has three subjects on offer through Irish – industrial relations, personnel management and economics – while science students can take mathematical physics, applied physics, chemistry, maths and biology through Irish.

At post-graduate level, NUI Galway also has an árd-diplóma i gcumarsáid fheidhmeach – teilifís agus raidió (higher diploma in applied communications – television and radio).

Students interested in pursuing a college course as Gaeilge might be interested in *An Dialann Chumarsáide*, a book which contains a comprehensive section of the third-level courses offered through Irish as well as courses that offer Irish as a subject. (Available from Cumarsaid Publications, 15 Bothar Belgrave, Ráth Maonais, Baile Atha Cliath 6.)

## JOURNALISM

Jobs in journalism are scarce. However, this does not seem to deter students from applying for the two undergraduate courses available through the CAO. The cut-off points for DCU's journalism degree were 460 in 1997 while students needed a minimum of 450 points to secure a place on DIT's degree course.

Another well-travelled route into journalism is via a postgraduate course in DIT, DCU and NUI Galway. These courses are open to graduates of any discipline. A number of Post-Leaving Certificate colleges also offer journalism courses. The NUJ estimates that more than 100 new journalists enter the market each year.

Would-be journalists must expect to work on a freelance basis for a number of years.

## SOME NEW OPTIONS

### German and historical studies

NUI Maynooth's four-year degree in German and historical studies includes one year in Germany. Dr Andrea McTigue, head of the German department, says first year students will study German, historical studies and one other arts subject. They drop this third subject in second year. The following year they leave Maynooth's leafy environs to spend the entire year at a German or Austrian university. In fourth year, they resume their studies in Ireland. Dr McTigue says that graduates of this 'specialised course will be absolutely fluent in German and also good historians'.

# Arts degrees

Students wishing to gain one of the 10 first-year places must apply through the omnibus arts programme.

*National certs in humanities – applied languages, applied language for communication and administration, and languages with heritage studies*
Tallaght IT has three new courses on offer in the humanities area this year. Ms Helen O'Connell, head of the department of languages, explains that all of these courses include modules in computer applications, business studies and marketing. The applied languages course and applied languages for communication and administration have a common first year. The purpose of all three courses is to produce students with a high level of proficiency in both written and spoken skills in two European languages – French and German. The plan is that graduates who want to continue will be able to proceed to a diploma in the future, says Ms O'Connell. It is also hoped that there will be an avenue where they proceed to degree level.

# *Business studies*

Where do you go with a business or commerce degree? The most likely answer is directly into employment.

The Higher Education Authority figures for 1996 business and commerce graduates (degree level) show that the bulk of graduates, 63 per cent, were in full time jobs by April 1997. Almost 30 per cent went on to further study, training or research. Only 2.6 per cent were actively seeking employment. Of those who gained employment in Ireland, 31.5 per cent entered the insurance, financial, business and commercial computer services sector while 30.1 per cent entered this sector overseas.

At certificate level, the pattern is somewhat different with two-thirds of 1996 graduates engaged in further studies. However, 29 per cent entered the labour market directly while 1.9 per cent were seeking employment at the date of the survey.

Slightly more than half of those graduating with a business studies diploma in 1996 were continuing their studies, presumably to degree level, while 38 per cent had entered full-time employment. Almost five per cent were seeking employment.

The dilemma facing most students interested in the business area is which course they should choose. Should they specialise in marketing, accountancy, finance, actuarial studies . . . or should they opt for a more general business studies or commerce programme? They could also combine their business studies with computing or law or a language – and a number of colleges offer international and European business programmes.

## Taking the broad road

If you are unsure which option is for you, a programme which offers a broad approach will allow you time to make up your mind.

For instance, the University of Limerick has a four-year business studies degree which exposes students to a variety of business subjects and some humanities subjects in the first two years. The objective is to give them a very general business background, explains Mary Sweeney, careers officer with UL. You specialise in third and fourth year and also do a work placement.

UL's business studies with a language (French/German/Spanish/Japanese) takes the same general approach. Sweeney notes that opportunities for business graduates have never been better. One factor is the boom in the computer industry which has repercussions right across the board, she explains.

UCC offers a commerce degree which is also very broad. Seamus McEvoy, careers officer with UCC, says it gives people lots of options and a little more exposure to IT than they may get through an arts degree. Traditionally graduates go into areas such as accountancy, and IT consultancy, where firms are looking for someone who understands IT and business, he says.

Professor Seamus Collins, dean of NUI Galway's commerce faculty, says that the first two years of the college's commerce degree are broad-based. 'In the final year, we ask people to select one major area or two minor areas from areas such as accounting, marketing, information systems, human resource management, logistics management, economics, business law (minor option only).'

Careers vary with about one-fifth of students going on to do post-graduate work of an academic nature or a specialised practical course such as information systems, marketing practice, accountancy.

NUI Galway's careers officer, Peter Keane, is concerned at the imbalance in the jobs market with most financial and language companies locating in the Dublin area. 'It hasn't quite transferred to the provinces in anything like the numbers we would like,' he adds.

NUI Galway also offers commerce with languages, which follows the same structure as the commerce degree. In the final year, students specialise in the language plus one other area. Language studies are very practical and related to the business environment rather than literature based as in an arts programme, stresses Professor Collins.

The booming job prospects for commerce graduates are borne out by figures for UCD's commerce and BBLS graduates which show sharply rising levels of employment over the past five years. The proportion of 1996 graduates in employment was 53 per cent, compared to 49.6 per cent of 1995 graduates. Compare this with 43.2 per cent of 1994 graduates, 38.8 per cent of 1993 graduates and 24.2 per cent of 1992 graduates in employment.

TCD's Business, Economics and Social Studies (BESS) degree has a common first year which includes economics, management, political science, sociology, statistics, computing and maths or law. This degree, which provides a broadly-based education, includes an option to study French or

German. TCD also offers direct-entry business programmes with French, German and Russian.

## Direct-entry

There is a vast array of direct-entry business programmes which allow students to specialise immediately in areas such as accounting, marketing, finance or actuarial studies. The following is just a sample of what is on offer. The main thing is to check the subjects offered, as direct-entry programmes can be very confining if you make a mistake. On the other hand, if you know exactly what you want, these programmes offer you the chance to begin specialising from year one.

## Finance at NUI Maynooth

NUI Maynooth's careers officer, Ms Loretta Jennings, says that the college's finance degree is a very popular and successful option. People go into areas such as insurance and stockbroking, she adds. It is not intended as a preparatory course for accountancy – it only gives minor exemptions.

## Accounting

There is now a very strong demand for professional accountants, according to the professional accountancy bodies. Increasingly, the trend is for students to do a third-level qualification and then to study for the accountancy exams. There are exemptions available from some of the accountancy exams for most business studies/commerce qualifications. For instance, DIT's degree in business studies offers good exemptions from the accountancy exams (see chapter on accountant as a career).

Athlone IT is the only college in the Republic which offers full-time accountancy studies up to and including the final examinations of the major professional accountancy bodies, according to Mr John Cusack, head of the school of business, management and general studies. The college's three-year national diploma in professional accounting allows substantial subject exemptions from the professional accountancy bodies. Holders of the national diploma may progress to a one-year degree which prepares them for the final accountancy exams (see chapter on careers in accountancy for further details).

## Actuarial studies

UCD's actuarial studies topped the points table in 1997 with 595* points (* means random selection applied). Six hundred is the maximum possible points attainable for six subjects in the Leaving Cert. However the 595* included UCD's bonus for higher-level maths so it may be slightly inflated for the purposes of comparison. In any case, you needed to be close to genius level to secure a place.

The points required for DCU's financial and actuarial maths programme were a more attainable 520 (see chapter on actuary as a career).

## Marketing

There are a huge number of marketing programmes available. DCU alone offers four international marketing with languages programmes while DIT offers degrees in marketing and administration with marketing (see marketing with languages chapter).

## Cert/diplomas

All regional technical colleges and institutes of technology offer business programmes. These range from the very specialised, such as DIT's retail marketing or meat management programmes, to the general.

## Business studies

Certs and diplomas are complete in themselves; however, most colleges offer add-on diplomas and degrees for those who wish to continue their studies.

### ADD-ON DEGREES

The following is a list of add-on degrees currently available in the business area. Each year, the list grows, so by the time students come to the end of their courses, there may be even more add-on options available:

Athlone IT: Bachelor of Business Studies (BBS); BA in accounting and finance; Carlow IT: BBS in services marketing; Dundalk IT: BBS; Galway/Mayo IT: BBS; Letterkenny IT: BBS; Sligo IT: BBS in finance, marketing and management; Tallaght IT: BBS with marketing and languages with options in French, Spanish and German and two other business degrees with options in accounting and management; Tralee IT: BBS with options in marketing and accountancy; WIT: BA in business and financial studies and a BA in legal and business studies; BA in financial services.

### SOME NEW OFFERINGS:

*Bachelor of Business Studies with German in WIT*
WIT already offers a BBS with French. The four-year BBS with German is a similar degree with students taking their language studies through the four years. The college's BBS degree with a language was designed to give students a broad range of business skills. In third and fourth year, students can specialise in accounting, marketing, human resource management or economics and finance.

## *National cert in business studies and national cert in office information systems*

Carlow IT has received approval from the Department of Education to offer these courses at its Wexford and Kilkenny campuses. The college reports good opportunities for graduates with a business studies certificate – surveys show that almost all of those entering the workforce find employment within six months of graduation. Students who opt for office information systems will do a work placement in year two. The course also includes continental languages.

## *BComm (European)*

UCC is offering five new BComm (European) degree programmes this year – commerce with French, German, Italian, Spanish and Irish. The programmes are designed to ensure students are competent in their chosen language and have a broad business studies foundation. The course has been introduced in response to the growing cultural, economic, and financial integration of Ireland within the European Union. Students (other than those taking Irish) will spend their third year abroad studying in appropriate universities.

'The year abroad will make a tremendous difference to the cultural experience and the level of language that the student would have to achieve,' says Mr Donncha Kavanagh of UCC's department of management and marketing. Students pursuing year three of the BComm (European) degree programme in Irish will spend a period in placement and must also complete and pass a series of projects/reports.

WIT has introduced a BA in Administration. This three year full-time degree course replaces the Institute of Chartered Secretaries and Administrators course and will equip graduates to function as professional administrators in industry, local government, the civil service and higher education.

# Business studies

## BA in economic and social studies

Students spend the first two years in St Angela's College, Sligo, and their final year in NUI Galway, which will award the degree.

In year one, students study economics, political science, sociology and information technology. In second year, they will concentrate on areas such as microeconomics, Irish economic history, classical social thought, modern political thought, techniques of analysis in the social sciences and European politics. And, in their final year, they will study a wider range of disciplines within this general framework.

## Economics and finance at UCD

First year subjects include accounting, mathematics, statistics and introductory economics. In their second year, students will be introduced to the principles of finance, taxation and business law, together with courses in economic theory, introductory econometrics and the Irish economy. In their final year there will be a range of specialised courses in finance, banking, economics and econometrics.

The degree is expected to provide good prospects for those students who want to pursue a career in banking and financial services.

## The B Comm International (Swedish)

Also in UCD, the B Comm international degree has added Swedish to its list of languages. Students now have the option of studying French, German, Spanish, Italian, Irish or Swedish.

Professor Frank Bradley, dean of UCD's faculty of commerce, says that it is one of the most popular degree programmes because 'it appeals to the students who want to maintain both sides to their life – the language, arts and literature as well as the business side'.

The Swedish option has been established in response to the number of Swedish companies which are now based here, explains Professor Bradley. UCD already has links with a number of Swedish universities.

## TCD Business and Chinese/Japanese

Meanwhile, the Orient is beckoning as TCD expands its business with a language programme to include Chinese this year (1998–99) and Japanese next year (1999–2000). The language emphasis is similar to TCD's established business programmes with French, German and Russian (under the BESS umbrella), with language taught for a specific purpose.

Business and language are taught in an integrated manner, explains Patrick McCabe, co-ordinator of the business and languages degree at TCD. 'Language is taught in the context of contemporary culture, society, economy and institutions.'

It will be a tough programme, he admits, with students having no previous exposure to Chinese or Japanese. 'So, we have set fairly stiff entry requirements. We're looking for two Bs at Leaving Cert in languages other than English. This is to signal that students need to be generally interested in language acquisition, enjoy language structure and the technical side of language.'

McCabe says Asia is opening up and is important to a small open economy like Ireland. Chinese will be alternated with Japanese over the coming years. It is hoped that a postgraduate offering in Asian studies or management may be available by the time the first cohort of students graduate with their primary degree.

## Business studies

*Postgraduate option*

Ms Mary Sweeney, careers officer with UL, says that students who are interested in business but do not get the points for a degree, can do another degree and a one year post-graduate qualification. 'Sometimes students think all is lost if they don't get their first choice. It may take a little time but they usually get into the area they want.'

## *Engineering*

College careers officers are reporting huge demand for engineering graduates. This is borne out by the latest graduate surveys. The survey of 1996 graduates, which was carried out on 30 April 1997, provides a fascinating snapshot of how the graduates fared in the marketplace.

Of the civil engineering graduates, 71 per cent of respondents were employed on the date of the survey, while 24 per cent were in further study, training or research and 4.0 per cent were seeking employment.

In other branches of engineering, a similar proportion, 71 per cent, were in employment, 21 per cent went to further study, training or research, while a slightly higher proportion, 4.5 per cent, were seeking work.

At national certificate level, the bulk of the engineering graduates, 64 per cent, went on to further study, while 28 per cent were in full-time employment at the time of the survey and three per cent were seeking employment.

At diploma level, 44 per cent went on to further study – presumably to degree level – while 50 were employed full-time and three per cent were seeking employment. The low proportion of certificate and diploma graduates seeking employment (overall graduate unemployment was 3.6 per cent) is a reflection of the demand for people with these qualifications.

## Engineering

The high proportion of students going on to further study both at certificate and diploma level provides a good illustration of the well-trodden route from cert to diploma to degree.

### COMMON-ENTRY ENGINEERING PROGRAMMES

TCD, UCD and NUI Galway all offer common-entry engineering programmes which allow students time to make up their minds before they opt for a particular specialism.

### DIRECT ENTRY PROGRAMMES

There is a wide variety of direct-entry engineering programmes on offer from electrical to electronic to electromechanical to civil to industrial to food engineering . . . The following is a sample of just some of these programmes. Students with a serious interest in engineering should read the college prospectuses – almost all colleges offer engineering.

### MINERAL ENGINEERING

Athlone IT, which offers the only mineral engineering programme in the Republic, reports good job prospects for students. There are opportunities to transfer to degree programmes in British universities for graduates who reach the required standard in the college's national diploma. Most students progress to degree.

### POLYMER ENGINEERING

Another unique offering from Athlone IT, the college is anxious to recruit students into its degree programme, which offers excellent employment opportunities.

### CHEMICAL ENGINEERING

Cork IT offers the only direct-entry chemical engineering programme in the Republic. Chemical engineering is also available through UCD's common-entry engineering programme while UL offers an industrial engineering programme which includes a fair amount of process engineering.

The job scene is very good for chemical engineers. Ireland has a stable chemical industry and chemical engineers can also find work in a variety of other areas such as food processing, brewing, distilling, oil exploration and waste minimisation.

### Food process engineering

UCC's food process engineering degree is offered jointly by the faculties of engineering and food science and technology. Students will learn about the design and implementation of processes and equipment for the conversion of raw materials into food ingredients and consumer-ready foods.

UCD offers a Bachelor of Agricultural Science in engineering technology which is intended to address a niche in the market between the professional engineer and the food scientist. Candidates apply to UCD's common-entry agriculture degree.

### Mechanical engineering with a language

Ms Mary Sweeney, careers officer in UL, says that there is a huge demand for mechanical engineers. Most manufacturing firms would have mechanical engineering requirements. Last year, the college introduced a new programme – mechanical engineering with a language, which proved very popular with school-leavers. Points soared to 530.

### Management engineering with a language

This is a new engineering programme being offered by NUI Galway this year. An enthusiastic Professor Jim Browne, dean of engineering, explains that management engineers are concerned with the planning, control and evaluation of work pro-

## Engineering

grammes and business processes. Job opportunities exist in the services and manufacturing industry, he says.

All students who begin an engineering degree in the University of Galway this year will do an industrial placement.

# *Science*

Scientifically inclined students need to do their homework when it comes to courses. There is a bewilderingly vast array of courses on offer, from earth sciences to food science to sports science to biotechnology and genetics.

Many students have problems identifying exactly which area they would like to specialise in. Common-entry programmes, such as science/applied science in UCD, NUI Galway, NUI Maynooth, DIT and TCD, afford students an opportunity to sample a number of subjects before they make up their minds. If you opt for a common-entry programme, it is essential to read the college prospectus to find out what subjects are offered.

Of course, if you know exactly what you want, it makes sense to head for a direct-entry programme. The following is just a sample of some of the direct-entry courses on offer.

### APPLIED PHYSIOLOGY AND HEALTH SCIENCE

Carlow IT's national certificate in science (applied physiology and health science) is an increasingly popular course which provides a good foundation for a variety of careers in the health sciences area. Last year, the cut-off points were 380* (* means random selection applied).

The college has produced a list which chronicles the transfer of 1997 graduates into universities in the UK and Northern Ireland. This includes eight students progressing to physiotherapy degrees; ten to occupational therapy; six to radiography; five to speech therapy; four to sports science/medicine, one to pharmacy and two to biomedical science.

## MATERIALS SCIENCE AT UL

UL offers a four-year degree in materials science. Materials studied range from polymers to ceramics to metals, composites, biomaterials and opto-electronic materials. Professor Martin Buggy explains that the main thrust of the course is to understand the structure-property relationships of materials so you can choose the right material for an engineering process.

UL's most recent graduate survey shows 10 of the 19 respondents (1996 graduates) had gained employment by April 1997. A further five graduates were engaged in research work or further study. Three were seeking employment while one graduate was not available for work or study.

## AGRICULTURAL SCIENCE AT UCD

Many urban students assume that agricultural science is aimed at farmers' sons. In fact, more than half of the students are now from non-farm backgrounds and 40 per cent are women. The faculty of agriculture in UCD offers nine specialisms under the umbrella of its agricultural science programme. Students take a common first year and then specialise in animal and crop production, animal science, agribusiness and rural development, agricultural and environmental science, food science, engineering technology, commercial horticulture, landscape horticulture or forestry.

UCD's latest graduate survey shows that 58.4 per cent of agricultural science graduates went directly into full-time employment. One-third of 1996 graduates went on to further study or research work while a low 2.1 per cent were seeking employment at the time of the survey (see chapter on ag science in UCD for more information).

### TOXICOLOGY AT ATHLONE IT

Dr Siobhan Finnegan, head of the school of science at Athlone IT, says the school has two departments – applied biology and applied chemistry. After four years, students can end up with a BSc in applied chemistry or toxicology. Athlone IT is the national centre for toxicology. Students progress via a certificate in applied biology to an add-on diploma in toxicology. And from there, if they do sufficiently well in their exams, they can do an add-on degree. Dr Finnegan says that the graduate unemployment rate is less than five per cent. 'You usually only hear about computer and electronics when it comes to skills shortages. However, there is a skills shortage in the chemistry area,' she says.

### MARINE SCIENCE AT NUI GALWAY

The Martin Ryan Institute in NUI Galway is a state-of-the-art facility devoted to the marine sciences. The college offers a degree in marine science (410* points in 1997. The asterix means random selection applied). Professor Michael Guiry says that 'our marine resources are very poorly developed. We need to build up a level of expertise. We need people out there with a good education who are prepared to work. We need innovators and entrepreneurs. Our aim is to give a good basic training in marine science, basic sciences, ecology and environmental sciences.' There are no ready-made jobs but it is a very exciting area, he says.

### FOOD SCIENCE AT UCC

UCC is the only Irish university which has a full faculty dedicated to food science. The college offers five food-related degrees from science and technology to nutrition, engineering (food process) and business. Professor Charlie Daly says that the science and technology programmes would suit students in biological sciences and their application to food.

Students who opt for DIT's applied science degree can also specialise in food science and technology. UL offers a four-year degree in food technology while students can study food science within UCD's agricultural science programme. At cert/diploma level, there are programmes available in DIT, Dundalk IT, Letterkenny IT and Sligo IT. Students interested in food science should also check common-entry science programmes for food science and related specialisations (see chapter on food science for more information).

## Sports and exercise science, UL

In 1993, UL introduced a four-year degree in sports science and exercise, the only such undergraduate programme in the Republic. Professor Phil Jakeman explains that what they have is 'a young and exciting degree which uses the vehicle of sports and excercise in order to study science'. There are three main strands – physiology, psychology and biomechanics. The multi-disciplinary approach is needed, he explains, as performers are integrated organisms and the various approaches make up a composite picture of how an athlete works or fails. Of the 24 students who graduated in 1997, the majority have gone on to further study. There are 35 places in first year and the cut-off points were 475* in 1997 (see chapter on sport science for more information).

## Applied physics

Professor Tom Glynn, of NUI Galway says excellent employment opportunities await applied physics graduates. These graduates are being 'hoovered out' into the software area, he says. 'Applied physics provides excellent training in a broad range of technical areas, and almost unconsciously, develops excellent computing skills in graduates also,' he adds. NUI Galway offers degrees in applied physics and electronics (with computing options) and experimental physics (with computing options). Students can enter via the common-entry science option or the denominated option.

And still with physics. Dr Norman McMillan of Carlow IT says the college's certificate in applied physics/photonics can be the first step towards a degree. Subject to exam results, students can progress to a diploma in photonics and, from there, they can transfer to the final year of a BSc in physical optoelectronics in Essex University, England. Dr McMillan is concerned that students labour under the perception that physics is extremely difficult. In fact, their course has one of the best pass rates in the country, he says. Carlow IT has produced a video entitled *Careers in photonics* which outlines the possibilities offered by the Carlow IT-Essex University route.

## THE FATE OF 1996 SCIENCE GRADUATES

Almost half of all 1996 science graduates (degree level) had gained full-time employment by April 1997, according to Higher Education Authority statistics. Just over one-third went on to research work or further academic study, while two per cent went into teacher training. The proportion seeking employment at the time of the survey was 3.5 per cent, which compares favourably with an overall graduate unemployment rate of 3.6 per cent.

Surprisingly, the most important sectors of employment for science graduates in Ireland were the insurance, financial, business and commercial computer services sectors (29.5 per cent). These were also the most important employment sectors for arts graduates. The next most important sector for science graduates was the more traditional chemical, pharmaceutical and healthcare sectors (18.6 per cent).

At national certificate level, 28 per cent of graduates went directly into full-time jobs while 62 per cent went on to further study, presumably at diploma level. There were 4.9 per cent of certificate graduates seeking employment at the date of the survey.

At diploma level, 48.9 per cent of graduates went on to further study while 42.5 per cent were employed in full-time jobs. The proportion seeking employment was 4.6 per cent.

### ADD-ON SCIENCE DEGREES:

Eight colleges offer students the opportunity to progress via the certificate/diploma route to degree level in the sciences. These are of equal value to ab-initio degrees and the free fees initiative applies as you progress up the ladder. So, do not write off certificates and diplomas, even if you are only interested in a degree. And, of course, certificates and diplomas are valuable qualifications in their own right.

Athlone IT: BSc in applied chemistry; BSc in toxicology; Carlow RTC: BSc in industrial biology; transfer arrangements with Essex University, England, for a BSc in physical optoelectronics and a BSc in environmental and industrial chemistry. Cork IT: BSc in biomedical science offered in conjunction with UCC; BSc in analytical chemistry with quality assurance; BSc in applied physics and instrumentation; Dundalk IT: BSc in food science; Sligo IT: BSc in quality assurance; BSc in environmental chemistry; BSc in occupational safety and health; transfer arrangement into the colleges ab-initio degree in environmental science and technology; Tallaght IT: BSc in applied chemistry; BSc in bioanalytical science; Tralee IT: BSc in analytical science with product/process development; BSc in health and leisure; WIT: BSc in chemistry and quality management; BSc in applied biology with quality management.

### SOME NEW OFFERINGS:

UCD's new Theoretical Physics course, which will have about 15 first-year places, is the brainchild of the departments of mathematical physics and theoretical physics.

Dr Peter Duffy, of the department of mathematical physics, says that graduates could go into areas as diverse as teaching, financial services or actuarial work. Employers are looking for people who have problem-solving skills in a whole lot of environments, he says.

In first year, students will study mathematical physics, experimental physics, maths and one other subject such as chemistry or computer science. In second year, they will drop this fourth subject. In third and fourth year, they will concentrate on specialist courses, such as astro-physics and nuclear physics. 'There will be a heavy emphasis on problem solving on computer,' says Duffy.

TCD introduced a degree in computational chemistry/computational physics in late 1997. Dr Sara McMurry, senior lecturer in the department of physics at TCD, explains that 'there is an enormous demand for scientists with good numerical and good computational backgrounds. There are very good employment prospects.' In the first two years, students study maths, physics and chemistry from the natural sciences programme. Then, in the final two years, they opt for physics or chemistry.

NUI Galway is bringing in a new degree in biomedical sciences which is essentially a combination of anatomy, physiology and biochemistry with information technology. It is not laboratory sciences and should not be confused with medical lab sciences. Equally it is not a backdoor into medicine. Jean

## Science

Folan-Curran, professor of anatomy, notes that anatomy was traditionally associated with the medical faculty. It is now being offered, in NUI Galway, as a subject within science and biomedical science.

# *Paramedical options*

Paramedical courses exercise a strong fascination on the minds of second-level students, particularly girls.

The number of places available in each career area is usually limited in an attempt to ensure the marketplace is not flooded with graduates. While this is a sensible approach, limited places and huge numbers of applications translate into high points and put the courses firmly in the preserve of the high achievers.

Last year, at degree level, there were six applicants for each pharmacy place, 11 applicants for each physiotherapy place and 6 applications for each other health care place. Physiotherapy, pharmacy and radiography all featured in the list of 21 courses which required more than 525 points. Meanwhile, at certificate/diploma level there were a staggering 30 applicants for each healthcare place.

## MEDICAL LABORATORY SCIENCES

Medical lab sciences is listed among the certificates and diplomas in the CAO handbook, but it is, in effect, a five-year degree course. Almost all students progress via the three-year certificate to the final two years of a biomedical sciences degree. The certificate is no longer recognised by the Department of Health as a valid entry-level qualification to the profession. A degree is now the minimum requirement.

## Paramedical options

Certificates in medical lab sciences are offered by DIT Kevin Street (425 points in 1997 with a higher C in chemistry required); Cork Institute of Technology (460 points in 1997) and Galway RTC (435 points in 1997). The certificate course comprises two years in college and one year in a training hospital.

Follow-on degrees are offered by DIT Kevin Street and CIT in association with UCC and Ulster University. It is also possible to progress from year two of UCC's biological and chemical sciences degrees into the two-year biomedical option offered jointly by CIT and UCC.

Most graduates will find work in hospital diagnostic labs. The first few years employment are likely to be in temporary or locum positions (see chapter on medical lab sciences).

### OPTOMETRY

There is only one course in the Republic which will allow students to qualify as optometrists (probably better known to most people by the old name of optician). It is a degree programme in Dublin Institute of Technology (1997 points: 515*).

There are excellent job prospects. The course includes six months supervised practical work in fourth year. There is also a course in optometry available at the University of Ulster.

### PHARMACY

TCD is the only college in the Republic which offers a pharmacy degree. There are 70 first-year places (1997 points: 545*). Dr Des Corrigan, head of TCD's School of Pharmacy, says that 'there is still a shortage of pharmacists. Although we've increased the intake (there were 50 places previously), it will be another four years before these students come into the jobs market. The situation in community pharmacies is extremely healthy jobs-wise. There is a particular shortage in hospital pharmacies, where they are finding it difficult to recruit basic grade pharmacists.' Dr Corrigan says that is a professionally rewarding career.

The intake into pharmacy, like most other paramedical courses, tends to be predominantly women. Over the past 20 years, we would have up to 70 per cent more females than males, says Dr Corrigan. After four years at TCD, graduates must spend a pre-registration year working before they are qualified as professional pharmacists.

This year, the School of Pharmacy moved from Ballsbridge to a new state-of-the-art building on campus. Based at the Westland Row end of the college, the building comprises four stories of pharmacy laboratories for teaching and research.

Occupational Therapy: Thirty people are taken onto the Occupational therapy course in TCD each year – the only degree programme in the Republic. The University of Ulster, Jordanstown, also offers a course.

Ms Geraldine O'Neill, director of TCD's school of occupational therapy, says that job prospects at home and abroad are very good. 'The degree is well recognised worldwide and they are ready to work in any area when they graduate. A lot go to Australia, America, English-speaking centres . . . in Ireland they get jobs in hospitals, based in physical therapy or psychiatry or in community day-centres.'

Cut-off points were 495 in 1997. Students spend half of third year and all of fourth year in clinical work-experience practice. Throughout the course, 'the key thing is that the person is reflective and a problem solver,' says Ms O'Neill.

### CLINICAL SPEECH AND LANGUAGE

This year TCD will take 26 on to its clinical speech and language degree course (1997 points were 480*) – the only

## Paramedical options

course in the Republic. Ms Margaret Leahy, head of TCD's school of clinical speech and language studies, says that 'there is a very strong demand for clinical speech and language therapists, as people become more aware of what can be done . . . Although there are good job prospects, the pay scale does not go as high as comparable professions.' She says, however, that a pay review has been granted 'so there is optimism about'. From second year, students participate in clinical placements.

The biggest employers of therapists are health and community care centres but therapists are also employed in special schools, hospitals and in private therapy. Since the course began in TCD in 1969 there have been three male graduates. This seems to be a tradition in Ireland whereas the situation in other countries is very different, says Ms Leahy. For students willing to travel, Ulster University also offers a clinical speech degree.

### PSYCHOLOGY

Psychology is another perennial favourite with school-leavers. Students can opt for direct-entry programmes, offered by TCD and UCC, or they can take the common-entry route through programmes such as science and arts. The catch with taking the common-entry route is that places in psychology are limited and you will have to do very well in your first year exams to secure a place.

If you want to work as a professional psychologist you will usually have to do a post-graduate qualification. In fact, many psychology graduates will end up working in other spheres.

### TCD

There are only 31 first-year places on TCD's single-honours psychology programme, so points are usually very high (in

1997 the cut-off was 515*). It is also possible to take psychology within TCD's arts programme but there are only 17 places available on the joint honours course and the points were even higher at 535* in 1997.

## UCC

UCC has 30 first-year places on its direct-entry degree in applied psychology. Last year, 500* points were the minimum needed to secure a place. Students take applied psychology in first year with two other arts subjects. In second and third year, students take a single-honours degree in psychology. 'Studies in psychology' may also be taken as a minor subject through an arts degree.

## UCD

In UCD, psychology is offered under the arts and science umbrellas. Altogether, up to 85 students are taken onto the psychology programme after completing first year – 70 from arts and 15 from science.

Professor Ciarán Benson, head of the college's department of psychology, explains that the university's three year programme provides a good liberal arts education. He says that the degree provides an excellent background for those who go on to work in personnel, research or the arts. Of course, it may also act as the first step on the route to a career in professional psychology. If you go through arts, you end up with a BA in psychology, while if you entered through the science route, you will graduate with a BSc in psychology. Both degrees are equally valid if you wish to become a professional psychologist.

## Paramedical options

### NUI GALWAY

Psychology is offered through arts with students taking psychology as one of their four first-year subjects. There are only 25 places available in second year, so, again, you must compete to secure a place.

### DENTISTRY

While the mere word dentist is enough to fill a large proportion of the population with horror, a substantial number of very bright school-leavers are fascinated. Of course, they want to be on the other side of the dental drill.

Unfortunately for these school-leavers, there is a limited number of first-year places in dental schools in the Republic – about 40 places in TCD and a further 30 in UCC. A number of Irish students usually apply to one of the 16 dental schools in Britain and Northern Ireland.

The limited number of places here and the high demand puts the points levels out of reach of the majority of the school-leavers. Last year, you would have needed 540 points to secure a place in TCD and 520* (* means random selection applied) to get a place in UCC.

Professor Derry Shanley, dean of dental affairs at TCD, says that 'it's a very intense course but people enjoy it. The course is a problem-based learning curriculum. We have moved away from the tradition of lectures. It's self-directed learning. They are given problems and they discuss the answers between themselves.' It is not an alternative to medicine, he warns, it is a very different kind of course and career.

Professor Denis O'Mullane, head of UCC's dental school and hospital, says that the first two years of the degree programme are spent studying basic clinical sciences – anatomy, physiology and biochemistry. The following three years are spent in the dental hospital learning techniques.

'At the end of second year students begin to look at pathology and then, in third year, they get involved in techniques working with phantom heads where they learn to be dextrous . . . Students treat patients for the last two years under supervision,' says Professor O'Mullane.

As for career options, he says that dentists go into general practice, into the health boards, and there are also opportunities in the defence forces, in dental schools and hospitals in Ireland and the UK.

There is a tradition for dental graduates to go the UK to gain experience. These graduates usually return after a few years.

### OTHER DENTAL CAREERS:

TCD offers a one-year certificate course in dental nursing, a two-year diploma course in dental hygiene and a three-year diploma course in dental technology. Applications should be made directly to TCD's admissions office. There are up to 20 places on the certificate course, six on the dental technology programme and a limited number of places open to Leaving Cert students on the dental hygiene course.

At UCC, there is a two-year diploma course in dental hygiene with at least eight places on offer. Applicants to this course must apply to the university's admissions office before Easter.

### DIETETICS AND HUMAN NUTRITION

This is another very popular four-year honours degree, which is run jointly by the Dublin Institute of Technology and TCD. There are 20 to 25 first-year places each year. Under an agreement negotiated in February 1998, the degree is recognised by the American Dietetic Association. It is also recognised in the UK.

## Paramedical options

A survey of past graduates, carried out by Ms Mary Moloney, course tutor at DIT, shows that 56 per cent are employed in the traditional clinical and community area; 17 per cent are in the academic area (teaching or pursuing postgraduate research); 16 per cent are working in the pharmaceutical and food industries and the remaining 11 per cent are dispersed among various other areas.

Some students will end up working in research while others may counsel people on a one-to-one basis. Communications is an important component of the course. In their final year, students spend 12 weeks working on a research project and 26 weeks on a placement in a hospital or community setting. 'So, they are very much eligible to start work when they graduate,' says Mary Moloney (see chapter on dietician).

### PHYSIOTHERAPY

There are between 60 and 80 first-year places in the two colleges in the Republic which offer physiotherapy. Another exceedingly popular course, points in 1997 were 560 in UCD and 530* (random selection applied) in TCD. Both courses are four years in duration and involve a substantial amount of clinical practice.

Students are advised to visit a local general hospital or other area where physiotherapists work to gain an understanding of the work. Physiotherapists usually work in hospitals, the community or in private practice.

Each year, a number of Irish students travel to Britain to study physiotherapy. However, there is also a very strong demand for courses there.

### RADIOGRAPHY

TCD has 12 to 14 first-year places on its therapeutic radiography degree while UCD has a maximum of 20 first-year

## Career choice

places on its diagnostic radiography course. Ulster University has a radiography course which allows students to opt for either specialism (see chapter on radiography).

## Teagasc courses

Agriculture is Ireland's largest single industry. Serving this industry, Teagasc offers full-time residential and non-residential courses in 15 colleges – 11 agricultural and four horticultural.

Courses include general agriculture, horse breeding and training, pig production, poultry production, forestry, farm machinery, production horticulture and leisure horticulture. Interested students should read the chapter in this book on agricultural science in UCD and the chapter on amenity horticulture.

Those unable to attend full-time courses can avail of Teagasc's three-year part-time certificate in farming (general agriculture) which is offered at more than 50 Teagasc centres.

Figures for full-time students in 1997 show a total of 160 students undertaking horticulture courses and 975 doing agriculture courses.

| Horticulture | Student numbers |
|---|---|
| Botanic Gardens | 50 |
| An Grianan | 40 |
| Warrenstown | 40 |
| Kildalton | 30 |

| Agriculture | Student numbers |
|---|---|
| Ballyhaise | 70 |
| Clonakilty | 90 |
| Kildalton | 90 |
| Mellowes | 75 |
| Gurteen | 85 |
| Mountbellew | 105 |
| Multyfarnham | 100 |
| Pallaskenry | 110 |
| Rockwell | 120 |
| St Patricks | 45 |
| Warrenstown | 85 |

TEAGASC MINIMUM ENTRY STANDARDS:
Age: At least 17 years of age on 1 October of year of entry or have completed senior cycle at a second-level school.

Women and agriculture: While farming is traditionally a male-dominated profession, this is changing and women are welcome on all Teagasc courses.

Pre-entry assessment: This may include a written test or interview or both.

## Teagasc courses

### CERTIFICATE IN AGRICULTURE

This is a one-year course offered at the 11 agriculture colleges. Successful graduates may continue in the certificate in farming – general agriculture, the main training programme for young entrants to farming.

### CERTIFICATE IN FARMING – GENERAL AGRICULTURE

Possession of the certificate is essential to obtain some farm development grants. It can be obtained in one of two ways.

College option: A person who has completed the certificate in agriculture can continue for a further two years on work experience on the home farm or another farm under the supervision of the local education officer. He or she undertakes project work and must do at least 12 weeks work experience on a farm other than the home farm. Eighty hours of formal course work on enterprise and financial management are provided at the end of year three.

Local option: This involves part-time course work at the local Teagasc training centre over the three-year period. The work experience, placement, projects and management course are similar to the college option. Apply to the local education officer.

### CERTIFICATE IN FARMING – POULTRY PRODUCTION

This two-year course is offered in Mellows College, Athenry. Those who complete the course may find work as head stock person or manager in a commercial poultry unit or as a poultry technician. Students spend from September to April on course work in the college. The second year is spent on supervised work experience in large-scale commercial poultry units. Students return to college in May and June.

Educational requirements: Students must have satisfactorily completed the certificate in agriculture or have the

Leaving Certificate and satisfactory work experience. The college can assist in arranging work experience in the summer prior to entry.

Apply to the principal of Mellows College.

### Certificate in horse breeding and training

This 15-month course is offered jointly by Kildalton College and Grennan College, Thomastown, Co. Kilkenny. It is designed for students who wish to pursue a career in stud management and young horse training or who wish to establish their own equestrian enterprise.

The first stage is a nine-month college-based course of classroom and practical work in topics such as breeding, nutrition, grassland management, young horse management, horse training, riding, and stud management. The second six-month phase consists of supervised work experience on a stud farm or training yard.

Entry requirements: Certificate in agriculture or Pony Club C or equivalent equestrian experience. Applicants must undergo a written entrance test and a riding test.

Apply to the principal of Kildalton College.

### Certificate in forestry

Forestry covers about eight per cent of the land area of Ireland at present and the Government aims to double this by the year 2030.

Teagasc's two-year forestry certificate is run jointly by Ballyhaise College, which does the course work, and Coillte, which provides the skills training. The course work takes nine months and is interspersed with six months skill training. There is a three-month work experience period in the private forestry sector at the end of the programme.

The course includes the study of botany, soil science, establishment, protection, maintenance, management, harvesting and conservation. Skills training includes planting, fencing, vegetation control, pesticide application, cleaning, shaping, chainsaw handling, pruning.

Past graduates of the course have found work with private forestry contractors, set up their own forestry contracting companies, and worked on their own farm forests. Some students have continued to diploma and degree level in the UK.

Apply to the principal of Ballyhaise college.

### CERTIFICATE IN HORTICULTURE

This one-year course is designed for school-leavers and is offered at four colleges – National Botanic Gardens, An Grianan, Kildalton and Warrenstown.

The course covers the scientific and economic principles underlying horticulture and the application of these principles. Soils, plant identification, production and use are studied. At the Botanic Gardens, the emphasis is on ornamental and leisure horticulture while the other three colleges cover both production and ornamental/leisure horticulture.

Admission is by order of merit on the results of a pre-entry assessment which may be interview or a short written paper or a combination of both.

Apply to the Education Section, Teagasc, 19 Sandymount Avenue, Dublin.

Diploma in horticulture – see chapter on horticulture.

### BASIC HORTICULTURE COURSE

This one-year full-time course is held in Multyfarnham and covers amenity and commercial horticulture. It also includes work experience.

Other courses offered by Teagasc include a diploma in pig management/certificate in farming – pig production at Mellows College. Prospective students must have completed the certificate in agriculture and the Leaving Certificate or have an equivalent standard of education and experience of pig production.

A diploma in operation, maintenance and repair of farm machinery is a follow-on from the certificate in agriculture and is offered at Pallaskenry Agricultural Centre.

A national certificate in agricultural science is offered jointly by Waterford Institute of Technology and Kildalton Agricultural and Horticultural college. It is aimed at people who wish to train for a career as field and laboratory technicians and sales personnel in off-farm agriculture. Apply through the Central Applications Office.

A national certificate in business studies (agri-business) is offered jointly by Galway Institute of Technology and Mountbellow Agricultural college. Apply through the Central Applications Office.

# *FÁS apprenticeships*

Up to 5,000 young people will begin apprenticeships this year. They will embark on the new standards-based apprenticeship, which usually takes four years. If they complete the apprenticeship satisfactorily, they will be awarded the national craft certificate which is recognised internationally.

To become an apprentice, you must first find an employer and then register with FÁS, the body responsible for organising, controlling and monitoring all aspects of apprentice training.

### THE MINIMUM REQUIREMENTS:

*Age: at least 16 years old*
Education: Minimum of grade D in five Junior Certificate subjects. (Increasingly, apprentices have completed their Leaving Certificate and this is the qualification sought by many employers).

If you do not meet the minimum education requirement you can still gain access to an apprenticeship by completing an approved preparatory course and an assessment interview.

People over 23 years of age can become apprentices if they have a minimum of three year's work experience relevant to their chosen occupation. They must also do an assessment interview.

# Career choice

Colour vision tests: must be passed by those wishing to enter the apprenticeships marked with an asterisk below.

The new standards-based apprenticeship applies to the following trades:

| | |
|---|---|
| Agricultural mechanic* | Metal fabricator |
| Aircraft mechanic* | Motor mechanic* |
| Bookbinder* | Originator* |
| Bricklayer | Painter/decorator* |
| Cabinet maker | Plasterer |
| Carpenter/joiner | Plumber |
| Carton maker* | Printer* |
| Construction plant fitter* | Refrigeration craftsperson* |
| Electrician* | Sheet metal worker |
| Fitter* | Toolmaker |
| Floor/wall tiler* | Vehicle body repairer* |
| Heavy vehicle mechanic* | Wood machinist |
| Instrumentation craftsperson* | |

The standards-based apprenticeship consists of seven phases of training both on-the-job with your employer and off-the-job in a FÁS training centre or a college.

FÁS makes every effort to provide off-the-job training in or near the apprentice's normal place of work but if an apprentice has to travel, subsidies for travel and/or accommodation are provided.

Phase one, which is on-the-job, consists of an introduction to apprenticeship, safety, and the world of work as well as introducing the new apprentice to the basic skills required.

Phases two, four and six are off-the-job where the apprentice gets full-time skills training and education and there is also time to put the skills into practice. The duration of the off-the-job phase is usually 40 weeks.

Phases three, five and seven are on-the-job where skills are further developed.

Apprentices are assessed on-the-job in terms of skill, knowledge and attitudes in performing specific tasks to required standards under working conditions. Each task must be carried out successfully. Repeat attempts may be undertaken with the agreement of the supervisor.

Assessment off-the-job is based on exercises and projects together with standardised tests covering practice and theory. Two repeat attempts are permitted.

Apprentices are paid during the four years of training with rates varying with different occupations and employers. The rate usually goes up as the apprentice progresses.

## WOMEN APPRENTICES

Less than two per cent of apprentices are women. However, it is FÁS policy to encourage women into apprenticeships through its bursary scheme for employers who recruit women apprentices. FÁS also offers preparatory training for women which should help them prepare to train and work in a traditionally male environment.

## THE JOBS

Tradespeople may have to work in dirty, oily or noisy conditions. Often they have to work outdoors, but the jobs bring their own reward in terms of job satisfaction. Many of the trades afford people the opportunity to be self-employed or to set up their own businesses.

You should try and spend a little time with a tradesperson before you decide on an apprenticeship, or at least talk to somebody in the trade in which you are interested.

Qualified tradespeople are among the people most in demand at present as the economy booms. Many of the trades are familiar to most people. However, not everyone knows what a fitter, sheet metal worker, or cabinet maker does. The following are brief descriptions of some of the standards-based apprenticeships, based on information supplied by FAS.

Agricultural mechanics repair, overhaul and maintain farm tractors and machinery: Their work may include the repair of agricultural tractors, heavy and light commercial trucks and vans, earth moving track machines, forklift trucks and farm machines such as forage equipment, balers, mowers, crop-sprayers, fertiliser applicators, combine harvesters, tillage and slurry handling equipment.

Agricultural mechanics may find work with garages or large agricultural contracting firms. Firms which deal in garage and factory equipment also recruit agricultural mechanics as their technical sales people and service engineers. The work is usually done in a workshop but there may also be some outdoor work.

Aircraft mechanics maintain light, rotary and large commercial aircraft. They inspect, maintain and repair airframe structures, engines, electronic and avionic systems. The increasing reliance of the aviation industry on computerised flight control and aircraft management systems means that the use of electronic and computer equipment is an important aspect of the aircraft mechanic's work.

Aircraft mechanics usually work at airports, on runways servicing aircraft before takeoff and landing. Work conditions may be noisy and dirty.

Bricklayers are mainly concerned with the laying of brick, hollow concrete blocks and similar building materials, including stone, in the construction of solid and cavity walls, partitions, fireplaces, chimneys, furnaces and other structures. They are usually employed in the building industry or they may be engaged in maintenance work in large industrial undertakings.

Bricklayers work on scaffolding when they are working at high level. They work outdoors and conditions are often dirty and dusty (see chapter in this book on Bricklaying as a career).

Cabinet-makers make and repair wooden furniture such as sideboards, tables, cabinets and chairs. The work includes shaping machined parts by cutting, planing and turning, trimming joints to make them fit neatly and fitting parts together accurately to make a complete unit. Cabinet-makers also apply veneers.

Many cabinet-makers work in a factory environment although some small businesses may be based at home or in a studio. Machinery is used constantly and this can be noisy, dusty and dangerous.

Carpenter/joiners are not confined to working in wood but may also work with metals, plastics and fabrics. They may work in joinery shops where they set out, produce and assemble items such as stairs, doors, windows and built-in furniture. They are also employed in site work where buildings are being constructed. Carpenter/joiners may carry out maintenance of public and private buildings.

The work environment varies – it could be on site, in a workshop or a person's home. It may be necessary to carry heavy equipment and work conditions can be dirty and dusty.

Construction plant fitters are usually employed in the construction and engineering industries. They maintain and repair engine transmissions, hydraulic systems and small plant. They may diagnose and rectify electrical faults and carry out welding and fitting repairs. On sites, the construction plant fitter may have to work in all weathers. The work can be dirty, oily and noisy.

Electricians install and maintain electrical circuits and equipment in plants and buildings. The work involves understanding complex circuits. Work places vary from houses to offices to industrial plants to construction sites.

Fitter's work concerns plant and machinery installation, maintenance and repairs. Broken or worn parts may have to be replaced, adjusted, serviced or checked. Parts may have to be fabricated using machine tools such as lathes, milling machines and grinders. Components may be repaired or fabricated using welding, brazing and soldering. The place of work is usually a factory or workshop but fitters may work on outside sites also. The work can be dirty, oily and noisy.

Heavy vehicle mechanics specialise in work on vehicles such as lorries, buses or trucks. The work may include routine servicings and tuning, replacing components, locating and correcting faults, fitting accessories or overhauling and reconditioning components. As new parts for heavy vehicles are expensive, the emphasis is on repairing rather than replacing worn parts.

Most heavy vehicle mechanics are employed by firms owning fleets of vehicles such as bus companies, haulage firms and electricity boards. The work is usually carried out in garages or workshops but occasional repairs may have to be done at the roadside.

Instrumentation craftspeople are usually employed in large chemical, food processing or textile plants. They maintain and repair instruments such as those used in the measurement and

## FÁS apprenticeships

control of process variables such as temperature, pressure and flow. The work would also involve the mechanical or electrical repair of indicators, controllers, recorders and flow meters.

Instrumentation craftspeople usually work in industrial plants and on construction sites. They may be exposed to cold and damp conditions and may also need to work at heights.

Motor mechanics service, maintain and repair cars and light vehicles. The work may include routine servicings and tuning, replacing components, locating and correcting faults, fitting accessories and overhauling and reconditioning components.

Many motor mechanics are based in garages or workshops but they may have to work in the open also.

Metal fabricators are involved in the forming and joining of semi-finished metal parts. For instance, sheet and plate metal and steel sections are fabricated into boxes, pipes or other shapes to assemble a finished product. Metal fabricators work mainly in factories or workshops with machines and welding and cutting equipment. It can be dirty, hot and noisy work.

Painter/decorators are usually employed by building or painting contractors, public authorities or institutions, or may be self-employed. The work includes the decoration and preservation of new and existing buildings. The work may be indoors or outdoors and can involve working on scaffolding or ladders.

Plasterers apply plaster to interior walls and ceilings to produce a fine finished surface. They may also apply protective coatings of cement, plaster and similar materials to outside building surfaces. Surface preparation may include fastening metal or wooden lathes to hold plaster.

## Career choice

Plasterers are less affected by the weather than most building trades since much of their work is done indoors. However, the work environment is often dirty, dusty and possibly damp.

Plumbers are concerned with the provision of water to buildings and the provision of piped services in buildings including hot and cold water, heating systems, soil and waste disposal systems and specialised piping services for industry. External work may include cladding, pipes and gutters.

Work conditions may be cold, wet and dirty. All plumbers have to work in cramped and uncomfortable positions.

Printers operate printing machines to produce books, brochures, magazines and so on. The use of computers and electronic control systems is now an important aspect of the work. Printers usually work in a factory environment, sometimes with noisy machinery.

Refrigeration craftspeople install, maintain and repair all types of refrigeration and air-conditioning equipment and systems. Think beyond your own fridge at home to items such as display cabinets, deep freezers, cold rooms, refrigerated transport and shop refrigerator. They are generally employed by dealers and contractors engaged in selling and servicing refrigeration equipment. Much of the work is indoors, although it may be necessary at times to work in half-completed buildings, for instance, when installing air conditioning in a new building.

Sheet metalworkers are usually employed by firms manufacturing ventilation equipment, roofings and weatherings, containers, catering and food processing equipment, computer and data communications hardware. They can also be involved in vehicle manufacture. Sheet metal workers work with sheet metal, galvanised steel, stainless, aluminium, copper, etc. They cut and shape the metals by forming, bending, beating or rolling, using manual and CNC machinery. The work is generally in a factory or workshop but may also be on site.

Toolmakers produce and maintain precision tools used in the production of metal, plastic and other materials. The work involves the interpretation of drawings and technical data to machine and assemble jigs, fixtures, mouldings, tools, dies and punches. Toolmakers use lathes, milling machines, drills and spark erosion equipment. The work is mainly indoors – varying from a small production unit to a large factory.

Vehicle body repairers are employed in the motor industry in specialised repair shops. Computerised and electronically controlled systems are now an important aspect of the job. The work involves the assessment of damage and preparation of estimates, panel repair and replacement, body alignment, spray painting and customised alterations. Vehicle body repairers are usually based in garages or workshops which can be oily, dirty and dusty.

Woodmachinists are employed in the furniture and building industries. Those working in the furniture industry cut and machine parts for sideboards, tables, cabinets and chairs. In the building industry, they are normally employed in joinery workshops.

## *CERT courses*

There are more than 42,000 people working in hotels and guesthouses in Ireland – an increase of more than 50 per cent in the past ten years. This phenomenal rate of growth means that tourism is about to overtake agriculture as the single largest industry in the State, according to David Harney, regional chairman of the Irish Hotels Federation.

'As the fastest growing industry in the country, however,' he adds, 'we are currently facing a major skills shortage.'

There is a perception of the tourism industry as offering low paid work with anti-social hours. In November 1996, the IHF, which represents 700 hotels and guesthouses around Ireland, launched the quality employer programme for its members. It outlines a code of practice with standards in place covering all areas of employment, including the recruitment and selection of staff, contracts of employment, training and development and career progression, rostering and the arrangement of working hours. It also sets out conditions of employment and makes recommendations on the provision of benefits including meals, uniforms and pensions.

Hotels and guesthouses complying with the standards are assessed by the IHF and, if successful, are awarded a certificate of accreditation which is subject to an annual review. This certificate will act as an assurance to people seeking employment in the industry, according to the IHF.

# CERT courses

There are a number of ways to enter the industry – starting at entry level and working your way up, training with CERT, or doing a third-level course. The IHF can be contacted at (01) 467 6459.

## CERT

All CERT courses lead to national certificates awarded by the National Tourism Certification Board. CERT training courses are available in 13 hotels and catering colleges and CERT hotel schools throughout the country. All courses are grant-aided and include a period of paid work experience. The grant includes tuition, lunch, a weekly training grant and uniform. These grants apply to CERT courses for chefs, restaurant skills, accommodation assistants, hospitality assistants, bartenders, tourism assistants and receptionists. Some student costs may be required by certain colleges.

Some practical experience of work in hotels, catering or tourism before training is helpful. It will also allow you to find out if a career in tourism is for you. In general, it is desirable, but not essential, to have completed the Leaving Certificate or NCVA level 2. The NCVA level 2 is a post Leaving Certificate qualification so you should look carefully at PLC courses, as these one-year courses can provide a route into CERT training.

*Career choice*

## GENERAL REQUIREMENTS
*(some courses have higher age or educational requirements):*

Age: 17 years by 31 December in year of entry.
Educational standard: Leaving Cert or NCVA level 2 is desirable but not essential.

Reserved places: Places are set aside for NCVA level 2 candidates and for those working in the industry who are nominated by their employers.

Contact: Your guidance counsellor, local FÁS office or CERT for an application form at the beginning of each year.
Preference will be given to candidates with work experience. CERT can be contacted at CERT House, Amiens Street, Dublin 1. Tel: (01) 855 6555.

## CHEF

CERT offers a two-year full-time college course in professional cookery or a part-time training option where you attend college for one day each week.

The course covers all aspects of food preparation, vegetable cookery, preparation of sweets and pastries, kitchen organisation, menu planning, hygiene, food costing, general life skills, new technology and language training.

When you have two years' experience after training, you may apply for CERT's advanced courses for qualified chefs. For those in senior positions, CERT offers a supervisory management programme.

# CERT courses

> **CERT'S CHECKLIST FOR WOULD-BE CHEFS:**
>
> To be a successful chef you should be:
> Creative and imaginative
> Fit and healthy
> Able to deal with finances
> Practical
> Willing to work as part of a team

## Hospitality assistant

As a hospitality assistant you will be trained to be 'multi-skilled' so that you can move easily from one job to another within a hotel, restaurant or guesthouse. The hospitality skills course covers food preparation, restaurant and bar service, office and reception techniques, new technology, accommodation services/housekeeping, lifeskills training, customer relations and hospitality skills, language training, personal and work hygiene and tourism studies.

CERT offers a two-year full-time hospitality skills course in a hotel and catering college. When you have completed the course and have worked for at least one year, you can apply again to CERT for further training.

> **CERT CHECKLIST**
>
> An important part of your job would be customer relations, so you should be:
> Friendly and outgoing
> Adaptable and reliable
> Genuinely caring for people's comfort
> Have a good deal of common sense

## Tourism Assistant

As a tourism assistant you could find work in heritage centres, historical sites, leisure centres, craft centres or information offices. Your job might include giving information, selling crafts, serving tea or coffee or taking bookings for local events.

CERT offers a two-year college course in tourism skills. The course covers tourism studies, tourism retail and service skills, language, visitor information and office skills, customer relations, local guiding skills, heritage interpretation skills and activity/leisure organisation.

### CERT CHECKLIST

Are you
Friendly and outgoing?
Adaptable and reliable?

Do you
Have a good deal of common sense?
Care for other people's comforts?
Have a knowledge of Ireland which you can pass on to visitors?
Have a knowledge of a continental language to Leaving Certificate standard?

In additional to the general CERT requirements you must have at least grade C in a continental language at Leaving Certificate or equivalent.

## Hotel Receptionist

The first person a guest comes in contact with is the receptionist. In addition to greeting guests, a receptionist may also be responsible for guest accounts, cash transactions, advance reservations and switchboard duties.

CERT offers a one-year full-time course at the Tourism College, Killybegs, Co. Donegal as well as a six-month full-time course at a CERT hotel school for those who hold a certificate in secretarial/computer skills.

You must be 18 years of age by 31 December in the year of entry for both courses and have a Leaving Certificate with grade D or higher in five subjects including English and maths. Preference is given to those with continental languages.

The course includes customer relations and salesmanship, hotel organisation, reception and business practice, hotel law, book-keeping and accounts, computer/typing skills, English, European language, speech and deportment.

> ### CERT CHECKLIST
>
> To be a successful receptionist you should:
> Have an outgoing, friendly personality
> Be a good organiser and feel confident dealing with figures
> Be capable of making decisions
> Enjoy dealing with people
> Look and dress smartly
> Be alert and willing to learn new skills
> Be able to handle complaints and compliments
> Have a knowledge of the locality which you can pass on to visitors
> Preferably speak a continental language

Other reception courses are offered by Athlone and Dublin Institutes of Technology.

## RESTAURANT SKILLS

A career in restaurant skills offers plenty of opportunities to move up the ladder, according to CERT. If you start by working as a waiter or waitress, you can follow an advanced course and later you may be chosen to train as a restaurant supervisor or manager.

CERT offers a one-year full-time course in restaurant skills in CERT colleges or a one-year full-time course in combined restaurant and accommodation skills at CERT hotel schools.

The two CERT courses include service of wines and alcoholic beverages, practical food service, customer relations and communications, basic restaurant and bar law, marketing and salesmanship, personal and food hygiene, customer and employee safety, new technology, general life skills training and language training. If you follow the combined course, you will also study professional room maintenance, cleaning equipment and procedures and room service techniques.

### CERT CHECKLIST

To be a successful waiter or waitress you should:
Take pride in your appearance and work
Have a good memory
Have a pleasant outgoing personality
Be trustworthy and reliable
Be active and in good health
Genuinely enjoy dealing with people
Be able to anticipate customer needs

## HOTEL ACCOMMODATION ASSISTANT

The job involves the day to day upkeep of rooms and equipment, service of meals in guest bedrooms and other room services such as laundry facilities.

## CERT courses

CERT offers a one-year full-time course in accommodation skills in Cork Institute of Technology, or a one-year full-time combined restaurant and accommodation skills course at CERT hotel schools.

The course includes professional room maintenance, room service, new technology, guest and employee safety, language training, guest relations, basic law, general life skills training, personal and food hygiene and methods of cleaning and caring for cleaning equipment.

> **CERT CHECKLIST**
>
> To be a successful accommodation assistant you should:
> Take pride in your appearance and your work
> Have a good eye for detail
> Be able to anticipate guests' needs
> Be trustworthy and discreet
> Be active and in good health

### BARTENDER

CERT offers a one-year full-time course in bar skills at a hotel and training college. You could also get a job as a bartender and attend a release course over three years at DIT Mountjoy Square (apply directly to the college) or contact your local Licensed Vintners' Association for details of other part-time or day-release courses in your local area.

The CERT course includes a knowledge of alcoholic and non-alcoholic drinks, bar food, opening and closing tasks, hospitality studies, safety, hygiene and licensing legislation, life skills, dispensing and service of all bar products, new technology, control of stocks and cash, and language training.

Applicants must be 18 years of age by 1 October in the year of entry.

## CERT CHECKLIST

A successful bartender will:
Have a pleasant, friendly personality
Have a good memory
Genuinely like dealing with people
Be versatile
Be physically fit and in good health
Have a neat appearance
Be able to cope with the technicalities of bar work

### HOTEL AND CATERING MANAGEMENT

CERT does not recruit students for college-based management courses so you should apply through the Central Applications Office. Courses range from two-year full-time certificates to four-year full-time degrees.

It is also possible to work as a trainee manger, following the trainee manager development programme. This release course leads to a management qualification which is recognised by CERT and the hotel industry.

## CERT CHECKLIST

To be successful in hotel and catering management, you should:
Be willing to accept responsibility and make decisions
Enjoy dealing with people on a daily basis
Have a good business head and foresight for changing markets
Look and dress smartly
Be physically fit and healthy
Be adaptable, reliable and enjoy a varied lifestyle.

# CERT courses

## THE PLC OPTION

*There are two PLC programmes available from CERT.*
Hotel and catering level 2 covers food preparation, hospitality and accommodation skills, and food and beverage service skills. Optional subjects include food preservation and processing, bedroom and bathroom service, and design and presentation skills.

Tourism level 2 covers tourism awareness, customer relations and a range of tourism-related options such as community-based tourism, rural tourism, tourism and leisure, tourism and travel and tourism, and retail services.

As part of your PLC programme, you will also study communications and one or more general subjects selected from the following options: European language, business calculations, exercise and fitness, tourism awareness, Irish culture and environment, design and presentation skills.

Contact your local PLC college for further details.

## The Defence forces

The usual way to join the army, navy or airforce is to become a cadet, an apprentice or a recruit. Your route of entry to the army will determine your rank after you have completed your training.

After training, cadets receive a commission as an officer. They start off as second lieutenants in the army or air corps or as an ensign in the navy.

Apprentices are trained for a trade as well as receiving military training. All apprenticeships in the defence forces are recognised by FÁS. On completion of training, apprentices can expect to progress upwards through the non-commissioned ranks.

Recruits, after training, are qualified as private soldiers or seamen. They may apply for courses to qualify for promotion to corporal or leading seaman. Recruits taken on in 1994 and 1996 were recruited for a fixed term of five years. A number will be offered the opportunity to extend their service.

In addition to the three methods of entry above, direct entry officers are also taken in to the defence forces from time to time to fill particular appointments which cannot be filled from within. They are usually doctors, engineers, or conductors in the army school of music.

## The Defence forces

### ARMY CADETS

All army cadets do a 21-month training course in the military college in the Curragh, Co. Kildare. There are three stages with the first stage consisting of basic military skills from weapons training to map reading. Physical fitness and leadership skills are developed. In phase two, cadets continue their basic training and tactical and adventure training are undertaken. The final phase includes the study of subjects such as administration, politics, economics, internal security and military law. Cadets also undergo a period of service with an operational unit and a course at the defence force's school of PE.

After commissioning, second lieutenants are posted to units throughout the country. They are encouraged to attend full-time third-level education, usually in NUI Galway. This education is funded and officers return to their units during college breaks.

Each year, about 15 to 30 cadets are recruited with competitions advertised in the national newspapers in the first half of the year. All eligible candidates undergo a preliminary interview. If they pass, they must also undergo a medical examination, a physical fitness examination and a second interview.

*General requirements:*
Age: Not less than 17 and under 22 years of age on 1 October of year of application with extensions for members of the FCA, An Slua Muiri with certain service, serving members of the permanent defence forces with certain service, and holders of third-level degrees.
Minimum height: 5 ft 5 ins.
Education: Minimum of grade C in three higher-level papers and grade D in three ordinary-level papers in a single Leaving

Certificate. Candidates must have a pass in maths or applied maths; Irish or English; a modern European language or Latin or Greek (these subject requirements do not necessarily have to be obtained in a single Leaving Certificate)
    or
a pass in a first year exam in a course leading to a recognised degree from the NUI or institution of similar academic standing
    or
a certificate or diploma with merit or distinction following a course of at least two year's duration, which is recognised by the NCEA.

## AIR CORPS CADETS

The 22-month training course is divided into two stages. The first stage is in the cadet school in the Curragh and takes about seven months. The cadet receives a basic military training including instruction in weapons training, tactical operations, map reading, communication skills and first aid.

The second stage, which takes place in Casement Aerodrome, Baldonnel, consists of elementary, basic and advanced flying training and takes about 15 months.

As with the army cadets, competitions are advertised in the national newspapers in the first half of the year. All eligible candidates undergo a preliminary interview. If they are successful, they are called for a medical and physical fitness test. Subject to the outcome of these assessments, they may be called for a second interview.

*General requirements*
Age: as for army cadets.
Education: as for army cadets.

## The Defence forces

Height: minimum of 5 ft 6 ins and a maximum of 6 ft 2 ins. There are also other limitations such as sitting height and thigh length.

### Naval cadet

There are two types of cadetship offered – executive/seaman officers and engineering officers.

The officers of the executive branch are responsible for the efficient running of a ship's routine and operation. If you want to become a ship's captain, you must train for this branch. The responsibilities of an executive branch officer include watchkeeping, gunnery, weapons systems, helicopter control, boarding operations, navigation and safety.

Executive branch cadets are trained for about two years before being commissioned. The initial training phase (about three months) takes place at the Cadet School in the Curragh. Subsequent training takes place in the naval base, Haulbowline, Co. Cork, and on board ship. Subjects covered include navigation, seamanship, gunnery, leadership and management. Qualified officers may be given an opportunity to do a BSc course in NUI Galway. This course includes oceanography, meteorology, maritime law, marine biology, ecology and management science.

Engineer branch cadets are trained to be responsible for everything which keeps the ship afloat, moving and habitable. This includes the hull and general structures of the ship, its main engines and auxiliary equipment, the main electrical generators, ventilation and heating systems, and the computer systems for communications, navigation and weapons control systems. Cadets undergo a two-year training which includes basic military and naval training at the Curragh and onboard ship. Initial training is shared with the executive cadets but, in second year, the emphasis is on introducing cadets to marine engineering systems and practice. Personnel who are suitably qualified may be given the opportunity to study for a BEng (mechanical) in NUI Galway. Subjects include workshop practice, computing, electrical and electronic systems, machinery and equipment.

*General requirements:*
Age: Not less than 18 years and under 22 years of age on 1 October of the year of application with extensions for members of the FCA, An Slua Muiri and the permanent defence forces, and for holders of third-level degrees.
Education: As for army cadets above.

## ARMY APPRENTICE

Apprentices are required to enlist in the defence forces for 12 years (nine years in the permanent defence force and three in the reserve defence force). Training takes place at the army apprentice school in Naas. The following trades are on offer: carpenter, motor mechanic, fitter (armourer), radio technician, electronic service technician.

Training usually lasts three years and includes military training. On completion of the training course, the apprentice is assigned to an army corps where theoretical and practical training is continued for a further year.

Recruitment is via newspaper advertisement.

*General requirements:*
Age: over 16 and under 19 on 1 September in the year of the competition.
Education: Pass in five subjects in the Junior Certificate to include Irish or English and two of the following subjects: metalwork, materials technology (wood), science, art, technical graphics, technology or equivalent qualification.

# The Defence forces

Radio technician apprentices must have a pass in science and higher-level maths.
Other subjects may be specified for particular trades.

## AIR CORPS APPRENTICE

The air corps services and maintains all of its own aircraft. Again, apprentices are required to enlist for a minimum of 12 years. Training, which takes place at the Air Corps apprentice school in Baldonnel, includes both technical and military training. The apprenticeship is standards-based and takes four years, with alternating phases of off-the-job and on-the-job training. The off-the-job training is carried out in the classroom by qualified military and civilian instructors.

Applications are invited by newspaper advertisement.

*General requirements:*
Age: at least 16 and under 19 on 1 September of the year of the competition.
Education: as for army apprentices above.

## NAVAL APPRENTICES

The navy maintains its ships both at sea and in port. You must enlist for 12 years. Naval apprenticeships are usually available in the following three trades: shipwrights, electrical artificer, engineroom artificer.

A shipwright is responsible for maintaining equipment to keep the ship watertight. This includes all ship's furniture, watertight doors, sinks and showers, inflatable boats and some deck machinery.

Electrical artificers are responsible for all aspects of electrical power on board ship from generation to distribution. Engine room artificers are responsible for the safe and efficient running of the ship's main and auxiliary machinery.

# Career choice

### VACANCIES ARE ADVERTISED

There are two ways to become a naval apprentice. You can apply to join the navy as an apprentice and attend a three-year FÁS standards-based course in Haulbowline. Then you will be posted to the navy and complete your apprenticeship with two to three year's on the job training. Or a serving member of the navy may be selected to train under a FÁS apprenticeship scheme.

The requirements are similar to those for an army apprentice except that the upper age limit for the FAS scheme is 20 years of age.

### ARMY RECRUITS

Recruits are taken into the army as required. In 1997, 400 recruits were taken on for a fixed term of five years in the permanent defence forces, followed by a further seven years in the reserve. At the end of the five years, some of the recruits will be offered the opportunity to stay on in the army.

Army recruits do a 16-week training, during which time they are required to live in barracks. Training covers foot drill, arms drill, fieldcraft, first aid, rifle marksmanship, tactical and physical training. The first three months are a probation period. On successful completion of training, the recruit becomes a two star private. On completion of a further eight-week course, he or she becomes a three-star private and is assigned to a unit. Three-star privates can apply for a variety of courses including courses which will qualify him or her for promotion to non-commissioned officer rank.

*General requirements:*
Age: Between 17 and 21 years with an extension for serving members of the FCA and An Slua Muiri.
Education: sufficient to satisfy the recruiting officer.

# The Defence forces

Height: at least 5 ft 5 ins.
Medical and physical fitness assessments must also be passed. Non-technical private soldiers in the Air Corps are transferred in from the army as required.

## NAVAL RECRUITS

Recruits are taken in as needed and the qualifications for entry are similar to those for the army recruits. Recruits are currently employed for a fixed term of five years in the permanent defence forces, with a further seven years in the reserve.

The initial 16-week training covers basic military training and naval subjects such as seamanship, boat handling, rope work and communications. The first three months is a probationary period. On completion of basic training, the seaman (male or female!) is assigned for further training and subsequent employment onboard ship in one of the following specialisations: seaman gunner, seaman radar plotter, mechanician, communications operator and catering or supply. A seaman can normally apply for courses in a range of areas including a course to qualify for promotion to leading seaman. It is also possible to be promoted to a higher non-commissioned officer rank, dependent on satisfactory service, further training, suitability and the existence of vacancies.

The army, navy and air corps have a range of very specific requirements for each position. The above is a general guideline. Requirements may vary with each competition. For specific requirements contact the Defence Forces Headquarters, Parkgate, Dublin 8.

# Part Two

# Careers

# NURSE

*Caring is what counts*

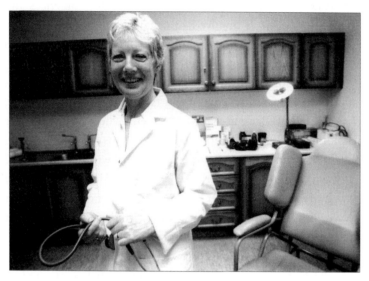

Marian O'Brien talks to Catherine Foley about her work as an occupational health nurse.

## Career choice

Working in a factory rather than a hospital, Marian O'Brien is one of the new breed of nurses. An occupational health nurse, she works in a large pharmaceutical plant, dealing with a workforce of over 300 who must be educated, informed, treated, monitored and kept up to date on all aspects of health and safety practices.

O'Brien must satisfy herself that the workers and any contractors on site are all well and aware of safety practices and regulations. She is involved in organising training sessions, monitoring the work environment and generally available to educate and prevent accidents or sickness occurring.

Today, nurses who want to work in an industrial environment are expected to complete a two-year diploma in safety, health and welfare at work. O'Brien, who completed her diploma in 1991, was among the first groups to graduate from UCD. When she started out in this kind of work in the 1970s, 'it was very much new territory,' she says. 'The emphasis then was more on treatment. If someone had a cut or a bruise, you dealt with it. There wasn't as much emphasis on prevention and education.'

Now, she says, in her role as occupational nurse at Eli Lilly SA, she 'would be involved in the training that is attached to areas such as manual handling, ergonomics, industrial hygiene, risk assessment, emergency planning and first-aid training. I do pre-employment medicals on all the people coming into the company. Also we offer periodic screening to individuals, for example, blood analyses and urine analyses and chest X-rays. We do audiometry tests as well.'

It's a very different type of work to the traditional hospital-based job but there is a growing demand for this kind of nurse, she explains. O'Brien says that more and more nurses are going to find themselves applying for jobs in this area.

Even hospitals are taking on occupational health nurses to look after their own staff.

She admits that she did miss the frenzy and busyness of hospital life in the early days when she started working for Ford in Cork, having trained and worked at the South Infirmary. 'Nowadays,' she says, 'I'm kept so busy, I don't miss it at all.'

As the plant's occupational health services co-ordinator, her day starts at 8.30am at the plant's medical centre. She must liase with all the other management groups on site. 'It's multi-disciplinary,' she says. Working outside the traditional nursing mode, O'Brien says that 'in occupational health, you are really dealing with those who are well, except for the occasional person.'

Part of her brief is to keep an eye on everything. 'We look at the work stations and make sure that the VDUs and chairs are positioned properly.' She recently completed a counselling and psychology certificate course through the Association for Community Counselling, Education and Psychological Training (ACCEPT). 'I would see counselling as part of any occupational nurse's brief,' she adds.

O'Brien believes that the right personality mix for nursing is the same across the board. Nursing is for 'somebody who likes dealing with people, somebody who is compassionate but reasonably strong and able to support people.'

Originally from Mitchelstown, Co. Cork, she has a number of cousins in nursing and for a while she was 'betwixt and between' about what she would do after school but 'once I started nursing, I loved it.' Graduating in 1971, she worked for a while in private nursing in Dublin. Then she returned to the South Infirmary to work as a staff nurse, spending time in the intensive care unit, casualty and X-ray departments. Then she was offered a job with Ford and her career took off in a completely different direction, and she has never looked back.

## Career choice

### CAREER FOCUS: NURSING

Nurse education has now completed the transition from an apprentice-style training to college-associated education. In 1998, there were 1,115 first-year places available. Of these, 754 were on general training programmes, 201 on psychiatric training and 160 in the mental handicap area.

Trainee nurses are no longer part of the hospital workforce but do hospital work as a learning exercise. Their time is divided between college and hospital. Students who complete the three-year programme will be awarded a nursing diploma from the relevant college and will be eligible to register with An Bord Altranais.

They are paid an annual non-means-tested maintenance grant of £3,000, an increase of £500 on previous years. Other expenses, such as uniforms and books, are paid by the health board or hospital.

Educational requirements include Irish, English and another language – essentially the NUI requirements. The recent Price Waterhouse review of the operations of the nursing applications centre recommends a reconsideration of the requirement for Irish and the third language.

Applicants are not given any additional credit for achieving grades in the Leaving Cert above the minimum requirements. Price Waterhouse raises the possibility of a sliding points scale and adopting CAO criteria; however, additional credit may not be given to students who score below 55 per cent at interview. The recommendations, if accepted, are unlikely to come into place for two years.

The current minimum educational requirements are set out in the Fact File (below). Applicants for general and psychiatric nursing sit a written assessment test and those placed highest are subsequently called to interview. The first round of offers should be made to coincide with the first round of

CAO offers. This coincidence with the CAO timetable should mean that students can consider all options simultaneously.

General nursing training has tended to attract more applicants than mental handicap and psychiatric training, according to the Minister for Health and Children, Brian Cowen. Only 91 of the 121 psychiatric places available in 1997 were filled.

Expressing his disappointment at the low levels of applications for these specialisms, he said 'there seems to be a perception that psychiatric nurses will not be required because of the move away from the old mental health institutions.' Mr Cowen spoke of the continuing expansion of community-based psychiatric care services and facilities, and said this presented young people with an opportunity to be part of a branch of nursing which is undergoing exciting change.

'The £30 million development plan for the mental handicap sector would enhance career prospects of nurses and other professionals working with the people with a mental handicap,' he added.

## Nursing Fact File

*Nursing Applications Centre:*
The Nursing Applications Centre which handles applications for general and psychiatric nursing can be contacted at the Office of the Civil Service and Local Appointments Commissions, 1 Lower Grand Canal Street, Dublin 2. Tel: (01) 661 5611

The National Applications Centre – Mental Handicap is at PO Box 3017, Dublin 15. Tel: (01) 821 7266.

*Education requirements:*
Six subjects in the Leaving Certificate (or equivalent examination) to include Irish (not foundation level); English; Maths

(not foundation level); one other language; a lab science subject (chemistry, physics, biology, physics and chemistry, agricultural science) but not home economics (social and scientific); one other subject which may include home economics (social and scientific) but may not include home economics (general). There is also a variety of prohibited subject combinations. Students must obtain a minimum of C3 in higher-level papers in any two of the subject combinations listed above and a minimum of grade D3 in ordinary-level papers in the other four subjects which must be achieved for entry.

Subjects and grades may be accumulated over two sittings of the Leaving Cert. An additional 10 per cent of the interview mark will be awarded to candidates who satisfy the Leaving Cert requirements in one sitting.

### *Schools of general nursing and associated colleges*

| | |
|---|---|
| Adelaide Hospital, Dublin | TCD |
| Beaumont Hospital, Dublin | DCU |
| Bon Secours Hospital, Cork | UCC |
| Cork Voluntary Hospitals, Mercy Hospital | UCC |
| James Connolly Memorial Hospital, Dublin | DCU |
| Letterkenny General Hospital | Letterkenny IT |
| Limerick School of Nursing | UL |
| Mater Misericordiae Hospital, Dublin | UCD |
| Meath Hospital, Dublin | TCD |
| Our Lady of Lourdes Hospital, Drogheda | Dundalk IT |
| Portiuncula Hospital, Ballinasloe | NUI Galway |
| St James's Hospital, Dublin | TCD |
| St Vincent's Hospital, Elm Park, Dublin | UCD |
| Sligo General Hospital through St Angela's, Sligo | NUI Galway |
| Tullamore General Hospital | Athlone IT |
| University College Hospital, Cork | UCC |

| University College Hospital, Galway | NUI Galway |
| Waterford Regional Hospital | WIT |

*Schools of psychiatric nursing and associated colleges*

| Eastern Health Board | DCU |
| Eastern Health Board | TCD |
| Mid Western Health Board | UL |
| North Western Health Board | Letterkenny IT |
| St John of God Hospital, Stillorgan | UCD |
| St Patrick's Hospital, Dublin | TCD |
| St Vincent's Hospital, Fairview | DCU |
| South Eastern Health Board | WIT |
| Southern Health Board | UCC |
| Western Health Board | NUI Galway |

*Schools of mental handicap nursing and associated colleges*

| COPE Foundation, Cork | UCC |
| Cregg House, Sligo via St Angela's, Sligo | NUI Galway |
| Eastern Health Board | DCU |
| Moore Abbey, Monsterevin, Co. Kildare | TCD |
| Stewart's Hospital, Palmerstown | TCD |
| St Joseph's, Clonsilla, Dublin | DCU |
| St Mary's, Drumcar, Co. Louth | Dundalk IT |
| St Vincent's, Lisagry, Limerick | UL |

# Doctor

## *It's all about liking people*

Dr Michael Collins talks to Catherine Foley about his life as a general practitioner.

Forget the romantic image of the doctor as healer and potent love figure. This was never part of the attraction for Michael Collins. 'It's not like that in reality. It's not the most glamorous of lifestyles . . . it's a people-based job, you're dealing with everyday problems.'

Doctors spend most of their days seeing patients over a desk or doing ward rounds, he says. 'People sometimes have the perception that what we do is well paid and prestigious – in many situations it's quite different and these factors should not be the prime motivators for choosing a career in medicine.'

Collins dismisses romantic notions that doctors, like those in *Casualty*, *Peak Practice* and *ER*, save the world and come to the aid of wan and beautiful patients. 'I had a realistic impression of what it was about. The responsibility and the decision-making is a huge part of the job. At the end of the day, half your decision can be pretty weighty and, if you miss something, the responsibility lies with you. Ultimately, that's really what leads to job satisfaction.'

He started taking an interest in medicine when he was studying for his Inter Cert in the Cistercian College in Roscrea, Co. Tipperary. 'Coming from a GP background, I'd a good insight as to what is entailed,' he says. His mother and grandparents were doctors.

Being a GP is 'very challenging and stimulating,' he continues. 'You can never get bored because you're in the front line. You need to be astute and vigilant, even in dealing with what may appear to be pretty straightforward symptoms. Your mind has to be acute. It's like detective work.

'There's a lot of human interaction and you discover you're interested in the person and not just in the patient.'

Today Collins is back home in his birth place in Co. Kildare, working in a busy practice with two other doctors. 'The variety involved is huge,' he says. 'You're dealing with people from the cradle to the grave. You can see a baby in the morning, the next minute you could be seeing a woman in a nursing home, or a pregnant woman or an elderly man who's had a stroke.

'You're not just dealing with their physical problems. You have to deal with physical, social and psychological problems. It's a holistic approach – there's no doubt about that.

'Being kind to people is a very important part of being a GP. You have to treat them with respect and give them time.'

After the Leaving Cert in 1986, he went to UCD the following year to study medicine. There were 109 students in first year. 'Your pre-med year is on campus in UCD. Then, first, second and third-year med are in Earlsfort Terrace. And then you go into fourth and fifth med – they're clinical years and part study and a lot of seeing patients.'

Looking back, he says that 'the academic side is tough enough but it's not tougher than any other course really. It's longer. It takes six years.' But the length, he figures, 'should not be a limiting factor to people who want to go to third level.'

Collins believes that young people, who may be a bit squeamish, should not be put off medicine. 'This is something that is dealt with gradually and in a subtle way,' he says. 'In pre-med, in ordinary biology, your dissections are on dogfish, frogs, locusts, earthworms and sheep heads. It's a pretty gentle, subtle transfer.'

He graduated in 1992. His first job was as an intern in Our Lady's General Hospital in Navan, Co. Meath. 'It's a huge learning curve,' he says. 'Once you start from being an undergraduate, once you come out from being on the ground as an intern, it's a pretty stressful time, probably the most stressful time in a doctor's career. It's the realisation that you now have a responsibility – and the hours are a big stress factor.'

After three months in Navan, he went to the Mater hospital in Dublin for nine months. After that, he did six months in St Luke's hospital in Kilkenny. 'It's a very demanding job and a very good learning job. There's good variety, you get very good exposure and it's very busy.'

After gaining experience in a range of disciplines, Collins went to Galway to complete a three-year programme to become a GP. General practice is now recognised as a specialism, he explains. 'You're working fully. During this period you do six months as a GP and then two year's hospital work and then six months as a GP again. You're called a GP trainee or a GP registrar . . . it's a good system.'

Summing up, he says, 'you need to be patient and even-tempered. You need to be a good listener and empathetic at the same time – and, one more thing. A GP has to be more business aware nowadays as well.'

### CAREER FOCUS:

The most controversial issue in medicine is career structure, according to Dr Geoff Chadwick, director of UCD's centre for medical education. After college, graduates spend one year in an internship in a hospital. Then, the two main avenues are into general practice or a hospital-based career.

There are about 3,000 GPs in the country and the numbers taken into the three-year post-graduate training programme are reasonably well linked with manpower requirements, says Chadwick. The only reservation is that it can be difficult in larger cities to get a GMS list.

'The real problem with manpower is in the hospital sector,' he says. 'There are 3,500 doctors in all grades – about 1,100 are consultants while 2,500 are in training. Typically, it takes 10 to 11 years, after medical school, to be appointed to a consultancy.

'So, most consultants are appointed in their mid- to late-30s . . . if there was to be a perfect balance there would be one trainee for every three consultants, whereas the ratio is one consultant for every 2.5 trainees.'

Doctors in training posts are not permanent members of hospital staff and may have to move frequently. Typically, they may spend up to half their time training abroad.

One-third of hospital posts are held by non-nationals, who are mainly in less desirable posts. In effect, they prop up the service. The 1993 Tierney Report recommended a change in the balance between consultants and trainees and there has been an increase of about 100 new consultancy posts. However, says Chadwick, the number of junior doctors has also increased.

Advice for anyone contemplating a career in medicine? 'It's still a challenging and rewarding career – there are very few unemployed doctors in Ireland. But, there are quite a few doctors in work they don't find satisfying. For every consultant you see in Ireland – and there are examples of consultants making a lot of money – there are at least a dozen doctors sitting in various countries around the world.

'If you want to do medicine, don't expect to spend the rest of your life in Ireland. I graduated in 1978 and there were 11 interns in the hospital. I'm the only one working in Ireland.'

For the undeterred, Dr Philip Kearney of NUI Galway's medical faculty says that the curriculum is being revised throughout the country. Clinical skills are being introduced at an earlier stage.

Traditionally, students would first come into contact with patients about half-way through their six-year education. There has been some criticism of doctors' communication skills. Now, they come into contact with patients much earlier in their education and they also study communication and interview skills.

'This is not the curriculum that their brothers, sisters or parents did,' says Kearney. 'A new shape has been given to it but it's no less demanding.'

In the past, the clinical experience was almost entirely hospital-based. Now, medical schools have professors of general medicine, he says. Students in NUI Galway also do an information technology course.

In common with the other medical schools, a substantial proportion of students in Galway are foreign. 'That enhances the quality of life for the undergraduate students. They learn about other cultures.' Students may also go abroad as volunteers to work in developing countries.

Kearney concludes: 'Medical education is heavy but interesting. It's a challenge.'

## THE ROUTE TO LIFE AS A GP:

If you want to work as a GP, the usual route is via six years in medical school, a one-year hospital internship and then a three-year structured training programme, explains Dermot Folan, director of management services with the Irish College of General Practitioners. Some 54 people are taken into GP training each year.

The three-year training breaks down into two years in hospital rotations – four six-month training posts, in specialisms such as paediatrics and psychiatry which are of relevance to general practice. The third year is spent in a designated training general practice. At the end of the training period, says Folan, doctors sit the ICGP membership exams.

If they are successful, they are eligible to apply for General Medical Services (GMS) posts – these allow them to treat medical card-holders who represent about 40 per cent of the patient population. While most GPs aspire to a partnership or their own practice, many will begin work as locums or assistants, says Folan. He advises would-be GPs to visit their own GP and find out what the work involves. The ICGP, which produces an information pack on a career as a GP, can be contacted at 4–5 Lincoln Place, Dublin 2.

## FACT FILE
*1997–98 cut-off points for medicine:*
TCD:           550
NUI Galway: 540*
UCC:           540*
UCD:           575
RCSI:          535

*random selection applied; not all applicants with these points levels were offered a place

## PLACES IN MEDICAL SCHOOLS:
The Higher Education Authority set a cap on the number of places in medical schools in the Republic in 1978 and this is still in place. There are 300 first-year places for Irish students in the five medical colleges.

UCD:           105
UCC:           55
NUI Galway     55
TCD:           60
RCSI:          25

The actual intake into the five medical schools over the past two years hovered around the 500 mark, as foreign students are also admitted.

### THE ROYAL COLLEGE OF SURGEONS:

is not in the free fees scheme but students are eligible to apply for maintenance grants. RCSI fees are tax-deductible at the standard rate. In addition, five bursaries (covering full fees and a £1,000 bursary) are awarded on the basis of Leaving Cert results and five on the basis of the college's entrance exam.

### BRITAIN AND NORTHERN IRELAND:

Chemistry is a must for students considering medicine in Britain and Northern Ireland. Many British colleges offer medicine as a five-year course only. These colleges do not accept the Leaving Cert as an entry-level qualification. Leaving Cert students must seek out colleges offering six-year courses.

Leaving Cert requirements vary but, typically, four As and two Bs will be required to be considered for a place and specific subject requirements usually apply.

# Social worker

## *It absolutely changed me*

Martin McCormack talks to Catherine Foley about his work as a community care social worker.

## Social worker

Eight years ago, deep in Co. Cavan, Martin McCormack's parents made a decision that was to change all of their lives. 'Nothing could have prepared us for what happened. In hindsight, it absolutely changed me. I was the eldest, I was 15 at the time, going along quite content with what I had.

'Suddenly Mam and Dad had been passed as foster parents,' he recalls, and the family became a foster home for children who needed to be in a happy, secure environment for different periods of time. 'The change was enormous. It absolutely changed me and it changed things at home in a big way.'

'The first week, we got a pre-adoptive baby for six weeks. It was unbelievable. I had no memory of when my brothers and sisters were born, and here we had a baby in the house for the first time. We had the neighbours coming in. The baby was premature, two pounds in weight. My parents were up in the night feeding the baby. It was lovely, and lovely in that the baby was placed for adoption.'

Then the McCormacks got three other children from the one family to foster. 'After a while, one went to another home but we still have one of them with us. We've had children for short periods also. The only way I can describe it is that we just celebrated things as a family.'

At the time McCormack was attending Cavan Vocational School, shuffling a range of career options. Gradually, as he met the individual social workers who had to visit their home and as he became familiar with terms such as 'natural parents' and 'signing consent forms,' he started getting curious about their work.

'I knew I had a good enough personality to work with people. I knew some of the things that could happen to children. I thought I was suited.' He did a four-year degree in social studies at TCD. Through this course, he also gained the necessary professional, internationally recognised, accreditation – the National Qualification in Social Work – when he graduated.

His work placements during the course gave him an insight into the job, he says, such as working in a geriatric hospital, St Phelim's Hospital in Cavan, in the summer after his first year. 'When you're working you soon see that there's a lot more to it than just being caring towards people.'

In second year, he did community care in the Cavan/Monaghan area. In third year, his studies included spending three days a week from September to February at St Vincent's Centre on the Navan Road, Dublin, where he worked with children and adults with learning disabilities. In fourth year, he worked on a neighbourhood youth project in Summerhill Parade, Dublin.

After graduating in 1997, McCormack started work with the Eastern Health Board, where he is a community care social worker. Based in Raheny, Dublin, he works over an area which covers a large part of north Co. Dublin from Kilbarrack to Balbriggan. 'Every day brings a new experience,' he says. 'It's never the same. I could be trying to catch up on paperwork and the next day there could be a crisis.'

A number of high-profile cases in the past few years have helped to highlight the need to protect children and the health boards are responsible for this, he explains.

'A lot of people don't know what child protection is. It's not just removing children from the home or dealing with a crisis situation. There's also a heavy aspect in our work that deals with preventative work. We place a heavy emphasis on the presumption that it's in the children's best interest to remain at home.

'A lot will be crisis situations initially. We are so pushed with resources, we work only with families where children are under 18 and where they are at risk of physical abuse, sexual abuse, neglect, domestic violence, rape, juvenile delinquency, criminal behaviour.'

It's so important, he explains, that people can call on someone for support. 'You never know what situation you're going to be put in. You need somebody who's going to be calm in a crisis, somebody who will be able to ask for supervision, to have confidence in yourself to ask for support – I don't know what I'm doing here, can you give me some help?

'You're not going to change the world but I wouldn't be in the job if I wasn't getting job satisfaction. You're helping families to help themselves. At the end of the period that you've been working with them, you see that the situation has changed for them and you know that the children in that household are going to be safe.'

Ideally, McCormack explains, the social worker needs to unequivocally accept whomever he's dealing with . . . 'you have to treat everybody as you would like to be treated yourself.'

## CAREER FOCUS: SOCIAL WORK

The employment scene for professional social workers is excellent. Robbie Gilligan, head of TCD's social work department, says that it's expected to remain buoyant for the next few years. 'Promotional opportunities, which were a weakness, are opening up and there are good opportunities abroad,' he says. He also points to the attractive starting salary for social workers (see Fact File).

The route to becoming a social worker varies. TCD offers the only undergraduate programme open to school-leavers, which qualifies graduates as professional social workers. This four-year course includes a substantial practical element, with 220 days of fieldwork.

It's very important to make an informed decision when it to comes to choosing social work as a career, says Gilligan. 'If students enjoy voluntary work with people in need, it's likely that they will fit happily into social work.' If an interest in current affairs, working with people or social needs has not surfaced by the time it comes to filling out CAO applications, it may not be the course for you. However, an important safeguard is built into the programme – students may be able to switch tracks after a year or two.

TCD also offers related degrees such as sociology and social policy and the Business Economic and Social Studies programme. However, these courses are not a back door into the social work course, where points are usually higher.

Not everyone who studies social work will end up working as a social worker – the degree provides a good general education, says Gilligan. Graduates have been successful in a variety of other fields.

UCC and UCD both offer three-year social science degrees and students must complete a master's programme to gain the professional social work qualification. Professor Gabriel Kiely of UCD explains that students of the three-year bachelor of social science who wish to do the professional qualification (a two-year master's programme) must take social policy and an introduction to social work in their undergraduate programme.

The master's in social science (social work) is a two-year professional training course with 30 first-year places. The demand for professionally qualified social workers is so high that the number of places was increased from 20, he says.

Students who do not meet the entry requirements may apply for a one-year transition higher diploma in social policy which includes the option to do the introduction to social work. This is open to graduates of all disciplines. 'What we tell students is to do whatever undergraduate programme they wish,' says Kiely. 'There is no preference given to one course over another.'

UCC introduced a transition diploma in social policy in 1997 and the level of interest this year is huge, says Fred Powell, professor of applied social studies. There were more than 100 applicants for 35 places on UCC's masters in social studies this year.

Demand is going up all the time, according to Powell. The implementation of the Childcare Act has generated a huge increase in the labour force so demand for graduates is equally intense. 'The problem at present,' he says, 'is that the colleges can't produce enough qualified social workers to meet the demand.'

As well as the three-year bachelor of social science programme, UCC offers a four-year bachelor of social work, which is open only to mature applicants. The college also offers a related programme – a master's of social science (youth and community work) which is open to social science graduates and other graduates with a year's relevant experience, says Powell.

## An area that welcomes maturity

Social work is an area which welcomes mature applicants more than most. Of its 100 first-year places on the bachelor of social science, UCC earmarks up to 40 places for mature applicants. UCC also offers a bachelor's in social work which is not open to school-leavers.

Professor Fred Powell says that applicants would need to have demonstrated a high level of commitment to social work and be active in a voluntary capacity. Alternatively, they might be employed in a related career such as nursing, teaching or a religious ministry. This is a limited route with 20 places every four years.

UCC also offers a bachelor of social science (youth and community work) which is targeted at community activists of mature years. 'There are many people active in voluntary and community organisations,' says Powell. 'It's a key objective of the department to target that group and to provide them with opportunities to receive education and training.'

In TCD, eight to 10 of the 30 first-year places on the four-year social work degree are reserved for mature applicants. Mature students bring their life experience to the course and their enthusiasm adds a lot, says Robbie Gilligan, head of the social work department.

Of its 150 first-year undergraduate places, UCD reserves about 15 places for mature applicants each year. Both UCD and UCC offer transition diploma courses which are open to graduates of other disciplines. These programmes facilitate transition to master's programmes, which allow students to qualify as professional social workers.

### Fact file

Salary scales: Professionally qualified social worker/medical social worker and psychiatric social worker: £22,151 to £26,620 in seven yearly increments, with additional increment after three years on maximum salary.

There are higher salary scales for senior social workers, head social workers and team leaders. For instance, head medical social worker salary scale goes from £27,193 to £31,725 in six increments. Salary scales supplied by Department of Health.

## Social worker

*1997–98 points for social science/social work courses:*
UCC – social science 415*; UCD – social science 425*; TCD – social work 485; sociology and social policy 450*; BESS – 450*

NQSW (National Qualification in Social Work): The NQSW is the national professional social work qualification awarded on successful completion of recognised courses.

Recognised undergraduate courses: UCC – bachelor in social work (not open to school-leavers); TCD – bachelor in social studies.

Post-graduate courses: UCC – Masters of social work; higher diploma in social work studies. UCD – Master of social science (social work); diploma in applied social studies. From report of the National Validation Body on social work qualifications and training (May 1995 – February 1997).

Useful addresses: Irish Association of Social Workers, 114 Pearse Street, Dublin 2 – phone (01)6774838. The association produces a leaflet explaining the various types of work a social worker may do. The National Validation Body on social work qualifications and training can be contacted at (01) 6766281.

Employment: Social workers may find work in hospitals and clinics, community care teams, child and family centres, probation and welfare service, housing departments, voluntary organisations, counselling services, community development projects and occupational welfare departments. Source: IASW leaflet.

# Radiographer

*You can't lie to children*

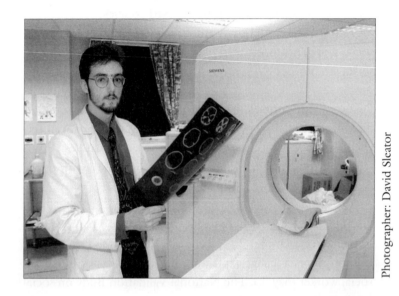

Brendan McCoubrey talks to Catherine Foley about his work as a radiographer.

## Radiographer

Down the corridor a 10-year-old boy rolls along in his wheelchair. He raises an arm to salute a friend. Brendan McCoubrey, a radiographer in Our Lady's Hospital for Sick children, Crumlin, Dublin, smiles back. As the two pass each other, they exchange 'high fives'. The boy, a regular visitor to the hospital, has cerebral palsy.

'I love working with children,' says McCoubrey. 'They're much easier, much nicer to work with. They are very genuine and very honest. They're funny too. They say you can never lie to children and it's very true.'

McCoubrey has been based in the hospital for the past three years. The children and young people who come to the X-ray department can be aged anything from a few hours to 20 years. Cases can vary widely. A teenage boy comes in on a spinal board after a car accident. An X-ray needs to be taken 'to make sure that the spine is not damaged'. Another case is a child who has suffered a cardiac arrest who 'needs a chest X-ray pretty immediately', says McCoubrey.

He leads the way to one of the X-ray rooms. Inside, there is a huge cream-coloured state-of-the-art CT (computerised tomography) machine. Around the walls there are little crayon drawings from the most regular visitors.

The regular visitors to the X-ray department, he explains, include children with cystic fibrosis, scoliosis and cerebral palsy, who have been coming for years. 'You do get to know them and they know the way the system works. We X-ray them on an ongoing basis for years.' McCoubrey loves his work. 'There's great job satisfaction. You get a lot of variety. You keep your hand in at everything. We are rotated around all the different areas.'

A three-month-old baby in a nappy is laid carefully on the X-ray table, its head cradled firmly in a sponge cut-out support cushion. Her crying ceases and the X-ray process is painless and quick. With older children, McCoubrey explains, you must be equally calm and reassuring. The parents are also present.

'It's very much hands-on,' he says. 'We would be involved in bringing the children in and setting them at ease. It's between you, the child and the parents. The child has to stay still and you have to get the best quality film that you can get with the minimum of investigation.

'You must convince them to keep still for the examination. You need common sense. You have to co-ordinate it. Some of the children can be agitated for no reason other than being in a hospital. Some of the long-term patients, even the one-year-olds, would know the ropes and be very content. The X-rays themselves don't hurt, it's just like a photograph.'

McCoubrey is the only male among the 16 radiographers working in Our Lady's Hospital. 'It has been seen in the past as a profession for women, but it's coming on very fast. Lots more men are starting now.'

He chose radiography because he 'didn't want to work at a desk. Pages of the CAO form didn't apply to me. Having a job was a big thing and the variety of the job appealed to me.' The job prospects are still extremely good, he says.

Having completed the Leaving Cert at De La Salle Secondary School in Churchtown, Dublin, in 1991, he was accepted on to UCD's radiography course at the school of diagnostic imaging. 'Very early on, you are sent to a hospital for two or three weeks at a time. I liked the way the training was very practical in its approach.'

He worked in the Meath Hospital, Dublin, which has an X-ray department with up to 40 radiographers. 'I was amazed at how many work in a hospital,' he recalls. 'I'd always thought that only one person worked in radiography.' After qualifying, he spent three months working at the Mater Private Hospital, and then started work at Crumlin.

'I'd recommend it as a career,' he says happily. 'It's nice working with the patients.'

### CAREER FOCUS: RADIOGRAPHY

Radiography is a perennial favourite with school leavers. The number of places on these courses is tailored to the jobs market, so the large numbers of applicants mean the points tend to soar to very high levels.

Last year was no exception. Students interested in a career as a radiographer needed 535 points to get on to UCD's diagnostic imaging course and 515 for TCD's therapeutic radiography course. Ulster University also offers a course in radiography, taking in more students than the Republic's two courses combined.

Students hoping to study at UU need a minimum of four As and four Bs in the Leaving Cert to be in the running. The UU course allows students to opt for either specialism – therapeutic or diagnostic. Both options require a total of 54 weeks' clinical placement throughout the four-year course. Each year, a number of Irish students travel to Britain to study radiography.

TCD, in association with St Luke's Hospital, Rathgar, Dublin, offers a four-year BSc in therapeutic radiography. There are between 12 and 15 first-year places. Therapeutic radiography is one of the main methods used in treating patients with cancer. Both UCD and TCD's course include periods of clinical experience in hospital departments.

Mary Coffey, head of TCD's school of radiography, says that the radiographer is the main contact with the patient during the course of treatment. He or she could be involved in various aspects of patient management. School-leavers interested in therapeutic radiography can contact the school and leave their name. When a sufficient number of enquiries is received, the school will organise a Saturday visit.

UCD has produced a careers leaflet on its diagnostic radiography course. It explains that X-rays are currently used in all body systems to assist diagnosis of patient illness. Most of the work is in the imaging department but the radiographer may also use mobile X-ray equipment in wards, intensive-care units and operating theatres. The range of imaging goes from simple skeletal examinations of body trauma to more complex investigations of organs and blood.

Computers, according to Kate Matthews, head of UCD's school of radiography, have had more impact, perhaps, on radiography than on any other aspect of medicine. Computed tomography combines computers with X-ray imaging to produce cross-sectional and 3D imaging. Other new technologies include magnetic resonance imaging, ultrasound and radionuclide imaging.

The careers leaflet shows three pie charts which detail where the graduates of UCD's course were in 1997. Two years post-graduation, more than 50 per cent of students were in permanent employment with the bulk of the remainder in temporary employment. Six years post graduation, about 50 per cent are employed at radiographer grade with more than one-quarter at a senior grade. Almost half had gained a postgraduate qualification and about one-quarter were pursuing post-graduate qualifications.

There is a worldwide shortage of therapeutic radiographers at the moment and TCD graduates in recent years have not had any difficulty getting employment.

# Radiographer

## A WAY WITH PATIENTS IS ESSENTIAL

So, what do you need to become a radiographer? The obvious answer is sufficient points in the Leaving Cert. However, Mary Coffey of TCD's therapeutic radiography school says that the job would suit 'somebody outgoing, who is able to communicate well and to empathise with people.'

'It's quite a physical job – some people with disabilities might find it difficult so it would be worth their while contacting the school to talk about it. There is a lot of pushing and pulling and lifting heavy weights.'

Kate Matthews, principal of UCD's school of diagnostic imaging, says that the best advice for school-leavers would be to visit an X-ray department. The job can accommodate people with a technical bent and those who are interested in communication and interpersonal relations, she says.

Unlike therapeutic radiography, you are not dealing with people over a long period of time. 'You must be able to establish a good rapport quite quickly. In many instances, you may be in contact with the patient for only 20 minutes.' She also notes that the job is quite physical and you must be able to give the patients physical as well as emotional rapport. While there is a perception that radiography is a woman's career, this is slowly changing.

Students who have visited X-ray departments and are sure that this is the career for them may be interested in contacting the College of Radiographers in London for details of courses in Britain and Northern Ireland. Write to the college at 2, Carriage Row, 183 Eversholt Road, London NW1 1BU, England.

## FACT FILE

*1997 points:*
TCD, therapeutic radiography, 12-15 first-year places – 515.
UCD, diagnostic radiography, maximum of 20 first-year places – 535
UU, minimum of two As and four Bs; 40 first-year places.

*Subject requirements:*
There are also specific subject requirements for each of these courses.
TCD – C in higher-level physics, chemistry, biology or physics/chemistry
UCD – Prospective students are strongly recommended to present physics as their lab science subject
UU – One higher-level science subject, ordinary-level maths and physics and ordinary-level biology or chemistry is required. Many Irish students go to Britain to study radiography as there are a limited number of places here

*Salary scale 1997:*
Qualified radiographers start at an annual salary of £16,460 which rises by 10 annual increments to £21,540.

# Medical Laboratory Sciences

*A huge and very important part of medicine*

Photographer: Paddy Whelan

Helena Reynolds talks to Catherine Foley about her work as a medical laboratory technician.

# Career choice

Arrows to the pathology and then the haematology department lead you down a long, white corridor. Heavy doors swing open and there they are: the medical laboratory technicians, working away in the background, heads down, backs bent, eyes scanning minute slides and test tubes. What do they do all day in their white coats sitting in front of microscopes and other complicated equipment?

'It's amazing how little the public knows about our work,' says Helena Reynolds, who works in the haematology department of St Vincent's General Hospital, Dublin. 'It's kind of in the back room, it doesn't seem to be seen very much but it's such a huge and a very important part of medicine.'

The work is absolutely vital in the running of a hospital, she say. 'Without the lab, there would not be diagnosis, patients could not be treated. It's crucial, especially where patients are extremely ill, where they are in intensive care or post-operative care. They need constant monitoring. The lab plays a huge role in that.'

Reynolds loves her work. 'You feel like you are making a difference, that you have a role to play.'

There on one counter ESR (Erythrocyte Sedimentation Rate) tests are carried out. In another section, she points to the ACL 1,000 (Automated Coagulation Laboratory) analyser – 'this is a huge section of haematology.'

The range of tests carried out in the lab include blood coagulation, full blood counts, diabetic monitoring and the study of blood under the microscope. 'It takes a long time to be familiar with all the different cell morphology types . . . cell size, colour, cell shape and the various granulations. Anything that looks abnormal has to be examined. A blood film has to be fixed and stained in order to be examined under the microscope. Looking at blood films is probably the most skilled part of the job – it's something that requires a lot of expertise.'

## Medical laboratory sciences

Reynolds had no idea what a med lab technician did until she visited the general hospital in Naas, Co. Kildare, as a student at St Mary's College in the town. 'Pat Flynn, the chief medical laboratory technologist, took me through every section and showed me the main procedures in each section. It really opened my eyes to what goes on.' She saw the five different disciplines of haematology, blood transfusion, histology, clinical chemistry and microbiology.

The visit awakened her interest and, as a result, she applied to DIT Kevin Street. 'You have to have honours chemistry for the (certificate in medical laboratory sciences) course and I had that. I was eligible. It was 415 points at the time. First year was a year to bring everybody up to the same level. We did the three science subjects, maths and a language. I did German.'

After three years, students, on successful completion of their exams, go on to study for a diploma in biomedical sciences at DIT and a BSc (applied sciences) degree from TCD. In her final year, Reynolds majored in haematology/blood transfusion. She also spent six months researching her final year project at the University of Uppsala, Sweden.

Reynolds graduated at the top of her class earlier this year. 'It's a very, very tough course. It's hard going. There are long hours as well as the practicals. Most practicals are three hours long. It's definitely not an easy trip to get through but at the same time, it's rewarding when you get to the end, when you have your qualification.

'The more familiar you become with technology and the tests you carry out, the better you are. You have to have your wits about you. You're dealing with people. What you say means you have a huge impact on the treatment that person receives. You see samples all day – you have to remember that what you say is extremely important.'

*Career choice*

### CAREER FOCUS: MEDICAL LABORATORY SCIENCES

The CAO handbook lists medical laboratory sciences as a certificate course but, in effect, the course is a five-year degree. Almost all students progress via the three-year certificate to the final two years of a degree programme. The certificate is a historical legacy and is no longer recognised by the Department of Health for purposes of employment as a medical laboratory technician in centres under its ambit.

A degree is the minimum qualification required so for new entrants, a degree is a must. You should think five years of study, not three. As with all third-level paramedical courses in Ireland, securing a place is no mean feat. In 1997, you would have needed points in the mid-400s range (DIT Kevin Street also has a requirement for a higher-level C in chemistry). First-year places are limited to about 20 in each college.

Although admission is purely points-based, college lecturers advise students to visit a laboratory before they list it on their CAO form. Even better, try for some work experience and find out what the job is really like. A number of hospitals offer Transition Year work experience programmes.

The certificate courses in the three colleges – Cork IT, Galway IT and DIT – follow the same basic structure. Students spend the first two years in college and the third year in a designated hospital lab. Colm O'Rourke, lecturer in DIT Kevin Street, explains that first year students will study the basic sciences – biology, chemistry, physics, maths – and a language (French/German in DIT).

In second year, they will begin to branch into areas such as biochemistry, physiology, applied physics and instrumentation, the medical lab sciences and statistics and computing. Third year is spent in designated teaching labs. Students will spend some time in each of the major specialisms –

haematology, clinical chemistry, transfusion, histology and microbiology.

Eamon Wall of Cork IT says that this programme is quite structured with students completing methodology projects and a library dissertation. They are also graded in each department and sit an exam in biomedical sciences at the end of the year. Third-year students are paid a training grant by the Department of Health for this year.

Then it's back from the lab to college for more study. Richard Delaney, lecturer in Galway IT, says that progression to the degree is automatic. Graduates of Galway IT's certificate compete on an equal basis for places on the degree programmes in DIT Kevin Street and Cork IT (which offers the programme conjointly with UCC). Each year, some students also go to Ulster University to complete the degree there.

Eamon Wall explains that the Cork IT degree is run conjointly with UCC and students attend lectures on both campuses. The degree itself is awarded by the National University of Ireland. There is a certain element of specialisation in the degree, he says.

In DIT Kevin Street, students select a specialist option as their major subject. They must also undertake a second specialist discipline as a minor subject. The specialist programmes include cellular pathology, clinical chemistry, clinical immunology, haematology/blood transfusion science, and medical microbiology. Final-year students must also complete a research project.

DIT Kevin Street has just introduced a taught master's programme in molecular pathology. This consists of two year's block release study and a project. Students can choose between specialist modules.

# Career choice

SALARIES ARE GOOD, BUT THE WAIT IS LONG

There are about 1,100 members of the Association of Medical Laboratory Sciences which represents 90 to 95 per cent of medical lab technicians and technologists in the Republic. As can be seen from the Fact File, starting annual salaries are good at almost £17,000. However, progress up to the maximum of almost £26,000 is slow and as medical lab science is a relatively young profession, opportunities for promotion may not be as plentiful as most basic grades would wish.

With the advent of the degree, career opportunities have broadened somewhat. A careers leaflet produced by the Academy of Medical Laboratory Sciences lists career opportunities in diagnostic labs in hospitals, blood transfusion service, virus reference labs, university research labs, veterinary labs, the pharmaceutical industry, public health labs, food industry and research institutes.

The reality is that most graduates will find work in diagnostic labs in hospitals. 'To work as a medical laboratory scientist in a modern hospital laboratory requires a knowledge of the pathology of disease and its investigation. It also commands an expertise in advanced forms of technology and computer literacy,' according to the Academy.

The hospital lab is divided into specialisms such as haematology, blood transfusion, histology, cytology, microbiology, immunology, and clinical chemistry.

The job scene is reasonable. Most graduates will first find employment in locum or temporary positions and it may take up to four years to secure permanent employment.

# Medical laboratory sciences

## FACT FILE

1997–98 cut-off points:
Certificate in medical lab sciences
Cork IT: 465
Galway IT: 435
DIT: 440

### FOLLOW-ON DEGREES

Offered by DIT Kevin Street and Cork IT/UCC. Galway IT offers med lab sciences to cert level only but graduates compete for degree places on an equal basis with cert graduates from the other two colleges. Ulster University also offers a degree in biomedical sciences and some cert students will transfer on to this programme.

It is possible for students of UCC's biological and chemical sciences degree to progress from year two of their degree into the biomedical option.

### LEAVING CERT SUBJECT REQUIREMENTS:

DIT requires ordinary-level maths and a higher-level C in chemistry. Cork, Galway and Mayo ITs require an ordinary-level D in a science subject.

### ANNUAL SALARIES:

Medical lab technician: £16,926 to £25,093 in 14 increments. An additional long-service increment brings the maximum to £25,595.

Senior medical lab technician: £22,442 to £26,238 in six increments.

Medical lab technologist: £24,158 to £30,261 in seven increments.

Chief 1: £26,786 to £35,745 in nine increments.
Chief 2: £28,730 to £37,724 in nine increments

*Career choice*

PROFESSIONAL BODY:
Academy of Medical Laboratory Science, 31, Old Kilmainham, Dublin 8. Phone (01) 677 5602.

# DIETICIAN

*A divinely inspired decision*

Mary Healy talks to Catherine Foley about her life and work as a dietician.

# Career choice

Her decision to become a dietician was 'divinely inspired', jokes Mary Healy. She may be exaggerating, but she still laughs at her own good fortune. She loves her work.

Healy is employed as a dietician at Cork University Hospital. Working in a busy regional hospital as a dietician is a satisfying, rewarding job. Directing patients back towards a healthier diet 'can be life-changing for them', she says.

'The patient-contact, that's definitely what I like most, seeing that you can make a difference. It's often a whole lifestyle change . . . there's a sense of satisfaction there.'

First and foremost, Healy is a scientist. But on top of having a definite interest in science, she explains that 'you have to be a communicator. You have to be interested in people. And you have to want to work in a hospital, that's a relatively obvious one.'

Listing off other important attributes, she says 'common sense is necessary'. She says, 'you have to be practical because all the theory is all well and good but it's about putting it into practice. And you are trying to make dietary changes. You have to be organised.'

Mary Healy is from Kanturk, Co. Cork. She went to the Convent of Mercy school there. 'I was always very interested in science. I always loved chemistry and biology at school but there was no astounding call to dietetics.'

She decided to give herself a chance to discover what her options were and so she signed on for a BSc hons at UCC. By third year, she had narrowed the field down and knew that dietetics was the discipline she wanted to pursue.

'I explored the different options that were open to me,' she recalls. The career guidance available at UCC was particularly valuable, she says.

In first year at university, she studied maths methodology, physics, chemistry and biology. In second year, she took nutrition, microbiology and biochemistry. 'Definitely nutrition was the most interesting. But I really liked microbiology as well.'

In third year, she took biochemistry and nutrition and in fourth year she studied nutrition. Although the degree is very much geared towards research and industry, Healy found her area of interest leaned away from the laboratory work. 'My colleagues took different routes to me. I decided to do a postgrad diploma in dietetics,' she says.

As a dietician, the route she took 'is definitely longer but it suited me quite well'. After graduation, Healy went to Glasgow's Caledonian University for two years. This included six months practical training at Belfast's Royal Victoria Hospital. There were eight in the class, including Healy and one girl from Co. Donegal.

Belfast 'was a great experience. It's a very large hospital. I was there with three more students. They have a very large dietician department. They have a staff of about ten dieticians. I'm one of five here in Cork. It's extremely practical – you're putting it all into practice.'

After Belfast she moved back to Cork and, after a few locums in some of the city's hospitals, she says, 'I was very lucky. I got a job here in November 1995. It's great'.

Today she works in the cardiology area. Her case load can include heart attack patients and diabetes and gastro-enterology patients. In spite of some misconceptions about what dieticians do, she explains that 'not only do I see patients about weight reduction, but I also see patients about increasing weight', such as those who need building up after surgery.

Her interest in the science of nutrition is as strong as ever. 'It's an area that is ever expanding,' she says. 'It's always busy.'

## Career choice

CAREER FOCUS:
Only one undergraduate course in the Republic provides the appropriate qualification to work as a dietician. Run conjointly by DIT Kevin Street and TCD, it is listed under DIT in the CAO handbook. Students attend lectures in both colleges and receive an honours diploma from DIT and an honours degree from TCD.

In common with other paramedical courses, human nutrition is much sought-after with a cut-off of 480* in 1997. There are about 20 to 25 first-year places and a small number are allocated to mature students.

DIT course tutor Mary Moloney says: 'The aims of the course are to provide an integrated undergraduate training in the science of nutrition and dietetics and to apply this training to the human being at an individual level and a community level. Graduates are also eligible to work in the food and pharmaceutical industries.'

The four-and-a-half year course includes six months practical training in a clinical setting. Students complete six placements in these six months. They are based in teaching hospitals in Dublin and they spend time in other hospitals and community settings around the country.

On the academic side, the first-year basic science courses are common with DIT's biomedical science students. Students also study communications, a foreign language, and food studies. Communications is studied throughout the course and students also take computer studies.

Students are first introduced to nutrition and dietetics in second year. These key subjects are supplemented by other sciences, such as microbiology, physiology and biochemistry.

Moloney says there is no unemployment among graduates but a lot of students go to Britain for their first job and return home after gaining some experience. 'In the past week, I've

*Dietician*

had half a dozen employers in Britain desperately looking for our graduates.' Graduates of the DIT/TCD course are eligible to apply for State registration in Britain.

Last year, a reciprocity agreement was signed with the American Dietetic Association which means that graduates are now recognised in the US. There is only one other country in Europe with a similar agreement, says Moloney. It opens doors to very interesting posts, she adds.

Moloney conducted a survey of graduate destinations in 1996. This survey, which covered the preceding 10 years of graduates, found that 56 per cent are employed in the clinical and community areas (the traditional areas of employment), with 17 per cent in the academic area (teaching and post-graduate research), 16 per cent in the pharmaceutical and food industries and 11 per cent dispersed among various other areas. Nobody was unemployed. Industry is quite attractive to graduates, she notes, usually offering higher salaries and fringe benefits.

More posts in the community and health promotion areas have been created recently, says Moloney. The proportion of students opting for post-graduate studies is also increasing.

## ULSTER UNIVERSITY OPTION:

There is strong competition for the University of Ulster's 30 first-year places on the BSc (hons) human nutrition. There were 393 applicants in 1996 for this four-year course. In addition to school leavers who apply through UCAS, the British central applications body, there is also some transfer provision (usually into year two) for students of relevant higher national diploma courses or courses in ITs in the Republic. This is at the discretion of the course committee.

For those lucky enough to secure a place on the course, there is a choice between two options leading to a BSc in human nutrition with a diploma in industrial studies or a BSc in human nutrition with eligibility for state registration in dietetics. The decision on which option to take is made at the beginning of second year.

The common first year includes science foundation modules as well as an introduction to management and sociology. Elements of nutrition, biochemistry and statistics are taught in all years. Students carry out an individual research project in fourth year.

The taught modules are almost the same for both course options. It is the placement which makes the difference. Dietetics students undertake six weeks' practical catering experience between second and third year and a 28-week clinical dietetics placement at an approved training hospital.

Nutrition students undertake a 48-week placement in third year. This may be spent in the food industry, nutrition research or in health promotion.

## FACT FILE

*Full-time undergraduate courses:*
DIT Kevin Street and TCD jointly offer a four-and-a-half year course in human nutrition and dietetics. Graduates are awarded a DIT diploma and a TCD degree.

The University of Ulster offers a four-year degree in human nutrition specialising in the industrial or clinical areas.

## ENTRY REQUIREMENTS:

DIT: The cut-off points in 1997–98 were 480* (random selection applied). Special subject requirement: C3 in higher-level chemistry.

UU: Minimum of one B and five Cs in the Leaving Cert including at least one higher-level science subject.

## *Dietician*

### NUTRITIONAL SCIENCE IN UCC:

UCC offers a nutritional science degree which trains nutritionists for the food and healthcare industries, mainly in research and development, quality research and consumer education. Graduates of this course who wish to work in clinical dietetics can then apply for an 18-month post-graduate course in UU or in a number of British colleges.

### BRITISH COLLEGES:

A number of British colleges offer courses in human nutrition which provide state registration in dietetics. Most of these colleges have specific subject requirements. Your guidance counsellor will have a copy of the official UCAS guide to university and college entrance in the UK.

### ANNUAL SALARIES:

| | |
|---|---|
| Dietician: | £17,835 to £23,659 |
| Senior dietician: | £20,513 to £25,259 |
| Principal 11: | £22,598 to £27,113 |
| Principal 1: | £23,847 to £28,988 |

# Food science

## *Creating new tastes*

Kate O'Donovan, research and development manager, talks to Catherine Foley.

# Food science

There are delicious smells coming from the kitchen-cum-laboratory area. Kate O'Donovan is in the inner sanctum, creating a new taste.

The ingredients that she may decide to add to this top-secret recipe are at her finger tips. Soya sauce, paprika, onions, herbs, garlic and spices are all ranged around. Aromas fill the air. Every new element to the mix is carefully measured and annotated. This is the research and development department of AllinAll Ingredients in Dublin. It is a laboratory where mouth-watering concoctions are made to specific, scientific calculations.

Kate O'Donovan, from Bishopstown in Cork city, is in the process of creating a new product or blend. She works in a company which supplies the food industry with new tastes, sauces, glazes and recipes.

'You really have to have a science background. That knowledge and a language also is a great bonus. I use French now, it's very helpful. We have to bring in spices, herbs . . . from all over the world. We deal with people from Japan. Ireland is getting so much into export, most people in industry will use another language.'

Her job involves working on different aspects in the development of new products, such as making a new type of crumb or adding value to meat products, developing new flavours, glazes, marinades. She is also involved in providing technical support to sales people in the food industry.

'All the industries are consumer lead, in every industry now there's a Research & Department department. It's a necessity now, it's not an luxury any more. A lot of industries would depend on suppliers to give them that bit of extra support in the area of R&D or technical area . . . we supply them with either a straightforward product or a blend.'

## Career choice

'My job would be to decide what ingredients to blend together to put into the final product,' she continues.

As to her background, O'Donovan points to the importance of the science subjects she studied at school. 'I built on the subjects I was good at. I always liked science. I was far stronger on science, maybe it was because I was from an engineering family. I always liked maths problems as well, I preferred them to writing essays. Maths was the strongest of all my subjects. I didn't come from a farming background,' she adds.

Having completed her schooling at the Convent of Mercy in Clonakilty, Co. Cork in 1988, she went on to the Food Science and Technology Department of UCC to study for a diploma in meat science.

After completing this course, O'Donovan went on to do a BSc in Food Business. 'It was very much an all-round degree,' she explains. 'The first two years (in the diploma programme) were very technical and based on meat science.' Her degree was, she recalls, 'a very good base for R&D'.

Her final year project involved developing a product for the market place. 'The projects are very realistic,' she offers. 'You have to go out and get the prices for products.' Four students worked on the project, doing market research, developing, financing, and producing it. 'It involved knowing how you are going to sell it. We did a low fat sausage replacing pork fat with a more healthy fat. We used the processing hall in the Food Science Department in UCC. They will allow you to replicate what's in industry.' In particular, she mentions the vital industrial perspective supplied by Eddie Twomey, owner of the Clonakilty Black Pudding Co., 'who was a great help'. The project won the IDA's Student Enterprise South West Regional Award.

After graduating from UCC, she moved to UCD to do a masters in marketing. This, she says, was a tough year but very useful. After completing this course, she started work in Anglo Irish Beef Processors (AIBP) in Rathkeale. After about a year she moved to Irish Country Meats, a division of Avonmore and worked in the R&D division for two years. Here, she says, 'I would have had a lot more to do with the area of production, I was more geared to the marketing,' she explains. 'I had to see all those products right through to sale.'

The move to her current job has, she says, given her 'a wider focus. I'm dealing with all industries here, meat, dairy, vegetarian.'

## CAREER FOCUS: FOOD SCIENCE

The only Irish university to have a full faculty dedicated to food science is UCC and Professor Charlie Daly is enthusiastic about the future for its graduates. Job take-up among the college's graduates is very strong, he says.

There are 40 full-time staff members in UCC's food science faculty, 100 contract research scientists and 250 postgraduate students. Research brings in about £4.5 million a year, says Daly. A new research building was opened in 1994 and the college has an extensive food-processing hall, which Daly describes as a major resource. The college offers five food-related degrees from science and technology to nutrition, engineering and business.

'Students have to be interested in food in the broadest sense,' says Daly. 'They must be challenged by and attracted to food.' The science and technology programmes would suit students interested in biological sciences and their application to food. 'They will understand food as a living system, safety issues . . . all of the programmes look forward to the consumer.' Consumer issues encompass sensory aspects such as taste, smell and visual presentation. We have moved on from 20 or 30 years ago when we were looking at how to process food, says Daly.

'Since the 1920s, our graduates have been going out into industry. We have a very close interaction with industry . . . we also place a major emphasis on work placement. It's an essential element in getting students to understand industry, the working environment and helping them to develop their skills.'

Students who opt for DIT Kevin Street's applied science degree can specialise in food science and technology. There is a heavy emphasis on chemistry and the physical sciences, according to course director John McEvoy.

In year one, students take chemistry, physics and maths. In year two, they drop maths and in year three they take chemical and biological sciences. The final year is devoted to food science and technology. This last year covers four areas – food chemistry, food processing, human nutrition and food microbiology. Graduates of the degree will be particularly strong in the physical sciences – food chemistry and processing.

At the end of the four-year degree, students spend six months on project work – most are placed abroad with prestigious companies, say McEvoy. The placement gives them great confidence, he adds.

Graduates may find work in the food or pharmaceutical industry. They usually go in at basic technical level – production, quality control or product development. From there, they may become managers, food engineers, sensory analysts, food microbiologists, nutritionists, or they may diversify into areas such as product development or marketing.

DIT Kevin Street also offers a one-year graduate diploma in food science and technology. This is aimed at students who have a three-year science course in any discipline and is of honours degree standard, says McEvoy. However, this course is being phased out and the college will actively seek an alternative conversion course.

Students interested in food science may not automatically think of agricultural science in UCD. But it's one of the nine specialisms offered under agricultural science. The first-year syllabus is common and students then specialise in areas as diverse as animal and crop production, commercial horticulture, engineering technology, agribusiness and rural development and food science. The advantage of going via this or any other common-entry programme is that students have more time to make up their minds as to what specialism will best suit them.

UL offers a four-year degree in food technology which includes an industrial placement. The first year and a half concentrates on basic sciences – biology and microbiology, maths, chemistry and physics – together with some introductory food technology. The third and fourth years constitute the professional part of the academic programme – food technology with biochemistry, microbiology, process engineering and agribusiness. Students can specialise in fourth year in topics such as advanced food chemistry, food microbiology, project management and energy management. A project is undertaken in the final year.

The college expects a strong demand from industry for this new degree. There is a continuing demand for graduates in the areas of food science, microbiology, new product development, non-food uses, process development, technical management, food ingredients, food safety and ready-to-use foods, according to the college prospectus. The first cohort of graduates from UL's food technology degree will emerge in 1998.

## COURSES AT ALL THREE LEVELS

Food science and technology is offered at all three levels – certificate, diploma and degree. Students who don't get the points or who don't want to commit to three or four years of study may find that the certificate/diploma route will suit them better. Last year 120 points would have secured a place on Dundalk IT's food science programme, while 100 points would have got a place on Letterkenny IT's programme.

Of course, the cut-off points tell you nothing about the quality of a course – they are merely the points obtained by the last person offered a place on the programme. Students who ignore certificate and diploma programmes are cutting themselves off from half of all available third-level courses. And, of course, students who do sufficiently well in cert and diploma exams can apply for degree programmes.

Sligo IT offers food science within its certificate in applied science. After a common first year, students can specialise in applied chemistry, applied biology or food science. Admissions officer, Padraic Cuffe, says that about 60 per cent of graduates of the certificate would usually continue their studies to diploma level. The college offers an add-on diploma in pollution assessment and control. Graduates of this programme are then eligible to apply for a degree in environmental science and technology.

*Food science*

## FACT FILE

*Cut-off points 1997–98*
Degrees:
UL: Food technology 380
UCC: Food business 415*; food science 405*; food technology 380*
DIT Kevin Street: applied science (food technology option) 365
UCD: agricultural science (food technology) 380*

*Some Certs/diplomas*
Dundalk IT: Food science 120
Letterkenny IT: Food science 100
DIT: Food technology 325; food quality assurance 160
Sligo IT: applied science (food science option) (* indicates random selection).

## COMMON-ENTRY PROGRAMMES

Students interested in food science/technology should look at the subjects offered in common-entry science and applied science programmes as it may be possible to specialise in food science. Students who take biological sciences such as microbiology and biochemistry, or who study the chemical sciences at undergraduate level, may decide to further specialise at post-graduate level in the food area, so it is not always necessary to start with a direct-entry dedicated programme.

# LAW

*It's not really as rarified as people make out*

Photographer: Eric Luke

Barra Faughnan talks to Catherine Foley about his working life as a barrister.

## Law

A stiff breeze outside the Four Courts has black gowns billowing majestically in the sunlight. Inside, along the cool stone corridors, men and women in wigs and gowns are walking purposefully to their desks at the Law Library. These are the hallowed halls where Barra Faughnan will spend the best part of his working life.

'There is a collegial atmosphere,' he says. 'The collective atmosphere is definitely attractive. It's very social. But it's not really as rarified as people make out. There's an awful lot of common sense involved as well. Ultimately you're dealing with people.'

There's a long and challenging road ahead for Faughnan. Having completed his devilling, now begins the hard part. He must establish himself as a barrister-at-law. 'You're not allowed advertise for work,' he explains. 'You're dependant on solicitors to give you work which is why being introduced to them is so important. They are the only source of our work. In the absence of solicitors, you get no work.'

Today Faughnan, like most young barristers, is working in the Four Courts, making contacts, meeting senior barristers and solicitors, drafting legal documents, researching cases, meeting witnesses and appearing in court for clients. 'One of the realities when you start is that it takes a number of years to establish yourself. There's a policy of open entry to the bar.

'You can give it a go if you satisfy the criteria. What's difficult is what I'm doing now. It's the fact that establishing a name for yourself is so hard.'

After graduating with a BA honours degree in English and classical studies from UCD, Faughnan went to King's Inns to study law. He spent two years studying at night for a diploma in legal studies. After finishing this course, he moved on to do the two-year barrister-at-law degree.

Last year he devilled, which involves working with a barrister as a kind of apprentice. 'It was a very, very productive year. Whom you devil with is important, it depends on the kind of pupil-master relationship you have. I was very lucky.'

His work is split between the paper work that is drafting, which a barrister has to do before a case comes to court, the research which may have to be done, preparation work and the actual time in court.

'It's an exciting environment to be in . . . but people nowadays would probably relate to something like *LA Law* whereas it's much quieter and more organised than that, and the wigs and gowns, the procedural aspect, makes it more formal and more dull to those outside.

'I do think you have to like words and like writing; you do more writing than anything else. The key is when you are drafting, you must set out what happened to your client. It's on the basis of the draft that you fight your case – you fight it out on paper before you go into court.'

Faughnan studied for his Leaving Cert at St Micheal's Secondary School in Ailesbury Road, Dublin. He started debating here. In 1991 he won the individual speaker award in *The Irish Times* Colleges Debating Competition.

'There are a lot of qualities that make up a good barrister,' he says. 'It's not just about being a good speaker or having a good knowledge of the law. You have to be very good with people – it's all very well to say you'll run this case but in order to do it right you have to have a good relationship with your solicitor, you have to relate to your client, you have to interact with any witnesses there might be. And you have to deal with the judge and they differ as much as anybody else. It requires varied talents. At the end of the day, you have to be thorough.'

At school, he says, he was very competitive. 'It helps to be competitive. There's no doubt about that.' Many people who debate go on to do law, he explains, and 'there has to be an element of the extrovert and the egotist to it.

'Debating was very good training. It has to help but at the same time being a lawyer is entirely different. It's helpful in terms of being able to speak fluently and being able to create arguments but there's an awful lot more to being a barrister.'

### Career focus: Barrister/solicitor

The list of desired professions for many second-level students is topped by barrister and solicitor. But, it's a long, difficult road to donning the wig and gown as a barrister or getting on the roll of solicitors. Most students find their way via a law degree. In 1997, cut-off points ranged from 435 to 570*.

Many degrees are available – some combine law with other subjects such as business, accountancy, a language or European studies. Others offer law by itself. NUI Galway also has a degree in corporate law. Only certain degrees are approved by King's Inns for entry to the barrister-at-law degree (see Fact File below).

On completing a law degree, further education and training is necessary to qualify as a barrister or solicitor. Graduates with a degree approved by King's Inns may apply for the two-year barrister-at-law degree. Professor Kevin Waldron, director of education, says that 50 per cent of places are reserved for graduates. Admission is very competitive and this year all who secured a place had a minimum of a 2.1 in their degrees, according to Waldron.

Remaining places are allocated to holders of the society's diploma, in order of merit (40 per cent of places) and by the education committee, also in order of merit (10 per cent of places). Those lucky enough to get a place then attend afternoon lectures from Monday to Friday, with evening tutorials.

There are 23 weeks of lectures, tutorials and practical exercises followed by an exam in May. Annual fees for the degree courses are close to £2,000. There are also some additional charges.

This all adds up to six years of study for graduates who have already put in four years studying for an approved law degree. But, the story is not quite over yet, as graduates of the two-year barrister-at-law degree must spend a further year devilling – essentially working as an apprentice without pay. After the year's devilling is over, Waldron says that 'no matter how good the students, pickings are very thin on the ground for the first few years'.

Quite a number of barristers will go into some other area, but they don't go there as failures, he emphasises. Two or three years at the bar is an asset that will stand to them throughout their careers.

For graduates of degrees other than the approved law degrees and for applicants without a degree, the route to the bar is even longer – they must travel via King's Inns two-year diploma in legal studies. Places are allocated on academic merit.

Each year of the course consists of 25 weeks of lectures followed by an exam. The annual fee for the diploma is £1,950. As already mentioned, 40 per cent of places on the barrister-at-law degree are reserved for diploma graduates and these places are awarded on academic merit.

The Law Society is responsible for the professional training of solicitors. Non-degree holders must first pass the preliminary examination. Very few people follow this route, according to education officer, TP Kennedy. The exam includes English, general knowledge, and government and politics. Certain people, such as law clerks with a number of years experience, may be exempted from the preliminary exam. Degree holders are also exempt.

The next stage is the Irish exam and the entrance exam to the law school. Graduates of some degrees were exempt from the entrance exam but after 1999, all graduates, of law or otherwise, will have to sit the eight subjects in the entrance exam – law of tort, law of contract, real property, equity, constitutional law, company law, criminal law and EU law. Of course, law graduates will have covered these subjects in their degrees. Non-law graduates tend to do a course such as DIT's diploma in legal studies, in order to prepare themselves for the exam.

Everyone who passes the entrance exam is entitled to train as a solicitor. There is no cap on numbers – there are now 6,000 on the rolls. There is a waiting list for the professional training course so it takes about a year at present for students to secure a place.

The course is full-time and lasts about four to five months. There is ongoing assessment and exams. On completion of the course, students spend a minimum of 18 months training as an apprentice. One of the many problems that students face along the way is securing an apprenticeship.

Then there is a further two months, advanced course and another exam and Irish test. When students have passed all of the exams and completed the training period, their names are entered on the roll of solicitors.

## Where law can lead

Many students study law and have no intention of working as solicitors or barristers. Law degrees are academic degrees, not professional training, so conventional career areas are open to graduates. The combination of law and another subject, such as accounting or European studies, may be attractive to students looking towards careers outside the courts or solicitors' rooms.

Seamus McEvoy, careers officer in UCC, says 'a law degree is a great degree to have. From a business perspective, it is very useful to have an understanding of law. A lot of students look at law and say but I don't want to become a solicitor or a barrister. In fact, it is a very good base degree. It is all based around the interpretation of English, so people gain very good communication skills. Last year, one of the six big accountancy firms took on six law graduates from UCC.'

Higher Education Authority figures show that the majority of 1996 law graduates (48.6 per cent) were engaged in research or further academic training. A further 22 per cent were in vocational and professional training while 26.8 per cent entered the labour market directly. This latter figure includes graduates who entered training as a solicitor. A small proportion, 2.1 per cent, were seeking employment in April 1997.

There is a variety of law degrees on offer, from corporate law in NUI Galway to law and accounting in UL to business and legal studies in UCD to law with languages in TCD. Graduates of degrees which combine the study of law with another discipline are more likely to enter the labour market directly. For instance, of UL's 1996 graduates, 21 had gained employment by April 1997, eight went on to research or further study, two to vocational or professional training, one was seeking work and one graduate was not available for work or study.

Legal studies are not just available at degree level. Waterford Institute of Technology and Letterkenny IT offer certificates in legal studies. Graduates of Letterkenny's certificate may find work as solicitors' assistants, legal executives and law clerks. They may also continue studies and complete add-on diplomas in legal studies in the college. Plans for an add-on degree are under way. Some diploma holders with a distinction or very high merit may be admitted to year two of UCC's BCL course.

WIT offers add-on diplomas in legal studies and in legal studies in internal trade. Graduates of either diploma may be eligible for the college's add-on BA in legal and business studies.

## FACT FILE

*Useful addresses:*
The Law School, Law Society of Ireland, Blackhall Place, Dublin 7 – phone (01) 6710200. The Law Society is responsible for training solicitors.

Director of Education, the Honourable Society of King's Inns, Henrietta Street, Dublin 1 – phone (01)874 4840. The King's Inns is responsible for training barristers.
Both King's Inns and the Law Society produce leaflets on entry requirements to their professional courses.

*1997–98 cut-off points for law degrees:*
UCC: law 460*; law and French 490*; law and German 455*.
UCD: law 490; business/legal 435.
NUI Galway: corporate law 455*.
UL: law and accounting 480; law and European studies 490.
TCD: law 515; law and French 570*; law and German 550*.

Law degrees approved by King's Inns for admission to the barrister-at-law course:

TCD: LLB, LLB (French), LLB (German). UCD: BCL. UCC: BCL, BCL (French), BCL (German). UL: BA (European studies, law option) and BA (law and accounting). QUB: LLB provided applicant also passes Irish constitutional law in Society's diploma course.

For all of the above degrees, the following six compulsory subjects must have been included in the degree (or the deficit must be made up by passing the appropriate subject in the diploma course): land law (including the law of succession), equity, law of torts, law of contracts, criminal law and constitution law.

# HAIRDRESSER

*I feel you couldn't just leave it*

Yvonne McKernan talks to Catherine Foley about her job as a hairdresser.

# Career choice

Two women sit at the back of the hairdressing salon as they wait to have their hair washed. In the front room, another woman is looking at herself in the mirror, checking to see how she's doing as her hair is styled and coiffed by Yvonne McKernan. 'Cool Blondes' says the poster overhead. 'Style, vogue, attitude, finesse, feeling.'

There's a nice homely feel to the salon where McKernan works. It's mid-morning but business is brisk. All hands are on deck and, unless there's a cancellation later on, there isn't a free half-hour left in the day.

'I love it here,' she says. 'It's just the people. Mothers and their daughters come in and their grand-daughters as well. Also we have a great staff here. We all get on pretty well. I just love the area. It's more a settled community but you get about 40 per cent young people coming in. And we're young ourselves so we know what styles are in.'

McKernan has worked in Hair by Roches for the past 10 years. The idea of leaving has never been an issue. She doesn't want to go to another salon or move away. 'I'm seeing the same faces here all the time. I'd hate to dump my customers like that and move on. I feel you couldn't just leave it.'

She is unashamedly enthusiastic about her job, and describes what she does in a quiet, gentle voice. 'You're creating something. They come in with flat hair and you change it. It's amazing what you can do. You listen. You don't always remember what they are saying but you leave your problems at the door. You put a smile on your face – nobody wants someone who is grumpy doing their hair. You look well and you feel better about yourself as well.

'I'd recommend hairdressing. It's artistic. You're changing people's image all the time. You watch it in their faces going out the door. From colour to blowdrying it's worth all the hard work to see them going out the door with a happy face.'

Located on Lower Kimmage Road on Dublin's southside, Hair by Roches has been doing business since 1942. It's a long-established salon with a loyal and appreciative clientele. It's situated over a barber shop, which is run by another member of the Roche family, and nestled in between a Chinese take-away and a pharmacy, not far from a busy crossroads.

'There's no whip but it's pretty tough work, like any other job,' says McKernan. She is happy to describe how she approaches her work.

'You look at the shape of the face, you have to be able to advise them. You're the expert. You'll be able to tell them exactly what suits them.'

Her mother was a hairdresser and she was 'always watching her' with a sharp, critical eye. 'My mother is convinced I'm always doing it wrong but all our fringes were crooked,' she laughs. From first year in St Anne's Secondary School in Milltown, she 'knew what she wanted to. I knew I'd leave in fourth year,' she says. 'None of the other girls knew what they wanted to do.'

Her guidance counsellor told her about the PLC course in Crumlin College of Business and Technical Studies. 'I got a full-time job out of it,' she says, smiling.

She did her work experience in Roches and then she was offered a job. Over a four-year period, she went on to do the Department of Education's Junior Trade Certificate exam and then the Senior Trade Certificate exam, working during the day and attending lectures and classes one or two nights a week throughout the term.

A hairdresser is constantly learning and doing courses, she says. McKernan has become an expert in wig fitting, which the salon has provided for a number of years. She now travels to many of Dublin's major hospitals fitting individuals who have lost their hair, perhaps due to chemotherapy, with a wig.

'I'd bring out about 10 wigs in the particular style they want. You have to be pretty sensitive and listen to them and not rush them, and consult them . . . I take my time with them. It's a different outlet for me.'

### CAREER FOCUS: HAIRDRESSING

Is the long-awaited revolution in hairdressing training about to happen? In 1994, the then-Minister Mary O'Rourke was pictured having her hair styled in celebration of the introduction of the standards-based apprenticeship training for hairdressers. Four years and much talk later, it appears that a pilot project is finally underway.

Some 12 first-year hairdressing students began their off-the-job training last week in the FÁS centre in Jervis Street, Dublin. They have embarked on a standards-based apprenticeship which consists of a sandwich-type training with alternating periods on and off-the-job. The off-the-job training will comprise 26 weeks in the pilot programme.

If the programme is successful, this will probably be increased to 40 weeks. This off-the-job training will be provided by FÁS training centres, Department of Education schools and colleges and approved industry-based training centres.

FÁS instructor Geraldine McKinn explains that the curriculum was drawn up in conjunction with FÁS, Peter Marks, the hairdressers' union, the Irish Hairdressing Federation and the VEC. 'I feel that the trade desperately needs something like this,' says McKinn. 'It's very, very difficult to get staff.'

Kevin Cahill, of Sankiev Salon, Dublin, one of the employers participating in the new pilot scheme, explains that the periods of off-the-job training are a new concept in hairdressing. He, and other employers, have to find replacement staff while their apprentices are off the job. However, he is philosophical and says that someone has to make a start.

'It's the way forward,' says Cahill. 'Up to now, there has been no real system. It depended on the salon owner and the apprentice and what they were willing to put into it.'

Anyone can open a salon, pay whatever they like (outside Dublin and Cork where Joint Labour Commission minimum rates apply), and train their 'apprentices' who may put in long hours sweeping up hair clippings and washing hair. On the other hand, there are salons which provide very well structured training for their apprentices. FÁS also runs a six-month hairdressing course and private schools of hairdressing offer course for which students pay fees.

The Irish Hairdressers Federation has long been lobbying for some form of standardised training. But, hairdressing is a hot potato, claims Cahill, with hundreds of salons out there nobody knows anything about.

Meanwhile, staff shortages are reaching crisis level as hairdressing seems to have lost its allure for school leavers. Salons are finding it increasingly difficult to recruit trainees who are put off by the common perception of a career with long hours and low pay but without structured training. The new apprenticeship may go some way towards redressing this.

Outside the pilot apprenticeship scheme, school-leavers should be careful when it comes to choosing a salon for training purposes. They should inquire in detail about training arrangements.

## Career choice

### Post Leaving Certificate courses:

An increasingly popular route into hairdressing is offered by the expanding PLC sector. These are mainly one-year courses which lead to an NCVA level 2 qualification.

Maura Clarke of Crumlin College of Business and Technical Studies, Dublin, says that a PLC teaches basic hairdressing skills as well as interpersonal skills – if students went directly into a salon they might not have the opportunity to do any hairdressing in first year.

Crumlin College has one of the biggest hairdressing schools in Dublin. It combines hairdressing with cosmetic studies and students spend one day a week on work experience. Most students sit the Department of Education's Junior Trade examinations as well as getting an NCVA level 2 qualification. They also sit the ITEC cosmetic studies qualification.

After graduation, most students return to the college at night for the Senior Trade Certificate. They can further specialise in subsequent years. The college has a guidance counsellor to help students make career choices.

Graduates may opt for hairdressing, cosmetic studies or possibly receptionist-type jobs in salons. If they go into hairdressing, they usually find work as a senior first-year apprentice in a high-profile hairdressing salon.

There are also opportunities to travel. 'If you have a scissors and comb in your hand, you can go,' says Clarke. 'Once you have the tools and skills, travel becomes a possibility.'

### Fact File

*Training:*
There is no standardised training programme for hairdressers. Trainees tend to follow one of four main routes:

# Hairdresser

Four-year time-served apprenticeship
PLC course
Six-month FÁS course followed by apprenticeship
Private schools of hairdressing

### PILOT TRAINING SCHEME:

This new scheme will pilot a standards-based apprenticeship. This will be sandwich-style training with three periods on-the-job and two off-the-job.

Phase 1: induction period with employer

Phase 2: six-module plan incorporating salon procedures (175 hours); blow drying and curling techniques (105 hours); perming and neutralising (140 hours); colouring (105 hours); styling and cutting (105 hours); salon experience (140 hours)

Phase 3: salon experience and competence assessment by employer

Phase 4: four-module plan including salon procedures (35 hours); perming (70 hours); colouring (70 hours); styling and cutting (105 hours)

Phase 5: salon experience and competence assessment by employer

### PLC OPTIONS:

A number of PLC colleges offer hairdressing alone or combined with other studies such as beauty care, cosmetic studies and enterprise studies. Contact your local VEC or PLC college for information.

# CONSTRUCTION TRADES

## *'The best job in the world'*

There's more to bricklaying than brute strength, George Kelly tells Catherine Foley.

He'll never work in an office. He smiles broadly at the idea of always being able to work out of doors. 'It's the best job in the world, in the summer it's excellent. If it wasn't for the bad weather I'd love it all year round. I'm never stuck in any one place. After two or three months at most in one place you're on to a completely different place.'

Having met a master bricklayer while he was still at school, George Kelly decided this was what he wanted to do. He left school after the Intermediate Certificate in St David's CBS Secondary School in Artane, Dublin, and started work on a building site. He will shortly finish a four-year apprenticeship at DIT Bolton Street. On completion of his exams at Christmas he will be awarded a national craft certificate in bricklaying.

'You're never finished learning, even the details. It's very precise. Just to break into it and get the basic things, like working with the trowel, is technical. There are skilful things about it . . . if you get satisfaction out of working with your hands and making something, and saying, well I'm proud of that, then you'll enjoy bricklaying.'

Before he started his apprenticeship, Kelly had already worked as a bricklayer and learned on the job. 'A man in his forties who worked beside me, he'd make a show of you, he's just tapping along at his own pace and he'll still do more than you.'

For Kelly, anyone who takes his job seriously should learn the theory behind bricklaying and study the rules and regulations. There are a number of families in Dublin who are regarded as master bricklayers, where the tradition goes back through generations, he explains.

At this stage, after four years at DIT Bolton Street on the apprenticeship course, having been recruited through FÁS, he is studying 'mainly theory', including craft science, craft calculations and technical drawing. 'You have to be able to draw something to be able to understand it. Stonework, wall tiling, floor tiling . . . it's essential to be good at maths. I did mechanical drawing at school and I enjoyed engineering and woodwork too.'

The apprentices study 'all the theory behind bricklaying, how to set things, how to do arches, ramps, curved brick work, splayed brick work and general decorative brick work and how to work with glass blocks.

'Back in the 1960s, they tried to build houses without bricklayers using prefabricated walls,' he explains. 'They were useless. Bricklaying is not about having muscles and throwing the blocks up.' Without the national craft certificate, Kelly adds, 'you could never travel, you could never have a union card, you could never apply for a visa . . . you can't emphasise it enough. It's not about physical power.

'You have to progress. It's like all the foremen we have on the building sites, they were all plumbers, bricklayers or plasterers. They went off and did the building technology course. The people we work for now, the builders, all started out as plasterers.

'I'd love to be a builder if I ever got the money together. You have to get a bit of money.' Next year Kelly hopes to start a construction technology certificate course.

This year he won the National Apprentice Competitions and was awarded the silver medal by the Department of Education. This summer he represented Ireland at the international Vocational Training Competitions, known as the 'Youth Skills Olympics' in Switzerland. Some 30 countries from all over the world took part. With 16 trades represented, Ireland came sixth in the overall result. Kelly was awarded a diploma of excellence.

## Career focus: construction trades

*Building boom means lots of jobs*
Urban skyscapes are dominated by cranes as the construction industry booms. Employment opportunities for the associated trades – electricians, plumbers, plasterers and bricklayers – are excellent. The Construction Industry Federation estimates that the numbers directly employed in the industry will reach 10,000 by the end of this year. The CIF has published a target schedule of apprenticeship intakes for the years up to 2000. Peter McCabe, CIF's business development director, is anxious that young people consider careers in the trades. 'You don't need to have all of those points,' he says. Entry into becoming an electrician and plumber is very popular so a good Leaving Cert is an advantage, he adds, but in other trades a good attitude and aptitude is as important.

In particular, he would like to encourage young people into the 'wet trades', becoming a plasterer, bricklayer or painter/decorator. Everybody wants to become a carpenter, electrician or plumber but there are good opportunities in other areas, he adds.

Robert Murphy, manager of apprenticeships with FÁS, says it would probably be wise for young people considering an apprenticeship to stay in education until the Leaving Certificate. At present, about 56 per cent of the 14,000 apprentices registered with FÁS have completed the Leaving Cert.

If you want to become an apprentice you must first find an employer who will offer you an apprenticeship and the employer must register you with FÁS. Murphy says that this is vital. 'We have come across the absurd situation where a person has been in a trade for many years but has never registered. De facto, they are not craftspeople' he says.

As to finding an apprenticeship, many large organisations advertise their apprenticeships in the local and national newspapers. You can also approach employers directly and Murphy says that approaches through informal channels have been found to be most effective. FÁS keeps lists of would-be apprentices which it makes available to potential employers.

All new apprentices follow the standards-based system of training. The older time-served system is being phased out, with about 4,500 apprentices completing this method of training.

New apprentices follow a sandwich type training with alternating periods on and off-the-job. The off-the-job training is provided by FÁS and institutes of technology. Skills are tested at all phases.

McCabe says that the Construction Industry Federation is happy with the new system of training but the delivery mechanisms have not been able to cope with the increased numbers. Location of courses is also a problem, with students having to travel considerable distances, in some cases, for their off-the-job training, he says.

'The skills-based system will eventually prove to be very good,' says Murphy. The award for the successful completion of the course is a national craft certificate. This is recognised throughout the EU.

The proportion of girls registering for apprenticeships remains less than two per cent. To help change this, FÁS offers bursaries to private sector employers who take on female apprentices.

Although the number of women registering for apprenticeship is low (61 on 30 June 1997) it is increasing. One of the key things is that it is increasing right across the trades – carpenter/joiner, toolmaker, fitter, painter/decorator, Murphy adds.

# Construction trades

FÁS also runs pre-apprenticeship programmes which allow people to sample the area before they decide to commit themselves. Check with your local VEC or PLC college.

### Fact file
Apprentices in the construction industry (20 October, 1997):
Bricklayer: 535
Carpenter/joiner: 1,468
Electrician: 2,160
Plasterer: 250
Plumber: 955
Painter/decorator: 249
*Figures supplied by FÁS*

### Minimum age requirements:
Age: at least 16 at the start of the apprenticeship.
Education: minimum of grade D in five subjects in the Junior Certificate (or approved equivalent) or satisfactorily complete a FÁS pre-apprenticeship course.
Bricklayers should be of good physique and have a head for heights. Painter/decorators and electricians must pass a colour vision test approved by FÁS.

### Standards-based apprenticeship:
The apprenticeship has seven alternating phases – three off-the-job and four on-the-job. Successful completion of a standards-based apprenticeship leads to a national crafts certificate.

## Career choice

### CIF PREDICTIONS:

*Standards-based apprenticeship intake 1997–98:*
Bricklayer: 250
Plasterer: 200
Painter/decorator: 150
Floor and wall tiler: 24
Carpenter/joiner: 850
Cabinet maker: 150
Wood machinist: 48
Plumber: 420
Metal fabricator: 250
Sheetmetal worker: 85
Construction plant fitter: 80
Electrician: 1172

# ACTUARY

## *The people who really count*

Dervla Tomlin talks to Catherine Foley about her work as head of actuarial and financial planning with Irish Life.

## Career choice

There is a rarefied atmosphere up on the fifth floor of the Irish Life Centre where Dervla Tomlin works. There are no honking horns, no screeching brakes. Far down below on street level, we can see the cars and the people rushing by in the early afternoon light.

If a quiet moment happens, Tomlin can gaze down in peace at the silent chaos underneath. Otherwise her head is bent over financial documents, computing and analysing figures, charts and reports. She is an actuary with Irish Life. This is where the company's assurance costs, possibilities, trends and patterns are analysed and priced.

'You do have to be accurate and pay attention to detail but at the same time we're quite involved in trying to design new products and it's important that we think creatively and think of new ways to do things,' she says. Products, she explains, mean packages, and these products include everything from pensions to savings plans for the customer. 'I would have to say that I really enjoy the variety and challenge,' she adds.

'We're selling products to individuals,' she explains. 'I work in the retail area.' Her current title is head of actuarial and financial planning at Irish Life. 'You do need to be numerate but it's not as technical, mathematically, as people might think. You have to be practical and like solving practical problems. I work in the life assurance areas, so communication skills are also very important. You do have to be able to communicate clearly and in layman's language.'

Her job is about pricing all the products, reporting on profits, estimating how much the company is going to make and the amount it will take to cover future claims. 'If somebody buys life cover, it would be the actuary who would price it.' The actuary also maps out 'how it's going to be sold, what claims we would expect, all the terms, and makes sure that it offers value to the customer and that it is profitable for the company.'

Looking back at her school days, she recalls that actuarial studies was not uppermost in her mind. 'When I did the Leaving Cert I didn't know what I wanted to do. I did have strong numerical skills, but I was equally interested in a lot of other subjects like English and history. I was leaning towards a job that was fairly practical. I decided to do maths and economics at UCD.'

Besides, she says, there were no actuarial courses in Ireland when she did the Leaving Cert. 'Now there are specific courses and post-graduate courses.'

She graduated from UCD in 1988. From a group of 10 who did honours maths in their arts degree, three, including Tomlin, went on to pursue a career as actuaries. Tomlin became interested in actuarial work because it would 'involve dealing with people, it had good career prospects and it involved practical problem solving'.

She got a job with Irish Life and was sponsored to go to City University in London to do a one-year full-time course as part of her training. When she came back, she only had to complete four exams in order to qualify and become a fellow of the Institute of Actuaries. 'You have to spend a couple of years both working and studying,' she says. 'It's quite pressurised but it's worth it.'

When she started out in her career, Tomlin says there were more men than women working as actuaries. However, the balance has since shifted and now it's about fifty/fifty. 'The intake would be fairly even,' she says. She does admit, however, that for the moment, 'at the more senior level in the profession, it's probably all men. But there's no sexism in the profession.'

For anyone who is thinking of becoming an actuary, she says the average time after finishing the Leaving Cert is seven years.

One of the key approaches of an actuary is to look at the long-term pattern, she says. 'We are taking on risks for maybe twenty years. You always look at the trends and what we would expect to happen.'

The job, she says, 'is much more pragmatic and practical than people think'. And finally, in answer to a question about a typical day for an actuary, she explains that 'as a professional working in a responsible, challenging job, you don't have nine-to-five hours'. But, she says, 'I like the variety'.

## Career focus: Actuary

The employment scene is very good for actuaries at present. The trick is finding your way in. Excellent mathematical skills – and a high grade in maths in the Leaving Cert – are a must. Qualified actuaries are fellows of the Institute of Actuaries, in England, or the Faculty of Actuaries in Scotland. There are a number of exams – now being revised – which you must pass to become a fellow.

There are three main routes into the profession. School-leavers can go directly into employment and, over a number of years, sit the exams of the Institute or the Faculty of Actuaries. You will usually need an A in higher-level maths as well as high grades in other subjects. Paul Duffy, chairman of the communications and public relations committee of the Society of Actuaries in Ireland, says employers are also looking for good communication skills.

Students can opt for the actuarial degrees at UCD or DCU, which offer substantial exemptions from the professional exams. Points are extremely high and likely to remain so.

The third route is a degree with a high mathematical content, for which you may gain some exemptions, explains Duffy.

Michael Marsh, chairman of DCU's programme board for the financial and actuarial maths degree, says the college's degree is structured as a maths degree. Some students will become actuaries while others will decide it is not for them. So, it's important that they graduate with a strong maths degree, he says.

In the third year of the four-year degree programme, students spend six months on industrial placement. This gives them a very good idea of what the job entails and many students find employment with the company with whom they did their placement, according to Marsh. In fact, employment prospects for trainee actuaries are 'embarrassingly good', he says. There is a growing awareness among employers of the value of an actuarial qualification. The success of the BSc programme has spawned an MSc in financial maths and demand for this is very high also.

Philip Boland, professor of statistics at UCD and director of the actuarial and financial studies degree, says they are looking for people with good quantitative skills. The course includes a substantial amount of statistics and maths so a liking for maths is a must. It is a pretty demanding course, he stresses.

About two-thirds of graduates go into trainee actuarial positions, about 20 per cent go into banking and finance while the remainder tend to go into accounting and management consultancy, says Boland.

The course is changing from a three-year programme to four years and will include a formal five or six-month work placement in third year.

When choosing an entry route, second-level students who want to train as actuaries may be attracted by the idea of going directly into employment, gaining experience and being paid while they train. And this route works well for many trainee actuaries.

On the other hand, these students miss out on the social and cultural aspects of university, says Boland. He also mentions the attrition rate among trainee actuaries which is about 50 per cent. If students have done a degree, they have something to fall back on. UCD's degree provides a good grounding in statistics, maths, economics and finance, he points out.

Each year, students call the college, saying that they are good at maths and want to do something in the business area, says Boland. If they want to do accountancy, they shouldn't do this degree, but if they want to go into insurance, finance or banking and use quantitative skills, actuarial studies may be the right degree, he advises.

### WHERE IT ALL BEGAN . . .

Many people are unsure what actuaries do but it is not a new profession. Its roots stretch back more than 240 years. It was 1756 when James Dodson, a fellow of the British Royal Society, was turned down for an insurance policy on the grounds that he was too old. His brain had obviously not slowed down and he set about putting together a table of annual premiums based on life expectancy.

From these beginnings, the profession began to provide solutions to a variety of problems in the life assurance and pension areas. In the recent past, actuaries have ventured further afield into areas such as general insurance, investment banking and management consultancy.

They are forecasters using probability theory to predict the future. While maths is obviously a requirement, actuaries also need good communication skills, as they must explain difficult concepts to boards of management and other interested bodies.

The rewards in financial terms are good (see Fact File) but Paul Duffy of the Society of Actuaries in Ireland says the career itself is also intellectually rewarding. 'It's very challenging and does make demands but it is also a very attractive career,' he says. 'Actuaries make sense of the future.'

## Fact File

1997–98 points for full-time degree:
UCD Actuarial and financial studies 595*; 30 to 32 first-year places
DCU Financial and actuarial maths 520; 20 to 25 first-year places
(* random selection applied; not all students at this points level were offered a place).

## Professional body:

The Society of Actuaries in Ireland, 5 Wilton Place, Dublin 2 – phone (01) 661 2422. There are about 190 qualified actuaries in Ireland and a similar number of students. The society is not an examining body – examinations are set by the Institute of Actuaries in London and the Faculty of Actuaries in Edinburgh

## Sample salaries:

Graduates of a full-time degree course, who find positions as trainee actuaries may earn up to £17,000 per annum. They may also be given study leave as part of their package. Newly qualified actuaries (depending on merit and experience) may earn between £30,000 and £35,000 per annum.

# Electronic Engineering

## *The happy troubleshooter*

Eimear Ní Dhonnchadha talks to Catherine Foley about her job as support engineer at Apple Computer's European base in Cork.

# Electronic engineering

We are lost in the murky depths of cyber space searching for the proverbial needle in the haystack. But there is help at hand – Eimear Ní Dhonnchadha is on the job. A problem solver, she delves courageously into the techno haystack. She is an ace trouble-shooter working for Apple Computers in Cork.

'Yes,' Ní Dhonnchadha agrees, 'I'm a bit like Inspector Morse or Poirot.' She spends her days picking up clues and vital pieces of information working to a deadline until she finally pins down the problem. Throughout the day as a technical support engineer at Apple's Cork base, the company's European centre, she handles technical queries and phone calls from 29 countries around Europe.

Ní Dhonnchadha deals with queries about software products. The queries come in from far-flung Apple users in Poland or Israel, from Turkey or Russia, not to mention more familiar places in France, Italy, Spain and Germany.

'We have to try and locate the problem,' she explains. 'Then we replicate it. Then we narrow it down to what file or what part of the software it is in. Then we go in and check if everything is all right and pin it down. Then we edit the actual code of the programme and we fix it.'

Even though her first view of a computer was in Leaving Cert, her interest in mathematical problems goes much further back, she says. 'We all had a leaning towards maths at school,' she says about her family.

Eimear Ní Dhonnchadha grew up in Co. Cork. She went to school at Scoil Mhuire, Kanturk. 'I had no particular *grá* for physics but I said I'd give it a shot. When I went into the Leaving Cert cycle, I took all the science subjects and by the end of fifth year, I had a fair idea that I'd like it. I preferred electronics to anything else within physics. I narrowed it down that way.'

## Career choice

Ní Dhonnchadha started the four-year Bachelor of Electronic Engineering in Cork RTC (now CIT) in 1992. The area is still male-dominated – there were just two females in her year out of a total of 35. In fourth year, she took part in the EU-funded New Opportunities for Women (NOW) programme, which tries to encourage women to go into new areas.

'The field of electronic engineering is so vast,' she says. On leaving college, the choice of job opportunities is wide. Graduates can decide to specialise in areas including software, hardware, communications and process control engineering.

The course at Cork RTC was 'totally different to what we had done at school. It was all new maths and new physics. I preferred that to what I had done. In first and second year, it was going great. In third year, the work started piling on – it was the amount of it rather than anything else. By fourth year, we were in the swing of it. It was much more practical.'

During the first two years, there were lab sessions and mini-projects. 'By fourth year, you had to do a project which was about 40 per cent of your final year. My project was designing a software licensing programme.'

Ní Dhonnchadha started in Apple as a quality engineer. 'My job was to test the quality of the products coming on the market. I was doing that up to last January. Then I designed a database for the Apple Localisation Group.' She is now support engineer to the group.

Her job is full of change, challenge and bouts of intensity. She enjoys her work 'because you're not stuck inside a computer all day. You're talking to people. You're not totally zonked at the end of the day. You're kept alert by all the things that are going on.'

Sometimes a problem arrives for which she knows the solution immediately . . . 'but most of the time you have to

## Electronic engineering

sit down and find the problem. You check it against other types of software. You're a troubleshooter. You pin it down. Then once you're sure, you delve into it and root around. It's technical. You have to use your head. When you start, you're so used to pinpointing it that you nearly know by instinct.'

### CAREER FOCUS: ELECTRONIC ENGINEERING

The demand for electronic engineering technicians is so overwhelming that the Government created an additional 500 third-level places in 1997 (1997–98 entry). A brochure produced by Forfás in recent months extols the career of technician in the electronics industry as 'very exciting . . . the job involves working on new designs, detecting errors and correcting microchips, installing and servicing new and complex equipment.'

With a recognised certificate or diploma, electronics technicians can expect to earn between £11,000 and £14,000 in their first year of employment, according to the brochure. But, the message is not getting through to school-leavers.

A glance at the 1997–98 CAO offers shows five electronics courses with vacancies. The cut-off points required for many electronics certificates and diploma, was also quite low. For instance, it was possible to secure a place on Dundalk IT's electronics course in 1997 with 110 points. This cut-off is not an indication of the quality of the course but of the demand for the course. School-leavers, especially girls, do not seem to be attracted by the idea of a career as an electronic technician.

Peter Lillis, manager of corporate development with the IDA, says that we need to attract a wider range of entrants to engineering education and that there is a particular need to attract women, who are currently very under-represented and who are eminently suitable for many engineering jobs. 'The reality is that technicians' jobs now are very clean, very interesting, very challenging, and very suitable for women as well as men,' he says. 'But that perception does not seem to have got through.'

For those interested, the institutes of technology offer a range of certificate and diploma courses. There is the possibility of progressing from certificate to diploma to degree or the possibility of transfer to degree programmes elsewhere.

For instance, you could start with a two-year certificate in Dundalk IT and proceed to a one-year add-on diploma in electronic manufacturing and service. And, from there, you could move into the degree programme in product design engineering.

Progression is not automatic and is dependent on exam results. To progress to diploma, students need a merit in certificate exams or a pass and one year's work experience. Some colleges are more flexible and will accept a pass alone. Students must gain a merit in the diploma to progress to degree. Not all students wish to progress to degree – a certificate or diploma is a valid qualification in its own right.

Meanwhile, there are moves afoot to persuade school-leavers of the value of a career in electronics. A taskforce on the supply of technicians to the Irish economy is expected to recommend a number of measures to increase the number of people applying and to increase throughput. The National Council for Educational Awards recently launched a new educational package promoting engineering as a career.

# Electronic engineering

## FACT FILE

*Direct entry degrees:*
NUI Galway: electronic engineering; applied physics and electronics; experimental physics; electronic and computer engineering
UCC: electronic and computer engineering
UL: electronic engineering; electronics manufacturing
DCU: electronic engineering; mechatronics; Euro electronic systems;
DIT: electrical/electronic engineering
Cork IT: electronic engineering
Waterford IT: electronics
Common entry degrees:
UCD, TCD and NUI Galway offer common-entry engineering programmes.

*Some full-time add-on degrees in related areas:*
Carlow IT: bachelor of technology in production technology
Dundalk IT: product design engineering
Galway IT: digital and software systems engineering
Sligo IT: quality assurance
Tallaght IT: manufacturing engineering
Waterford IT: computer-aided manufacturing

## CERTIFICATES AND DIPLOMAS:
All institutes of technology offer electronic engineering at certificate and/or diploma level. Some offer electronics combined with telecommunications and mechanical engineering.

## POST LEAVING CERTIFICATE COURSES:
A number of PLC colleges offer courses in electronics or related areas. Check with your local VEC or PLC college.

## Career choice

### CHOOSING A COURSE:

At degree level, there is also a tremendous demand for electronics graduates. Leaving Cert students attracted to electronics who are not quite sure if it is exactly what they want, might consider a common-entry engineering degree programme. This has been the approach in TCD and UCD, with students sampling various areas of engineering before making up their minds to specialise. NUI Galway has also adopted this approach and is now offering a common-entry engineering programme in addition to its two electronics degrees.

In TCD, students spend a common two years before deciding on one of the college's five specialisms: civil, structural and environmental engineering; mechanical and manufacturing engineering; electronic engineering; computer engineering; electronic and computer engineering (joint programme). There is no quota system in operation so students know that once they secure a place in first-year, they are guaranteed a place in third year in the specialism of their choice.

Both NUI Galway and UCD operate quota systems so students have to compete for places after a common first year. UCD offers specialisms in agricultural and food engineering, chemical engineering, civil engineering, electronic and electrical engineering and mechanical engineering. Chemical engineering is on offer only in UCD and CIT, which operates a direct-entry programme.

NUI Galway offers specialisms in civil engineering, electronic engineering, industrial engineering and information systems, mechanical engineering, electronic and computer engineering and management engineering with a language.

Employers often remark on the usefulness of a work placement. It's also useful from a student's point of view, giving them an opportunity to see exactly what the job entails before

# Electronic engineering

they graduate. A number of colleges include work placements in their programme.

For instance, students in the electronics manufacturing programme in UL spend from the end of January to the end of September in placement while students who have finished second year of the college's electronic engineering programme spend their summer and the first term of third year in work placement.

### THE FATE OF ENGINEERING DEGREE GRADUATES

A glance at the Higher Education Authority's engineering statistics shows a very high proportion of engineering graduates in employment – over 70 per cent in all branches of engineering – reflecting the buoyant demand for engineers. This compares very favourably with 54 per cent of all graduates.

Of the electrical/electronic engineering graduates, 79 per cent were employed – 68 per cent at home and 11 per cent overseas. Fifteen per cent went to research or further study while one per cent went into teacher training. Two per cent were seeking employment (compared to an overall graduate unemployment rate of 3.6 per cent) and the remaining three per cent were not available for work or study.

### SOME UNUSUAL OPTIONS:

*BEng/MEng in electronic systems*
DCU introduced this innovative five-year programme in 1996. Students spend the first four years in DCU studying engineering, business and a language while the fifth year is spent in a European engineering school. Graduates receive a BEng at the end of the four years and an MEng on successful completion of fifth year.

Mechatronic engineering: At Athlone IT, a new national diploma in mechatronics is on offer. Dr Eliathamby Ambikairajah, head of the college's school of engineering, explains that mechatronics 'is the integration of mechanical engineering, electronic engineering and computer control'. Mechatronic products include washing machines, camcorders and robotic devices. 'There's a real need in industry for people who have this multi-disciplinary technology', according to Dr Ambikairajah. The programme was introduced in response to contact with companies such as Hewlett Packard and Analog Devices.

Two years ago, DCU introduced a degree in mechatronic engineering and it is possible that diploma graduates may be able to transfer on to this programme. Dr Lisa Looney of DCU's School of Mechanical and Manufacturing Engineering says that the college's policy is to encourage this type of cross-transfer. DCU's course has a very strong design element and there is a six-month work placement in third year.

### No higher-level maths?

All ab-initio engineering degree programmes require maths at higher-level in the Leaving Certificate. However, students who take ordinary-level maths can still work their way towards a degree if they take the certificate, diploma, degree route.

### Good news for students taking biology:

Students seeking places on UL's Bachelor of Engineering programmes (computer, electronic, mechanical, production, industrial, aeronautical) should be pleased to find that the college's list of required Leaving Certificate science subjects has been expanded to include biology and agricultural science. This should make the programme more accessible to girls, according to the admission's officer.

## Electronic engineering

Prospective engineering students at UL now need a higher-level grade C3 in maths and an ordinary-level D3 in any one of the following science subjects: physics, chemistry, physics/chemistry, engineering, technical drawing, biology or agricultural science.

# Careers in Film

*What excites me is the process*

David McLoughlin talks to Catherine Foley about his work as a film producer.

Here's the story. Frame one rolls: a Cecil B de Mille type flashing a toothy smile and puffing on a big Cuban cigar walks onto the set. Minions quake. Actors' mouths drop open. The producer has arrived.

'Wrong picture!' cries David McLoughlin. 'That's not the reality.' OK, frame two comes up – enter a soft-spoken, casually-dressed manager who walks quietly behind the cameras to chat with the crew, check some details and move on.

McLoughlin explains: 'You're like a manager. You're responsible for the entire operation. The producer spends his time with the crew, the financiers, the distributors, the sales agents, you have to keep all of those people happy.' A film producer has to have good interpersonal skills, he explains.

'It's a combination of persuading on the one hand and motivating on the other. A good producer needs to have a reasonable commercial sense, an instinct that tells you if this is going to make money at the end of the day. You have to have that. If you don't have the confidence that tells you that people will go and see it, financiers won't go for it.'

In a matter-of-fact tone, he declares it's a job at the end of the day. 'People who work there are not dazzled by the glamour. What excites me is the process, knowing that you're in the middle of a project and you can see the final results at the end of the day.'

McLoughlin was always interested in film production – in particular 'in the business end and the organisational side of the industry, the co-ordinational side'. But, he explains, 'producers are not book-keepers. Being able to read budgets and set budgets is important but it's more the feeling of team work, of coming up with an interesting idea, of seeing whether it's feasible and getting around you a very good team bringing the thing to fruition and then seeing the thing on screen.'

# Career choice

After school at Blackrock College, he graduated from TCD with an economics degree in 1990. In hindsight, he says, 'I would have preferred if I'd learned more about law and more accountancy but it's still a very useful degree to have.'

His route into film production was circuitous. 'Entry is very undefined, particularly in terms of producers. It's a skill you have to acquire yourself. As the industry has expanded, it has become very obvious that there's a lack of producers.'

McLoughlin wrote film reviews for college publications and other magazines. Later he worked on a film set in Canada when he was a student. Then in 1991, he became full-time manager of the Dublin Film Festival. He was there until 1996. 'There are parallels between managing a film festival and managing a film – co-ordinating, the operational knowledge and raising finances.'

During this period, he had his first assignment as a producer, working with director Alan Gilsenan on a small film, *All Souls' Day*, which was screened at the Cork Film Festival in 1997.

'It was a small but very committed crew. We all just worked for nothing. It's kind of a subversive theme, it's a psychological drama.'

In 1996, he had the opportunity to work as a trainee producer on *The Boxer* which was being produced by Jim Sheridan and Arthur Lappin's company. 'It gave me a lot of freedom to learn and it's very rare that you would be given an opportunity like that, to have access to information like that on such a big operation. You get a good feel for the numbers and the whole event.'

After this, McLoughlin worked as assistant director on *Dancing at Lughnasa*. 'As assistant director, I had more responsibility and I was more heavily involved in the production of the film. It was a good extension of the training. I was on the set far more than *The Boxer*.'

Although directing was not his ultimate goal, McLoughlin explains that 'the reason I wanted to do it was I knew it would be a continuation of the training I was getting. To work on two very big productions is very good. People need to work on the floor of a film and see how it happens and the numbers involved. You get an appreciation of what people do. It's more than book-keeping. You have to be a good motivator.'

Having completed post-production work on *All Souls Day*, McLoughlin is also in the process of setting up his own production company.

'It's exciting on the one hand but also a challenge,' he says. 'I'm becoming my own boss. I have to pay the rent and come up with projects that are viable, that will be capable of raising finance. There are a few projects that I've been told about.

'That's the thing about the film industry. It's unique in that you rarely see them advertise in newspapers. That's why people are daunted by it. It's a mystery, in particular in terms of production. But, if you can get your foot in the door, you're started.'

### CAREER FOCUS: THE FILM INDUSTRY

Finding employment in films is not simply a matter of picking the right third-level course. Working your way up is an equally valid route, so it's difficult to advise on the most appropriate way in. Film is a diverse employer with jobs ranging from actors to camera people to production assistants to marketing people.

The industry fits into the audio-visual industry which encompasses film, television, multi-media, corporate video and information programming, explains Tony Treacey, education officer with the Film Institute of Ireland. Film costs much more than video, he says – it's also much more labour intensive and there is far less room for error.

'That's probably why the traditional way in was via an apprenticeship-type route with people beginning, for instance, as trainee clapper-loaders and working their way up.' For the uninitiated, a clapper loader takes film out and puts it in, he explains. A trainee clapper-loader helps the clapper-loader.

'When I first became interested in film, I was in the US,' says Treacey. 'I got a job on a set as a runner. From there, I moved to product placement. On small budget films, this means getting as many free props as possible; on larger films companies will pay to have their products showcased. I finally ended up working on distribution for Miramax, distributing films to film festivals. I then did the MA in film studies in UCD and ended up as education officer with the FII.'

Treacey talks of a non-traditional career path. 'You don't know where you'll be in five years. There's no guarantee that you'll have a job and you won't work regular hours. An average film shoot lasts four to six weeks and you may be working 15 hours a day.'

Pay? At the lower end, you may be getting little or nothing, he says. At the top end, technicians may earn £800 to £1,500 a week but they may do that for only 12 weeks in the year.

A range of third-level options are open to students, from certificate to diploma to degree. There are also PLC courses, notably in Ballyfermot Senior College and Coláiste Dhúlaigh, both in Dublin. These courses usually fill early.

Muireann Ní Dhuigneáin, DCU careers officer, says that the rationale behind the college's three-year communications degree is to offer a broad range of subjects, perhaps more so than any other BA, and also, to develop technical skills. 'The first year after graduation is like the fourth year of a programme for other people,' she says. 'We don't have work experience to the same extent.' She sees the jobs prognosis as good, although graduates may start with short-term contracts.

The 55 students who graduated in 1996 found work in a wide variety of areas – research in TV, public relations, telesales supervising, computer graphics, marketing, video production and banking.

Nora French, head of DIT's department of communications, says that Aungier Street's four-year communications degree is divided between study and production work in broadcasting and film. 'After the four years,' she says, 'we would hope that students would be able to produce work of an acceptable standard.' Work experience is built into the summer after the final exams and students must report on this experience before they graduate.

Most of the graduates find work in the private production area, in a variety of careers from the skills end, such as camera operator, to producers, directors and film writers. Students beginning the course in 1998 will be awarded a DIT degree at the end of four years.

Dun Laoghaire IT offers a range of courses in film and television, from a two-year certificate in TV production to a three-year film and video diploma to courses in model-making and make-up. Michael McNally, who co-ordinates the TV production certificate and the film and video diploma, says that the cross-linking dynamism in the college is very important, with the courses influencing each other.

Graduates of the various courses have generally done very well. 'There are loads of opportunities for people with a bit of get up and go,' says McNally – but people should think in terms of work not jobs.

The college also offers a one-year add-on degree programme and, usually, each year, five or six graduates of the diploma in film and video will continue their studies to degree.

## OTHER ROUTES ARE OPEN

Many people enter film and television, having completed a degree in a completely different area. DIT offers a post-graduate diploma in film production which would suit students with a degree in another area, says Nora French, head of DIT's department of communications.

The college's evening course in media studies was originally aimed at teachers, but now attracts a wide range of students. It's expected that this course will soon become an MA.

DCU's MA in film and television is primarily concerned with appreciation and criticism. There is very little practical content, says Muireann Ni Dhuigneain, DCU careers officer.

UCD has an MA in film studies covering the history, theory and practice of film-making in Europe (with particular reference to Ireland) and the US. UCD's school of film also offers an intensive summer course. A number of centres, including Film Base in the Irish Film Centre, the Nerve Centre in Derry, Galway Film Centre and the Cavern in Cork offer specific skills training, according to Tony Treacey, education officer with the Film Institute of Ireland

## FACT FILE

*Full-time ab-initio degrees:*
DIT Aungier Street: communications – film & broadcasting. 1997–98 points 465*(random selection – not all students at this points level were offered places).
DCU: communication studies. 1997–98 points: 465.

## Careers in film

*Full-time certificate/diploma courses:*
Dun Laoghaire IT: Design – communication – film/television. 1997–98 points 915
Dun Laoghaire IT: Make-up for film & theatre. 1997–98 points 760
Dun Laoghaire IT: TV & video production.
Dun Laoghaire IT: Model-making. 1997–98 points 650
Tallaght IT: Audio/visual communications. 1997–98 points 420

### ADD-ON DEGREES:
Dun Laoghaire IT: one-year add-on degrees in film/video and production design. Applicants must have a merit or distinction in a national diploma in design – communications or art or equivalent. A pass diploma may be considered if relevant work has been completed in the appropriate specialised area.

### DIRECT EMPLOYMENT IN FILM INDUSTRY 1995:
Total employment 17,890; feature films/major TV dramas 15,904; independent TV productions 1,780; animation 206.
From: 1995 IBEC report on economic impact of film production in Ireland. This report records 12 major film/drama productions in 1993, 13 in 1994 and 22 in 1995.

### EMPLOYMENT:
Total employment in the film industry in Ireland grew from 3,812 in 1993 to 15,904 in 1995. Of these, the number of Irish people employed rose from 3,435 to 14,123 in the same period. The number of Irish producers, directors and technical production people is also growing.

# Garda

*Some of the bars give off strange smells*

Detective Garda Noel Clarke talks to Catherine Foley about his life on the force.

He spreads the contents of his Gladstone bag across the table. There is a kilo of paki black, little bags of shrunk seeds, quantities of rock heroin, a spoon, some hubble bubbles, little bottles of poppers, grams of Chinese rock, some ten spots and a few chocolate bars. Some of the bars give off strange smells.

These are the oddly named stock-in-trade of drug dealers and addicts. It's a sad business, says Detective Noel Clarke, as he examines the packages. As a major part of his job in the Garda National Drug Unit (GNDU), Clarke visits schools, hospitals and community centres to brief people on drugs. He talks to parents, students, teachers, community groups and trainee gardai.

'We bring a certain amount of drugs to show them,' he explains. During his talk he explains each item in his bag, what it's worth in the street, how it is used by addicts. He talks about the tell-tale signs of drug abuse, about how to identify drugs with a run-down on what to look for.

Parents are 'exceptionally keen to come and see what it's like,' says Clarke. They want to be in a position to deal with it in their own homes and be able to nip it in the bud, he says.

Noel Clarke has been in the force for the past 33 years. He arrived at Templemore, Co. Tipperary, as an innocent young lad from Ballymote, Co. Sligo. He hoped for a rural posting but fate sent him to Donnybrook Garda Station in 1964 and he has spent all of his working life in the city.

'From the first time I went out on the beat in Donnybrook, I loved every moment of it,' he says. 'I got a different insight into Dublin people – they were always very genuine, the salt of the earth.'

After four years, he moved to the Special Detective Unit in Dublin Castle until the late 1960s. His work at that time involved protecting and escorting VIPs, working at Aras an

## Career choice

Uachtarain and some investigative work into subversive activity.

Later, as a detective garda, he joined the GNDU when it was set up in 1972, and was involved in surveillance work, searches and investigations. Yes, he says, this kind of work can be dangerous. 'We're dealing with people who, after getting drugs, come down and the euphoric feeling is gone,' he explains. 'It makes them depressed and angry.' Colleagues have been stabbed with syringes, bitten by dogs and beaten up. 'But generally the majority of people don't want to cause harm.'

Clarke recalls his early days on the drug problem: 'When I joined the drug squad, the greater percentage of drugs activity was at the top of Stephen's Green. It was mainly young people who came in around town, smoking dope. It was all part of the hippie regime. They were mostly inoffensive people. Cannabis was the most popular drug. There was a very small amount of hard drug users then. They were easy to deal with – they never had any animosity towards the police.'

Today, as the longest serving member of the Drug Squad, with uninterrupted service since the early 1970s, he can look back and compare that scene with today's crime levels. 'In later years, a different breed has come along,' says Clarke. 'They've made fortunes out of the misery of others. They don't mind who they hurt.'

His saddest memory was discovering the body of Garda Michael Reynolds, who had been shot, in St Anne's Park, Raheny. 'I knew him. We were often on patrol at the same time. We'd always stop and have a chat. He was an excellent policeman. That was one of the down parts.'

Noel Clarke has seen the terrible destruction and death that drugs cause but 'a feeling that you're doing something worthwhile' has sustained him. In 1994, he was awarded a

Divisional Merit Award for 'his caring attitude and humane approach to drug addicts and their families.

'There were failures, but it's great to see someone get motivated and go to get treatment. We wanted them to do something with their lives, not to end up in the gutter.'

### Fact File

Pay Scales: £12,040 to £19,159 per annum.

Pay and allowances for trainees prior to attestation (end of phase 3 of training): £83.35 per week when in Templemore or on annual leave plus an allowance of £42.80 per week towards food and accommodation.

The food and accommodation allowance is increased by £10 per week when trainees are on work experience.

Boot allowance: £2.08 per week; uniform allowance: £2.93 per week.

### Education requirements:

Grade D in at least five ordinary-level Leaving Certificate subjects to include Irish, English, Maths or Leaving Cert Vocational.

A grade not lower than D at ordinary level in at least three subjects, including English, together with a grade not lower than B at foundation level in maths and a grade not lower than C at foundation level in Irish in the Leaving Certificate or the Leaving Certificate Vocational programme or a merit grade in the Leaving Certificate Applied or similar grades in other exams of equal standard such as university matriculation, NCEA national certs and diplomas. Candidates with these qualifications must have the required standard in Irish, English and maths.

It is heartening to see recognition being given to all three Leaving Certificate programmes – the traditional Leaving

Cert, the Leaving Cert Vocational and the Leaving Cert Applied. In addition, the acceptance of foundation-level maths and Irish will aid many candidates who may be excluded from other courses.

AGE/HEIGHT/HEALTH REQUIREMENTS:
Candidates must be between 18 and 26 years of age with extensions for applicants who have served in the permanent defence forces or An Forsa Cosanta Áitiúl or An Slua Muiri.

Men must be at least 5 ft 9 inches in height.

Women must be at least 5 ft 5 inches in height.

All candidates must be in good mental and physical health and of good character. The vision standard required of a trainee Garda is 6/9 in one eye and not less than 6/12 in the other eye, unaided by glasses or contact lenses, with normal colour vision. The following conditions may be a bar to entry: varicose veins, overweight, albumenuria, dental caries, defective hearing, hypertension.

The mission of An Garda Siochana is 'to protect life and property, to safeguard the liberties of the individual and to preserve the public peace; to prevent and detect crime; to provide guidance for young people as they seek to become caring, law-abiding citizens; and in so doing to provide a quality service to the public while maintaining the highest standards of integrity, professionalism and efficiency'.

The two-year training period includes classroom instruction, physical education and work experience.

Selection for Garda training is on the basis of written tests, medical examination and interview. Recruitment is announced periodically and there are always far more applicants than places. You do not need to do any special preparation for the written exam – there is no syllabus and no past papers are available. Those placed highest in the written exam are called for interview.

The training programme breaks down into five phases. The first 22-week phase, the third 12-week phase and the fifth six-week phase are spent at the Garda College in Templemore, Co. Tipperary. Phases two (24 weeks) and four (36 weeks) are experimental learning phases where trainees go on work experience at selected training stations throughout Ireland.

Teaching facilities at the Garda College include a court room, a 'scene of the crime' room, television studio, computer room, printing unit, gym and tactical training facilities such as a driving school, abseiling walls and a firing range.

Phase one includes legal, social and technical studies as well as policing, communication, Irish and French or German and PE. Phase two is on-the-job training where trainees experience the reality of police work. Back in college for phase three, the knowledge and experience gained in the first two phases are put together. At the end of this phase, successful trainees are attested as probationer Gardai.

In phase four, the probationers operate as Gardai for the first time. They also complete a 10,000 word dissertation on a police-related topic. The final phase integrates all of the studies areas by means of case studies and simulated exercises.

After their final exams, successful probationers are awarded the national diploma in police studies, a National Council for Educational Awards qualification.

Gardai may further develop their careers by applying for positions in specialist units such as the drugs squad, the emergency response unit, the woman and child unit, the underwater unit and the dog unit. Gardai may also become teachers and trainers.

A Garda must have three years service (from the date of attestation) to be eligible to sit the sergeant's exam. But, if a

Garda has a degree, he or she may sit the first promotional exam after the two-year probationary period. In addition, Gardai who have certain third-level qualifications are entitled to a number of increments in their pay at the end of the probationary period.

# AMENITY HORTICULTURE

*I started work the day after graduation*

Martina Gormley talks to Catherine Foley about her work as a parks superintendent with Dún Laoghaire/Rathdown Co. Council.

# Career choice

The sun slants across the park on a bright, cold November day. Martina Gormley scans the work that has been carried out since her last visit. She takes note of the trees, the hedges, the lawns, the borders and the pathways. She walks on. Any deviation from the plan is noted. Any problems are jotted down.

Her job as a parks superintendent with Dún Laoghaire /Rathdown Co. Council involves drawing up and implementing designs for a range of public open spaces, including parks, sports amenities and facilities and also current work on the Southern Cross Motorway and the South-Eastern Motorway. She is also working on the restoration of the walled garden and the period house in Marley Park, both of which date back to the Georgian period between 1764 and 1837.

This is one of the most challenging and exciting projects at the moment, says Gormley, her eyes lighting up with enthusiasm. 'Two of us are working on the research and design of the walled garden. Our job primarily is to get all the relevant material together and to have it look as authentic as possible. It's very interesting.

'I spoke to members of the La Touche family who lived there over 100 years ago and also the Love family who lived in the house until 1973. They were able to give us photographs. It will be restored to the Georgian/Regency period.'

She is uncovering further details by reading through old documents at the National Library and the National Archive in order to discover the horticultural background of Marley House.

Gormley is one of a team of 10 parks superintendents with the council. 'We are project-based rather than area-based,' she says. Her job title 'comes from way back – it's an

## Amenity horticulture

old traditional name.' The European equivalent would be a landscape architect.

'You don't spend all the time outdoors,' says Gormley. 'The project will dictate how much time you need to spend outside. Generally, you'll do a lot of the design inside.' The parks department has 2,500 acres under its wing.

Her interest in this work goes back to her father, Eamon Gormley, she explains. 'He used to take me with him when he travelled to different farms . . . he was an agricultural officer with the Department of Agriculture. He used to inspect crops. I'd go with him during my summer holidays – I'd walk the drills with him sometimes. He was definitely the inspiration behind my decision to do this work. That's where it started. It's in the blood.'

Her first job was with Tipperary North Riding Co. Council – she was responsible for urban and village renewal projects, such as those at Toomevara and Killoscully. There old Mass paths were incorporated into the design. 'There were nine different projects – I was responsible for seven. I started work the day after graduation.'

After finishing second-level at the Holy Faith De La Salle College in Skerries, Co. Dublin, Gormley was offered a place on the BAg science in landscape horticulture at UCD. She deferred for a year and did a Teagasc certificate in amenity horticulture at the National Botanic Gardens in Glasnevin, Dublin. 'I found that a great help,' she says. 'It's very hard to know what way to go and that gave me an idea of what the work involved.'

She carried on to UCD then and began her studies in agricultural science. 'After two years at UCD, you decide what area you want to go into. There's a wide choice, including forestry, agricultural engineering, environmental science, commercial horticulture, animal science.' There were 11 in the group when Gormley graduated. 'It's very good because the class is so small.'

She found some of the subjects quite broad. 'You spend a lot of time doing design. It's very time consuming but I realised when I went to Tipperary how important it was. You can't have too much design. It helps if you enjoy learning how to draw and if you enjoy the design aspect but drawing is not a requirement.'

As part of her studies at UCD, she went to Wageningen University in the Netherlands for three months. Then she went to the Szarvasi Arboretum in Hungary for three months. 'I'd strongly recommend students to get experience abroad. You can see what other countries are at. I found the design in Holland to be very functional – a lot of planning would be in straight lines.

'In Ireland, although design would be very individual, in general we would be functional. We try to encompass as much nature as possible. Here you see nice curves. Theirs are very rigid.'

### CAREER FOCUS: HORTICULTURE

The Botanic Gardens' plant collection is a major resource for students. 'The gardens are the college not the buildings as in other courses,' says Dr Paul Cusack, co-ordinator of the diploma in amenity horticulture in the College of Amenity Horticulture at the National Botanic Gardens in Glasnevin, Dublin. A new library, herbarium and computing facilities have recently been built in the gardens.

Places on the three-year full-time diploma are awarded on the basis of an aptitude test, which involves horticultural knowledge, basic science and general knowledge. No past papers are available – the reason for this selection method is that the college wants to identify students with a genuine interest in the area, says Cusack. Ideally, prospective students would have spent some time working in a garden centre in the summers or part-time.

There are usually about four applicants for each of the 50 first-year places and there is generally a good mixture of mature students and school-leavers. 'There is a fair range of ages on the course. Some people are changing careers while others have been working in the horticulture area and want to formalise their qualifications,' says Cusack.

Second year of the course is spent on placement, usually with Dublin Corporation parks department. Students may also arrange their own placement, provided it is acceptable to the college. There are no fees for tuition throughout the three years and students receive a maintenance grant, which varies depending on the distance of their home from the college.

The course is more 'hands-on' than UCD's landscaping option. Job opportunities for graduates of the horticulture diploma are good, according to Cusack. Graduates may find work in the parks department, on private estates or with landscaping bodies.

Application forms for the course are available from the College of Amenity Horticulture and all Teagasc offices from May. The assessment test is usually held at the end of June, after the Leaving Cert and candidates know, by mid-July, if they have a place. So, there is no waiting around for Leaving Cert results.

In contrast, the landscape option within UCD's agricultural science degree is offered through the CAO. Last year, you would have needed at least 380 points to secure a place. Increasingly, students from an urban background are opting for agricultural sciences. The four-year degree includes a substantial element of design, allowing students to combine art with science.

# Career choice

Agricultural students take a common first-year which includes the basic sciences and computer science. Between 15 and 20 students usually opt for landscape horticulture in second year, where they begin to study the more applied areas – agricultural and environmental biology, plant physiology, soil science, agribusiness and landscape design.

In third year, students do a six-month placement. This may be in Ireland or abroad. The course has good links with Germany, England and the United States, says course co-ordinator Karen Foley. French and German are offered as elective languages. Under an EU exchange programme, students and staff may also participate in intensive two-week exchange programmes with 10 other universities in Europe.

At the moment, job opportunities for graduates of the landscape horticulture course are very good, says Foley. Students who wish to continue their studies may opt for an MSc in landscape architecture in UCD. There are about 10 places on this two-year programme which is also open to graduates of allied programmes such as architecture or other agricultural specialisms.

Graduates of other programmes may have to take pre-requisites. An arrangement is in the offing whereby graduates of the landscape programme will be able to go directly into second year of the master's programme.

### INTENSIVE ONE-YEAR GREENING

Horticulture is not an area you might associate immediately with PLC colleges in Dublin. However, for the past five years, Ringsend Technical Institute has offered an intensive one-year course in amenity horticulture and grounds maintenance.

Subjects studied include plant science, soil science, communications and horticultural science and engineering. This latter includes the Health and Safety Acts and the safety and

## Amenity horticulture

wiring of tools. Students also learn about the business side of horticulture; they study communications, computer studies and business administration.

Course co-ordinator Gwen Dolan explains that 'an integral part of the course is work experience. One advantage of NCVA accreditation is that work experience is taken very seriously. This gives students a link with the world of employment before they graduate.'

Graduates may continue their studies by doing the Teagasc diploma in amenity horticulture or they may go to British colleges, with Writtle and Ottley being particularly popular. Alternatively, they may find work directly, usually with garden centres or landscapers.

### Fact File

*Full-time undergraduate third-level courses:*
UCD: agricultural science, landscape horticulture option. Four year full-time course. 1997–98 points: 380* (* random selection applied so not all at this points level were offered a place).

Teagasc: The college of amenity horticulture, National Botanic Gardens, offers a three-year full-time diploma. Places are allocated on the basis of an aptitude test.

### Post Leaving Cert courses:

A number of PLC colleges offer amenity horticulture and greenkeeping courses. These are usually one year in duration and admission is generally by interview and a minimum of five passes in the Leaving Cert is required. Check with your local VEC or PLC college for details.

MSc in landscape architecture: Offered by UCD, this programme is open to graduates of related programmes, such as geography and architecture, as well as agricultural science graduates.

### Related courses:

Commercial horticulture courses concentrate on the production of plants and crops while amenity courses concentrate on landscape design, construction and maintenance.

There is a commercial horticulture option within UCD's agriculture degree and Teagasc offers a diploma in commercial horticulture in three colleges. Teagasc also offers a horticultural skills programme which is aimed at people seeking work as skilled operatives in nurseries, garden centres and parks. In addition, craft courses in horticulture are provided by Teagasc and sponsored by FÁS.

# Marketing with Languages

*It's not Curly Watts you'll meet*

Kyle Clifford talks to Catherine Foley about his life as a regional trainee manager with a supermarket chain.

# Career choice

'If you go in to see any good manager, it's not Curly Watts you'll meet,' says Kyle Clifford with a twinkle in his eye, rising to a claim that the bungling soap character is a true representation of today's retail manager. Yes, he nods, the Curly Watts syndrome does exist in the minds of some people, but nothing could be further from the truth.

'It's very challenging and it's very hard work. You're not swanning around in a suit and tie all day. It's a team effort.' After graduating from UL with a degree in business studies with a modern language, Clifford started working with the Musgrave Group for six months on the shop floor of Supervalu in Killester, Dublin. He worked in the meat department, the delicatessen section and the fruit-and-veg areas. He soaked up the sales strategies, store procedures and incentives and the overall heave and swell of the selling game.

As a regional manager trainee with the Musgrave group, which owns the Supervalu and Centra franchising chains, as well as a chain of cash-and-carry outlets, Clifford is enthusiastic and excited about his job. 'I find I can't just walk into a supermarket,' he says. 'I'm watching for every new idea, I'm criticising, analysing.'

On completion of the training programme, he expects his knowledge of the retail trade to be wide-ranging and detailed. For the past year, he has worked in many of Musgrave's departments, including purchasing, store design and engineering, accounting, finance and marketing.

During this time, he carried out research and implemented various projects as part of his preparation for the retail environment. Next year, when his trainee's umbilical cord will be cut, he will work as a regional manager with Supervalu. By then, he says, his mind will have to be focussed on 'going in and empathising with the retailer'. He will be at the coalface of retailing, in the shops dealing with retailers throughout a region as well as dealing with departments in head office.

'I knew when I went to the University of Limerick that I would enjoy marketing. I didn't know then that I would work in retailing.' Nor did he know that he would become addicted to the variety, challenge and excitement of the retail front. 'It's particularly exciting just now with the UK multiples entering the market.'

From Annacotty, Co. Limerick, Clifford did the Leaving Cert in 1992 at St Clement's Redemptorist College. 'I wanted to be in a people-orientated business,' he recalls. He decided on business studies with a modern language at UL.

He majored in marketing and studied Spanish as his minor subject. One year of his degree programme included work experience. He worked in a clinical research company in California and spent a further six months with Esso Ltd in Stillorgan, Dublin.

Studying Spanish at UL opened up that country's culture and business practices to him. This was particularly useful, since the Musgrave group owns two Spanish cash-and-carry companies.

'The regional manager's role is unique in that you interact with all the personnel from management and head office and you are on the road, meeting all the retailers as well,' says Clifford. 'If you're an out-going, ambitious individual who enjoys meeting people and dealing with issues, being on your feet, being out and about, interacting with different people and different personalities, and if you like being in an environment that is fast moving and changing, then the retail environment is for you, then you would suit retailing. You have to be open-minded and be able to work on a range of issues.'

# Career choice

## CAREER FOCUS: MARKETING WITH LANGUAGES

The recent explosion in marketing, business and commerce courses which include a language continues this year with the advent of a new international commerce degree with Swedish in UCD and a new business with Chinese degree in TCD (Chinese and Japanese will be alternated over the coming years). Catherine KilBride, education director with the Irish Marketing Institute, quotes the old saw about marketing people being in demand during a boom and accountants being in demand during a recession. To be fair to accountants, they are much in demand at present also.

This is definitely a boom time for the economy. For students who wish to take advantage of it by specialising in marketing, KilBride says that a third-level qualification is a must. A glance at the Fact File shows that there is no shortage of courses on offer from certificates to diplomas to degrees.

The points needed to secure places on the various degrees (1997 entry) ranged through the mid-300s up to mid-500s. At certificate/diploma level, 110 points would have secured a place on Sligo IT's marketing and Spanish course, while 125 points was needed to get a place on their marketing and German option.

Students who are not sure whether marketing is right for them, should eschew the direct-entry programmes and opt for a general business or commerce programme which will allow them to specialise later. These programmes allow students to specialise in marketing and languages to various extents.

Many students will also specialise at post-graduate level. It's important to read through the various subjects and options offered in each year of the undergraduate programme so you know exactly what you are opting for.

For instance, students opting for the University of Limerick's four-year degrees can specialise in a variety of areas –

those who take marketing will typically team it with a language, entrepreneurship or law, says Mary Sweeney, co-operative education manager at UL.

'The job scene has been very good for them,' says Sweeney. 'Of the 1996 graduates, about 90 majored in marketing. When we surveyed them in April 1997 about 88 per cent were employed, 10 per cent were doing further study and two per cent were seeking employment.' The 88 per cent who were employed breaks down into 76 per cent who found work in Ireland and 12 per cent who were employed overseas.

'The kinds of jobs are very varied,' she says. Some of the graduates are in customer support operations, working with companies such as IBM and Oracle. There is an interest in taking on graduates with a language because of the new European call centres, says Sweeney. Some graduates go in to banking or the financial services area while others will end up in export marketing with major food companies, such as Dairygold. The job list also includes marketing research, public relations, sales and advertising executives, retail management, purchasing and merchandising planning.

DCU offers four direct-entry international marketing and language degrees. Students take two European languages or Japanese and all students spend one year abroad. Careers officer, Muireann Ní Dhuigneáin says that graduates of this degree continue to do exceptionally well. Of the 1996 graduates, 85 per cent went directly into employment. The remainder went on to further study. Of those who were employed, more than half were working at home with the rest employed overseas. Some of these latter graduates are working on behalf of Irish companies abroad.

The international business and European business programmes are broader courses which also include some marketing.

## The cert/diploma option

Students who do not get the points for ab-initio degree programmes or who do not want to commit themselves to four years' study may consider a certificate or diploma in marketing or business with languages.

These programmes are offered by the institutes of technology (see Fact File).

For instance, Waterford Institute of Technology offers a national diploma in business studies (French/German and marketing). Half of the course is devoted to language studies and students may be able to study abroad under the EU Socrates programme. As well as their major language, students will also gain a good working knowledge of a second language.

Career opportunities are primarily in export promotion, marketing, sales and administration. Diploma students who get a merit or distinction are eligible to apply for a place on the college's BA in applied languages or the bachelor of business studies.

The advantages of going the cert/diploma route to a degree is that students can opt out after the cert or diploma and still have a valid qualification. They can also return to education at a later stage if they so desire.

## Fact File

*Degrees*
DCU: international marketing with French/German, French/Spanish, German/Spanish or Japanese; international business with French/German, French/Spanish, German/Spanish or Japanese; European business with French/German/Spanish
UL: business studies with French/German/Spanish/Japanese
UCD: commerce (international) with German/French/Spanish/Italian/modern Irish/Swedish

WIT: business studies with French
NCIR: European business and languages
UCC: European commerce with French/German/Italian/Spanish/Irish
TCD: business studies with French/German/Russian/Chinese or Japanese
NUI Galway: commerce with French/German/Spanish

Certificates/diplomas
WIT: business studies (French/German with marketing)
Carlow IT: business studies (international business and French/German)
Dundalk IT: business studies (marketing with language)
Letterkenny IT: business studies/languages with European studies
Sligo IT: business studies (languages and marketing with French/German/Spanish); business studies in European business with French/German/Spanish
Tallaght IT: business studies (marketing and languages)
Tralee IT: business studies/French/German
DIT: business and languages (French/German/Spanish)

PROFESSIONAL BODY:
The Marketing Institute, South County Business Park, Leopardstown, Dublin 18. Tel: (01) 295 2355. The Institute has more than 5,000 members and students. It offers both part-time and full-time courses.

SAMPLE STARTING SALARIES:
1996 graduates of degree programmes employed in Ireland: £11,000 to £13,000 a year. In general, graduates who found work in computer companies or abroad earned more in their first year.

# Polymer engineering

## *Two or three women in a group of 80 men*

Photographer: Peter Thursfield

Patricia Ryan talks to Catherine Foley about her career as a polymer engineer.

# Polymer engineering

'You name any industry and plastic is used in it,' says Patricia Ryan, with the look of a zealot in her eye. 'That's the thing about plastic, people just don't realise where it is used.' Take nylon, she argues – 'today, it's used for gearing huge pieces of machinery.'

With a quick glance around her office for confirmation, she says that plastic is all around us. In the Irish Ropes factory next door, for example, where she worked until recently, 'it's all plastic . . . all the rope, all the twine, all the strapping. They're just 100 per cent plastic.'

Ryan is a rarity. She's a polymer engineer. On top of that, she's the only woman working in a predominantly male world. 'You go to a conference and you will definitely be unusual. You might have two or three women in a group of 80 men.'

There was some disbelief among her friends when she expressed her intention back in the mid-1980s of pursuing a career in plastics. 'People thought I was doing plastic surgery,' she says. 'Polymer engineering was unheard of at that stage.'

With the shrewd know-how that comes from being the youngest member in a family of siblings who have already 'gone into the working world', she studied the jobs pages in the newspapers each week to see 'the industries that were up and coming' and quickly narrowed the field down to 'plastics and computers'.

Because she had 'a hankering for science even in Inter Cert' and because she always liked physics and chemistry and biology, she decided to study polymer technology at Athlone RTC (now Athlone Institute of Technology). After finishing the Leaving Cert in 1985 at the Sacred Heart School in Tullamore, Co. Offaly, Ryan started the four-year BSc course 30 miles away in Athlone. There were 19 in the class in first year including six girls.

'As I was going through, I found that there were aspects of it that I didn't like – I wasn't too keen on the lab work. You could take a job that would be purely polymer chemistry which would be just R&D but I love the industry aspect of it.

'First year was quite enjoyable and not that tough. People who didn't have honours maths had to work that bit harder. They were bringing people up to standard in first year. Then it just got tougher. But, because the class was so small, you had great rapport with your lecturers.'

Ryan did her work experience in third year with Bayer, the chemical giant based in Germany. 'I loved it,' she says. 'It was so hands-on. It was being out where real people have real problems and these are day-to-day problems. There was no such thing as making the answer fit what the lecturer wanted.'

After graduation with an honours degree, she went to Abbot Ireland based in Sligo, which made catheter devices. 'That was Abbot's main product at the time. I was there for about a year and a half. In Abbot you are actually working on a product that went to market. There's an enormous sense of satisfaction to see it going into manufacture from the design stage.'

In November 1990, she moved to Irish Ropes in Newbridge, Co. Kildare, as quality manager. Then in 1992, she was offered a job at a sister company, Sealcon, as technical and quality manager.

'Irish Ropes and Sealcon are on the same site but we do completely different products,' she explains. Sealcon produces packaging for the food industry, in particular a number of butterspread companies. 'It was a big change. It's a very different process that we use here.'

With the steady hum of big machines in the background, Ryan is happy, working in a world that she loves. 'That's the beauty of it,' she says. 'No two days are the same.'

Of course, she'd love to see more women working in the business – 'but I have to say that the guys treat you as an equal. The problem is that it's difficult to get young people into the industry.'

### Career focus: Polymer engineer

The polymer industry employs about 16,000 people in Ireland. Between 10 and 20 per cent are in the technical area, according to Reg McCabe of the Plastics Industry Association (PIA). The industry has grown in the past five years, particularly in healthcare.

Most school-leavers are unaware of the opportunities so the PIA and Athlone Institute of Technology have produced an introduction programme for Transition Year students – 'the message is that there are exciting and challenging opportunities and it's very well paid.'

Athlone IT, the national education centre for technicians and engineers for the plastic industry, offers a number of courses. The University of Limerick also offers a degree in material science which includes the study of polymers.

Dr Eliathamby Ambikairajah, head of Athlone's school of engineering, says that two four-year ab-initio degree programmes are being offered this year – polymer technology and polymer engineering.

'Students must have higher-level maths for the engineering programme or they must pass the special maths exam set by the college,' he says, 'whereas there is no higher-level maths requirement for the BSc in polymer technology.'

The higher-level maths requirement has been causing a problem with recruitment. There were only ten students in first year in 1997. To increase numbers and to fulfil industry needs, the college is re-introducing its BSc in polymer technology. About 30 degree graduates and 30 to 40 technicians are needed each year.

'There is less design on the technology programme,' he says. 'Industry will be able to choose between graduates who are more technically orientated or more design-orientated.' Athlone also offers a national certificate in plastics engineering from which students can progress to a diploma and from there to a degree.

Final-year degree and diploma students undertake industry-supported projects. Degree students also spend three months on industrial placement, many of them abroad. Plastic engineering students are virtually guaranteed jobs, according to the college, and they can earn salaries significantly ahead of those with general engineering qualifications.

A four-year UL degree in materials science covers all materials from polymers to ceramics to metals, composites, biomaterials and opto-electronic materials. 'The main thrust of the course is to understand the structure property relationships of materials so you can choose the right material for the right engineering applications,' explains Professor Martin Buggy.

Polymers are increasingly being used for biomedical applications, he says. For instance, drug carrier systems for timed release of drugs are often polymeric as are bio-absorbable materials. Boston Scientific employs graduates of UL and Athlone IT.

Buggy says that employment for UL graduates is very buoyant – about one-third go to electronics companies, one-third to new healthcare companies and one-third to engineering companies. The last available figures show an average starting salary in the region of £15,500 per annum.

McCabe, of the PIA, notes that entry to the industry is not necessarily via a degree. 'We're about to introduce traineeships for moulding technicians in conjunction with FÁS. We'll be looking for people already working in the industry who want a change.'

### FACT FILE

*Full-time third-level courses:*
UL: four-year materials science degree
Athlone IT: two-year certificate in plastic engineering; one-year national diploma in engineering (plastics); four-year degree in polymer engineering; four-year degree in polymer technology

### USEFUL ADDRESS:
Plastics Industry Association, Confederation House, 84–86 Baggot Street, Dublin 2. The association publishes *Platform*, a polymer science and technology resource pack for Transition Year. Copies available free of charge to teachers.

### THE INDUSTRY:
New applications are constantly being developed for industrial sectors as diverse as computers and electronics, automotive, aerospace, healthcare, packaging and consumer products. Ireland is now a leading centre for healthcare production in polymers. Source: Irish Plastics Association

# Estate agent

## *It's all about contacts*

Ronan Webster talks to Catherine Foley about his work as a property consultant.

Well before most offices in Ballsbridge, Dublin, have opened for business, Ronan Webster is at his desk. Even as he drives into work, he is scanning the hoardings, billboards, For Sale signs and empty lots. Interesting properties comes on the market all the time.

'I was always very curious about what was going on about town,' he says, 'always asking my mother about who worked where and who owned what.' Today, as director of investments at Gunne's Property Consultants in Ballsbridge, his youthful curiosity has translated itself into more than just a passing fancy. In these boom days, the role of the property consultant is crucial.

A bit like a marriage broker, Webster explains how a knowledge of the commercial world allows him 'to put proposals to clients and find opportunities for them. Initially it takes time to build up that knowledge but that's the interesting part of it because it's a people business. You're not just matching figures with faceless institutions.'

Webster worked in the United States for two years before returning to work for Gunne's. 'There is one big difference between working here and working in Silicon Valley in California,' he says. 'While you may be looking at bigger deals and more complex transactions in the US, you're not getting the same satisfaction. Here you're dealing with more interesting clients – and each has a different way of dealing. It's very bureaucratic in the US and there's a lot of procrastination. Here you'll get an indication of whether someone is interested or not very quickly.'

Originally from Blanchardstown, Co. Dublin, Webster went to Coolmine Community School, where he remembers being interested in architecture – 'but I didn't have any real talent for drawing'. However, he was always passionate about building and property.

## Career choice

'My first choice was economics in TCD,' he says, 'but then I went to a night-time lecture for sixth-year students at DIT Bolton Street on quantity surveying. I was quite impressed. I talked to one of the lecturers and then I decided to go for that. I hadn't any idea what it was all about.'

After the Leaving Cert, he did the four-year diploma in property economics in DIT Bolton Street. It was 'reasonably intensive', involving up to 30 hours a week of lectures. He graduated in 1990 with the diploma from DIT and a bachelor of science (surveying) from TCD.

His professional career started at Sherry FitzGerald. 'I joined at a good time. Up to that most graduates had to go to London.' Like all graduates, he had to complete 'a kind of probation period where you have to do exams and keep diaries. Then you sit an exam. After two years, you become a chartered surveyor. You're working during those two years.'

The first few years in the business can be difficult, says Webster. 'You have to get to know who owns what buildings and also know the contacts.' Today, he says, the business is very much contact-based and the pace has changed substantially – 'there is a whole new layer of people who were not there before.'

Like many other industries such as banking or accountancy, the property business has opened up to those who were not born into the profession. Today, he stresses, estate agency is an information-based industry.

For anyone thinking about this kind of career, he believes the key qualities needed include an 'ability to think quickly. And you need to be broad-minded in your ideas. A lot is based on someone coming up with an idea.'

After another quick breath, he adds another professional requirement: 'You have to be a self-starter – it's a business where people are very open to ideas.'

A successful property consultant also needs a good memory. 'And you need to be fairly adept with figures. The maths are not very difficult but you need to be numerically adept. And you also need to be able to relate to people, to communicate clearly and concisely when presenting an idea to people, and not talk on the basis of what you know but on the basis of what they will understand.'

Webster explains: 'At the end of the day, you're an agent managing a process. You have to understand that it's the clients on either side who are taking the risks . . . yes, ultimately, you're marrying people with property.'

## CAREER FOCUS

The booming property market means excellent job prospects at present for auctioneers. But, the Irish Auctioneers and Valuers Institute (IAVI) warns that employment in the property profession is cyclical and cautions students considering enrolling in auctioneering courses to take account of the future.

'In the current frenetic state of the market, jobs in estate agency and valuation business are readily available,' says Julie Creedon, IAVI education officer, 'but job placement follows the upwards or downwards movement of the property market, with this usually following a three- to four-year cycle.'

The Institute is concerned that jobs are not guaranteed in three or four year's time when students enrolling this year will be entering the jobs market. 'Too many graduates may be produced and, whereas in the forseeable future these may very well be gobbled up by employers, natural market conditions are usually cyclical and will dictate employment opportunity levels. There are only a certain amount of jobs in the industry.'

This caution may well be advised in view of IAVI estimates that the number of queries it received about third-level property courses rose by 40 per cent in 1997. For the undeterred, a range of full-time courses is on offer spanning the PLC and third-level sector.

At third-level, DIT Bolton Street offers a diploma in auctioneering, valuation and estate agency and diploma in property economics/BSc in surveying. Limerick IT offers a degree in valuation surveying and Galway-Mayo IT offers a diploma in business studies (estate management).

Tom Dunne, head of the department of surveying and building technology in DIT Bolton Street, explains that there is a certain amount of overlap between the college's two courses but they differ in their emphasis. The auctioneering diploma is more marketing and business-orientated while the property economics degree emphasises investment, urban economics and planning.

Dunne says that Ireland has traditionally produced more estate agents than the market would absorb. On the plus side, it's an exciting career, a great career, he adds, even in the bad times it's exciting. Dunne notes that would-be auctioneers should be 'extrovert, numerate, literate and entrepreneurial'.

Limerick IT has a four-year sandwich degree which includes one year's work placement. Peter Ronan, head of the college's department of the built environment, explains that students spend their third year in placements with employers such as estate agents, valuation offices and local authorities.

'The placement is of huge benefit to the students,' says Ronan. 'They're more mature when they return. They can relate their knowledge to practice and they know what pieces of information they're missing. In the first two years, we drive them, but in the final year the process is reversed.'

Galway-Mayo IT offers a three-year full-time diploma which educates students to practise as auctioneers, estate agents, valuers, property managers and assessors. Graduates find work with professional auctioneers, valuers and estate agents and within the corporate portfolio property management of insurance and banking institutions. Many graduates continue their studies to degree level in other colleges.

### PLCs OFFER PROPERTY COURSES

Two PLC colleges – Cork College of Commerce and Senior College Dun Laoghaire – offer two-year certificates from the Institute of Professional Auctioneers and Valuers. Liam O'Donnell, IPAV executive secretary, explains that students who go this route don't have to compete on Leaving Certificate points for places. About 40 places are available in each centre.

Graduates of the course must do a further two years work experience to qualify for full IPAV membership. The Cork College offers a one-year follow-on diploma, from the University of Glamorgan and graduates of the diploma may then travel to Glamorgan to do a further one year full-time to qualify for a BSc in estate management surveying. This year, 25 students are on the degree, according to O'Donnell.

Not all graduates will end up working in estate agencies per se. O'Donnell says that there are also opportunities with insurance companies and semi-state companies which have property portfolios.

For students with an interest in fine art and auctioneering, the IPAV has a one-year full-time course in fine and decorative arts. This includes the history of furniture, paintings and silver.

### FACT FILE

*Full-time third-level courses:*
Galway-Mayo Institute of Technology: National diploma in business studies (estate management); 1997–98 cut-off points – 330

Limerick Institute of Technology: Degree in chartered surveying (valuation management); 1997–98 cut-off points – 330

Dublin Institute of Technology: Certificate in auctioneering valuation (one-year follow-on diploma available). 1997–98 cut-off points – 365 (random selection; not all students at this points level were offered a place)

Property economics degree: 1997–98 cut-off points – 395 (random selection)

Some PLC colleges offering auctioneering/estate agency courses:

Ballsbridge College of Business Studies, Dublin
Cork College of Commerce
Dun Laoghaire Senior College
Plunkett College, Whitehall, Dublin

### Professional bodies:

Irish Auctioneers and Valuers Institute (IAVI), 38 Merrion Square, Dublin 2 – phone (01) 661 1794

Courses approved by the IAVI for the purposes of full membership include: four-year degree courses at LIT, DIT and UU; three-year diploma courses at DIT and Galway-Mayo IT.

Institute of Professional Auctioneers and Valuers (IPAV), 39 Upper Fitzwilliam St, Dublin 2 – phone (01) 678 5685. Two-year IPAV certificate courses are provided by Cork College of Commerce and Dun Laoghaire Senior College. One-year follow-on diploma in Cork College of Commerce and further one-year follow-on degree in Glamorgan University, Wales.

# Secondary Teacher

*You need to be less rigid, more open*

Catherine Foley talks to Éamon Ó Dochartaigh about his life as a teacher.

## Career choice

Some are laughing as they come through the school gate. Some are frowning. More are shivering. It's another school day in January, just coming up to 8.30 am. The students and teachers of Coláiste de hÍde, an all-Irish second-level school in Tallaght, Co. Dublin, are making their way to their classrooms. When the bell rings, the great migration of teenagers weaves once again through the corridors. The day is underway in Coláiste de hÍde.

Éamon Ó Dochartaigh, who teaches Junior Cert science, jokes with some of the students as he walks to the science room. 'Bím faoi bhrú ag tús an lae ag ullmhú rudaí,' a deir sé. 'Bím an-gnóthach sula thosaíonn na ranganna, caithfidh tú gach rud a bheith reidh. Ansin bím ag caint le daoine ag súil isteach, ag magadh le daoine. An chéad rud a deirim nuair a théim isteach is dócha ná 'tógaigí amach na leabhair' agus ansin déanaim marcáil ar na rolaí.'

Generally he tries to find out what the students think about whatever he's going to talk about . . . 'if you start from what they know, it links you up with them. Otherwise you're not connecting with them.'

Ó Dochartaigh sees teaching moving in a different direction. 'It's very difficult to get young people to accept the old rigid, traditional form of classroom control. Quite a lot of teachers like myself are happy to see that change and to move towards new ways of working with young people, ways that are less confrontational and more productive.'

The key to being an effective teacher, he believes, is that you 'need to be less rigid, more open, less defensive, able to listen to the kids'. Over the years, his style of teaching has changed as he changed. 'You have to be developing as a person. It's very, very rewarding as a job.'

At the moment, the class is learning about light. They have just finished learning all about pollination. 'I love teaching,' he says. 'I just really enjoy the crack with the pupils. It can be really wonderful, especially times when it's going well, it's magic.' He also teaches technology and environmental studies to the Transition Year class.

The college is just five years old. It has up to 200 students and 14 teachers and is getting bigger each year. Ó Dochartaigh, whose degree from TCD is in theoretical physics, taught in a number of Dublin schools before he moved here.

His first teaching job was in inner-city London. He had a class of about 20, aged between 15 and 16. 'It was pretty mad,' he recalls. 'I had a class that was really wild. It was a bit stressful. I was just out of college. They were good kids but really, really wild. They came from a very poor black community in Clapham. They had huge problems.'

Ó Dochartaigh grew up in Belfast. He went to Edmund Rice primary school and then attended St Malachy's College between 1971 and 1978. After sitting his A-levels, he left to do a four-year honours degree course in Dublin. After four years, plus a two-year stint working with the university's students' union, he graduated.

He then went north again, primarily because he was awarded a grant, to complete a post-graduate certificate in education at Queens. 'They had quite a good system in terms of subject assessment and practical examples, including how to structure classes . . . it was all about structuring knowledge.'

Later, because he did not complete the H. Dip in Education, he had to apply to the Registration Council when he returned from London so that he could get official recognition in the Republic as a teacher. 'They really scrutinise all your qualifications. I eventually got registered. I had to attend a series of lectures in TCD on the history of Irish education over the course of a term and then write an essay at the end.'

He then spent three years in Senior College, Ballyfermot, teaching physics and engineering to Post Leaving Certificate students. After that, he taught in O'Connell's CBS on North Richmond Street, Dublin.

At the moment, he is availing of a job-share which is becoming more common, he says. 'Tá na páistí óg agus tá mé ag iarraidh a bheith sa bhaile leo.' arsa sé.

'The real challenge of teaching is the relationship that you form with a group of young people. Often that's what you are not prepared for. And then when you're not prepared, you act according to the model you know, you act like the teachers you know.'

'It's a two-way process. For me it's about giving them access to the right learning experience. You can't go in with a rigid attitude.'

### CAREER FOCUS: SECOND-LEVEL TEACHING

The statistics for 1996 higher diploma graduates tell the story. Most graduates are not going to get a permanent pensionable teaching job in the first year or years after they leave college.

A degree followed by a higher diploma in education is the main route of entry into second-level teaching. The Higher Education Authority's snapshot of graduate destinations, taken in April 1997, shows only 3.8 per cent of H. Dip students with permanent teaching jobs. But, 57 per cent did have part-time, substitute teaching posts while 8.9 per cent were teaching abroad.

About one-eighth of the graduates found work outside the teaching sphere, while 8.9 per cent were teaching abroad. One tenth of graduates went on to further study or training. Almost three per cent were not available for work or further study while 5.1 per cent were seeking employment. This compares unfavourably with an overall graduate unemployment figure of 3.6 per cent.

Ten years ago, the picture was much brighter for would-be second-level teachers when 9.5 per cent of H. Dip graduates found permanent work within the first year after graduation. For the past few years, the number of higher diploma places has been capped at 800 by the Higher Education Authority and demand for H. Dip places consistently exceeds the number of places available. In recent years, second-level schools have had difficulties in finding trained teachers in a number of key subjects. Because of this, the Minister has agreed to the raising of the current cap on H. Dip places from 800 to 940 for the coming academic year. 100 of these additional places will be specifically for teachers of Irish, Religion, Italian, Spanish and key sciences. In addition, a H. Dip through Irish for 40 students will be introduced at National University of Ireland, Galway. A central applications office has been set up for NUI colleges offering H. Dip courses and this will be in operation for students applying for courses in 1999. TCD will continue to operate its own admissions system.

The other main route into second-level teaching is via a concurrent teaching degree. These degrees – which are offered in areas such as music, religion, PE, home economics, metal/engineering technology, and wood/engineering technology – include teacher training in the primary degree so there is no need to do a higher diploma.

Graduates of these concurrent programmes generally tend to fare better in the marketplace. For instance, statistics from UL for 1996 PE graduates show that of the 47 students who responded to the survey, five graduates were in permanent whole-time teaching in Ireland and one was teaching abroad. Only one graduate was seeking employment.

Indeed, looking at the combined statistics for UL's concurrent teaching degrees in PE, general/rural science, metal/engineering technology and wood/building technology, there was only that one PE graduate seeking employment. Of the 111 survey respondents, 13 found permanent teaching positions in Ireland, 81 found part-time or temporary teaching work at home and two were teaching abroad.

Having got the bad news over with, second-level students who are still hoping to become teachers should think carefully about the job and what it entails. John White, deputy general secretary of the Association of Secondary Teachers Ireland, which represents 15,500 teachers says 'the first thing they would want to ensure is that they have a liking for young adolescents and a desire to help them both emotionally and educationally. They must also have a good knowledge of their subject. Those are the two key things.'

Teachers can have a great influence on young adolescents, he says. 'It's at the level of saying 'hello' in the corridor or asking how a student is doing on the football team. That kind of level of concern is very important for adolescents. Of course, what goes on in the classroom is equally important.'

Rose Malone, education officer with the Teachers Union of Ireland, which represents 8,500 teachers in vocational, community and comprehensive schools, notes that lifelong learning is becoming a significant factor in education. This means that teachers will not necessarily be employed in a traditional school setting for all of their teaching career and that they may be teaching adults rather than adolescents.

Stamina is also needed, she adds wryly. New programmes are coming on stream and teachers will be called on, not just to implement these programmes, but also to develop them. That kind of flexibility and understanding is required, says Malone. 'It can be quite demanding on teachers. Students should not expect to spend the next 40 years teaching out of the same book.'

White draws attention to the fact that schools can vary widely. 'A young person coming from a tightly-run school may find it difficult to cope in a school with some discipline problems. Some young teachers can get quite a shock. Having said that, it's a matter of adapting and being flexible.'

## You needn't be stuck in a classroom

One of the criticisms of teaching is that there isn't a great promotional structure, says John White. In fact, well over 50 per cent of teachers have posts of responsibility, he points out.

'The problem really comes when a teacher is promoted to a principal or deputy principal post and he or she is essentially being promoted out of the classroom. It's a problem nobody has been able to come to grips with satisfactorily.'

Outside of straightforward promotion, White says there are quite good opportunities at present for experienced teachers to become involved in other education-related activities. For instance, there are now three Leaving Certs – the traditional Leaving Cert, the Leaving Cert Applied and the Leaving Cert Vocational. New subjects are being introduced and new curricula revised. Quite a number of teachers have been seconded to help introduce these programmes.

White points to the new English curriculum which will be introduced in 1999. Ten teachers will be seconded to travel to schools to help teachers introduce the new programme. All of this means that you will not necessarily spend your entire teaching career in the traditional classroom setting.

# Career choice

## FACT FILE

*Annual salary*
Salaries as 1 April 1998: £13, 989 to £27,191 in 25 increments. There are additional allowances for various academic qualifications and posts of responsibility. Principals earn between £3,805 and £15,368 a year extra, depending on the number of teachers in the school. *Source: ASTI*

### ARE WE TRAINING TOO MANY TEACHERS?

Student enrolments are falling. However, demographics could prove a dividend rather than the end-of-the-line for teacher recruitment. The ASTI notes that 77 per cent of students who enter second-level education now complete the senior cycle. Government policy is that, by the end of the decade, at least 90 per cent of the 16- to 18-year-olds will complete the senior cycle. The White Paper on Education proposes that the school-leaving age should be raised to 16. The ASTI points out that reducing the pupil teacher ratio from 19:1 to 17:1 in second-level schools would require an additional 1,200 teachers.

# Primary teacher

*'You're sad to see them go'*

Deirdre Foy talks to Catherine Foley about life as a primary school teacher.

# Career choice

After a quick *a haon, a dó, a trí*, Joceyln, up like a flash to the top of the class, leads with a rhymthic swing of her hips and a clap to the right, then to the left. The rest of the class stand by their chairs and sing with gusto. 'Down in the jungle where nobody knows, there's a googie, woogie washin' woman, washin' her clothes . . . yea.'

Deirdre Foy is by the blackboard, singing along with her class. In a short while, the bell goes and 32 little girls file out. Another day at Presentation Primary School, Warrenmount, Dublin, draws to a close.

'I didn't think I'd love teaching as much as I do,' she says. 'You become so involved with the pupils. Although I'd be giving out sometimes, by the end of the year, you're sad to see them go.'

Tomorrow morning after prayers in the assembly hall, her class will file in again. It's still early days in the term but already the class has been divided into groups, each with its own name – Spice Girls, Ginger Spice, Baby Spice, Swans and Girl Power – otherwise known as G1, G2, G3, G4 and G5. 'They are prouder when they vote for their own names . . . I think Swans is from the Children of Lir which we were reading about.'

The first 15 minutes of the day are taken up with homework, calling the roll and taking notes from parents. The first subject is Irish – 'they love it,' says Foy. 'There's a lot of drama and they get up and act it out. It's active so they enjoy it.' After an hour, they break. They sing songs at various intervals throughout the day, because 'it's good for breaks during subject changes.'

To be a teacher, she says, it's essential to be patient. 'You have to be fond of children and you have to be patient or learn to be patient. I never regarded myself as patient until I started teaching. You have to expect different levels within a class and expect them to come on within their own levels.'

# Teacher

Deirdre Foy has been teaching here for three years. Whatever about patience, energy is something which primary teachers must have in abundance. This is Foy's first year teaching third class. 'It's not as exhausting as first class,' she says. 'The younger the children are, the more you find yourself on your feet all day.' Generally, she says, with third class you can give them a certain bit of responsibility.

On Wednesday afternoons, the class is quieter than usual. Only the strains of Mozart waft around the room as children busy themselves with arts and crafts. 'During art, they listen to classical music. They forget about talking. The girls love pieces such as *The Nutcracker Suite* and *Swan Lake*.'

Her own happy memories of St Angela's National School in Castlebar, Co. Mayo, started her thinking about becoming a teacher. 'I was interested in the music part of it as well.' She studied at St Patrick's Training College, Drumcondra, Dublin, and got an honours B Ed in 1994.

She spent a year teaching in Chico, California, on an exchange scholarship which is awarded each year by St Patrick's. She completed a Masters in health education during the year.

After teacher training, it was the little things – 'like filling out a rollbook and crowd control when you don't know how to get them into groups' – which proved most difficult about being in a classroom. Recalling her first days at Warrenmount, she says, 'I didn't smile at them for the first month but once you have the control, they respect you'.

Tomorrow's homework is already on the blackboard. 'It's important to have a structure. You need to be organised. It helps. Children are like that. But you can't be so rigid that you can't go out of it.'

## CAREER FOCUS: PRIMARY TEACHING

There are five colleges offering teacher training courses which qualify students to work as primary teachers. These are St Patrick's College, Drumcondra, Mary Immaculate College, Limerick, Coláiste Mhuire, Marino, Froebel, Blackrock, Dublin and the Church of Ireland college in Dublin.

Each college has two admissions codes in the CAO handbook, reflecting the fact that 10 per cent of places are reserved for Gaeltacht applicants.

Last year, the cut-off points ranged from 470* (* means random selection applied) for St Patrick's College, Drumcondra, to 410 for the Church of Ireland college. The points required were lower for Gaeltacht applicants, ranging from 420* to 440.

Graduates of the bachelor of education programmes fared better on the jobs front than their H. Dip counterparts. Almost one-quarter of 1996 graduates had secured permanent full-time teaching positions by April 1997, according to HEA statistics. The bulk of graduates, 74.5 per cent, were in temporary, substitute or part-time teaching positions. The Irish National Teacher's Organisation says that there is a shortage of qualified substitute teachers. This is borne out by the fact that none of the graduates were seeking employment.

There is another occasional route into primary teaching. When the supply of qualified teachers is low, a post-graduate course may be sanctioned by the Department of Education. However, this is not a route that school-leavers should bank upon.

The Minister announced that over 1,000 places will be available in the primary colleges of education during the coming academic year. This represents a doubling from the 1996 figure. This entry will include 730 students who will be admitted into the standard B Ed courses of colleges of education.

## Teacher

### Fact File

Annual salary: £13,909 to £21,737 after 13 years and to £26,789 after a further 11 years. There are various additional allowances for qualifications and posts of responsibility.

### Teacher training colleges:

St Patrick's College, Drumcondra
Mary Immaculate College, Limerick
Coláiste Mhuire, Marino
Froebel College of Education, Sion Hill, Dublin
Church of Ireland College of Education, Dublin

All of the above colleges offer qualifications which are recognised by the Department of Education. Only Church of Ireland students are accepted by the Church of Ireland College. Froebel offers a different but equally valid approach to education.

Students at Coláiste Mhuire, the Church of Ireland College and Froebel take some courses in their own college and others in Trinity. All three colleges offer an ordinary B Ed degree which can be upgraded to an honours degree by spending a further year in Trinity. St Patrick's College, which is associated with DCU, and Mary Immaculate College, which is associated with UL, both offer honours B Ed programmes.

# VETERINARY MEDICINE

*Most of my class emigrated*

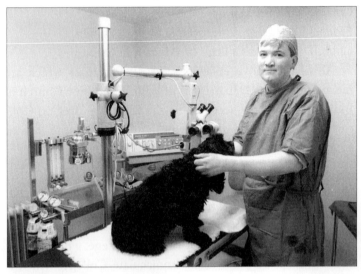

Photographer: David Sleator

Michael Woods talks to Catherine Foley about his work as a veterinary surgeon.

## Veterinary medicine

His large expressive eyes peer out from a fibre-glass cage in the corner of the surgery. There is no mistaking the canine sentiments. 'I want to go home,' he seems to say as he waits patiently for his mistress to come and collect him. 'Where is she?' he whines. This lovely King Charles spaniel is mending nicely and will go home today. Michael Woods, the vet, is happy with his progress.

'Yes,' Wood agrees, 'you have to love animals to like veterinary surgery but not in a fragile way.' He bends down to pet the dog's head. 'You must have a feeling for animals but not in a soppy way because you also have to diagnose and treat. You get an extra sense if you're with animals all the time. Your bites tend to happen in the first year.

'Some people think because animals don't talk that they can't let you know what's wrong with them. The pet is now an integral part of the family. We're all so much more educated, and with the vet programmes coming from the UK, people are seeing for the first time what vets actually do.'

Woods qualified from UCD in 1984. There were 60 in his class – 45 men and 15 women. 'Most of my class emigrated,' he says.

Before UCD, he went to St Fintan's CBS in Sutton, Dublin. 'My interest in veterinary science came from growing up beside a farm in Kilbarrack. I watched dogs dying from strychnine powder – that lead to an interest. When I got my Inter Cert, I really started thinking about it. Then when I decided to go for it, I repeated my Leaving Cert to get the points to get in.'

Today he runs his own practice in Dun Laoghaire. His days are as exciting as they are demanding, challenging and long. 'The day is so varied, you just don't know what's going to happen next,' he laughs. 'I start work at 8 am. I come in and do office work for an hour. Then the practice opens at 9 am. I do consults until 10 am and then I operate until lunch.'

## Career choice

His clients include dogs and cats but there is also the odd snake, cockatoo, budgie, lizard or iguana. Woods, as a veterinary ophthalmologist, has the only eye referral practice in the country and he now sees animals from all over the country, including horses, which are sent for diagnosis, treatment and sometimes operation.

His first job after he qualified was in the west of Ireland in 'a real James Herriot type practice', he remembers. It was a large animal practice – mostly cattle, sheep and horses. He was based in Kilrush, Co. Clare, and then in Ballina, Co. Mayo. The hours were long and the days hectic. He recalls doing up to 25 calls on Saturdays and having to cover a large area in his car.

'Now, it's different,' he says. 'The hours are quite considerably reduced. The west of Ireland is a practical type of environment and the veterinary practice is in accordance with the environment. There are disadvantaged areas. A lot of part-time farming. Small herds between five and 30 animals. You're in a car doing 50,000 miles a year. Your work routine is 90 hours a week. It's very physical.'

After two and a half years, Woods left to take up a job in England. 'My motivation for leaving Ireland was to further myself as a vet,' he says. He worked in a practice that concentrated on 'small animal work' in Luton. Then he moved to Hertfordshire on the Welsh border. 'A lovely rural practice, very different. The order and organisation of the practice was very different, with calls coming in by 10 in the morning. You could schedule your day.'

He worked with a veterinary ophthalmologist, one of the top eye surgeons for animals in Britain, for four years. He also studied for a certificate in ophthalmology and got that in 1990 from the Royal Veterinary College.

# Veterinary medicine

Back in Ireland in 1994, he took over a small practice in Dun Laoghaire and he has gradually built it up. 'You're beating a path forward and also introducing the concept that a referral is a positive thing to do,' he says. 'It's not negative. People are a bit afraid that you have to hand a case on.'

Of the vet's life, he says: 'You're dealing with different situations. The new puppy, the old dog being eased out of this life. There's a lot of emotion tied up with animals. They're often the most important aspect of a family. You're dealing with people as well and their sadness. With older people, the dog or the cat is often their only companion. You're treating the owner as much as the animal at times. They're often the last link a family has with someone who has died.'

Woods believes that veterinary medicine in Ireland is moving forward at a great pace. 'There's a great feeling of everything moving forward, of change. I feel our practice is being swept along.'

To youngsters thinking about this career, he says 'you would want to be very, very dedicated, and prepared to do a 12-hour day. I try and get an hour's break in the afternoon – it's a long day. Just like medicine, it takes a while to come up through the ranks. You're basically 10 years developing and then you see where to go but it's a progression. You have to be prepared to educate yourself.'

## VETERINARY MEDICINE

UCD is the only college in Ireland to offer veterinary medicine. There are 70 first-year places and a number of these are reserved for students from Northern Ireland.

You would have needed 570* points to have secured a place in 1997. With the abolition of bonus points for higher-level maths, this year's points may appear somewhat lower.

However, the maximum bonus was 40 points for an A in a higher-level paper, so don't expect massive drops.

UCD's graduate survey for 1996 graduates shows 71.4 per cent of veterinary medicine graduates in full-time employment in Ireland and 22.9 per cent in full-time employment overseas. A very small proportion – 2.8 per cent – went on to research work or further study or training while the remainder were not available for employment or study.

# SOFTWARE ENGINEER

## *Where logic rules supreme*

Photographer: Eric Luke

Rebecca Johnson talks to Catherine Foley about her work in the telecommunications industry.

## Career choice

If you listen carefully, you can almost hear the click – it's the sound of thoughts moving sequentially from one logical step to the next. Brains are working at a furious pace. There is no laughing or talking. Only an occasional whisper breaks the hush on the third floor of Hambleden House.

Technological problems are being solved. In the open-plan office, heads are hidden behind partitions, everyone within the department at Logica Aldiscon on Lower Pembroke Street, Dublin, is focussed on developing new codes which will run enhanced telephone paging services.

This is where new telecommunications software products are designed. It's the cutting edge of the business. Rebecca Johnson smiles. 'It's probably the hardest job in here,' she says demurely. Yes, it's exciting, she agrees. There is a thrill in knowing that you are creating technology which will soon be used to create a product for use in modern everyday life.

'Messaging would be the biggest product that we have,' she explains. A short message service allows brief messages to be exchanged between mobile telephones and elements in a fixed or mobile network.

Since Johnson started working with the company over two years ago, her interest and enthusiasm has grown. 'I enjoy my work,' she says. 'Trying to find a better way to do something in telecommunications is quite relaxing. I find that I come in the next day sometimes with a new idea, and I'm eager to try it, because something will have popped into my head at home, and that's because I've gone home and relaxed for the evening.'

The work is marked by lots of responsibility early on, she says. 'You get an awful lot of experience. You have to be quite organised. You have to have your mind very focussed all the time and be able to be multi-tasked as well. It's very, very methodical.'

## Software engineer

Johnson always wanted to do engineering. 'I wasn't sure what type of engineering. What really pushed me was the fact that I would get a job at the end of studying.'

After studying at Scoil Chríost Rí, an all-girls convent school in Cahir, Co. Tipperary, she went to Dublin City University to do a BSc in computer applications. The course was tough, 'but it gets easier as you go along and you learn to deal with the work-load and that helps you to be organised and get used to meeting deadlines'.

In first and second year, subjects included physics and maths. 'If I hadn't done physics at school, I would have found that very difficult . . . I did like the course. We had maths and science subjects and business subjects and pure computer subjects as well. It was all very new at the time. There was a lot of practical work, people help you along. There's an awful lot of help there.'

Project work during her four years at DCU involved, she explains, 'sitting down and coming up with an innovative product, designing it, coding it, testing it and then demonstrating it which is basically what you do in the work place.' For example, in her third year, Johnson, over a four-month period, designed an interface for teaching children how to read.

Before graduating, she had already been recruited by Aldiscon. Today, she says, 'the amount of jobs going is astounding, especially in telecommunications'.

In her experience, women are in the minority both at college and in the workplace. However, she says, working in a male-dominated environment 'is not an issue for me. It's not a matter of whether you're male or female but whether you're going to like what you're doing or be good at it. I was never very technical at school but college changes that – you develop the skills you need, you're taught how to think logically and you get better and better at solving problems.'

# Career choice

## CAREER FOCUS: SOFTWARE ENGINEER

By now almost everyone must have heard that there are lots of well-paid jobs in computing. But students should also consider whether the job will suit them. There is no point in going into an area that is well paid but you will not enjoy.

On the other hand, many girls fail to pay computing even the most cursory of attention when making career choices, thereby cutting off an option which they may well enjoy and which offers excellent prospects.

Ireland is the fifth largest software producer in the world. Five of the world's top ten companies have major operations here and a significant number of Irish companies have been highly successful internationally. There are 7,000 people employed in Irish-owned software companies and 8,000 in overseas companies. Employment in the industry here is expected to rise from 15,000 to 20,000 over the next three years.

Skills shortages have led to the creation of additional third-level places so points levels should remain accessible.

The enthusiasm of Seamus Gallen of the National Software Directorate is catching. 'The ability to get on with people and to work in a team is as important as technical ability. Software is very much a young person's industry – most software developers are in their 20s or early 30s. Bill Gates, the head of Microsoft, is still in his 30s, and is the world's richest man.'

Gallen notes that software companies occupy 'the very best office accommodation and provide top-class working conditions for employees'. The industry in Ireland exports most of its output, creating opportunities for travel abroad. And you don't need higher-level maths for software. Only TCD's computer science and engineering degrees have a requirement for higher-level maths in the Leaving Certificate. But, Gallen says 'it is an advantage if you don't hate or abhor maths'.

## Software engineer

The best route into the industry is via a third-level education, preferably a degree, he says. As there are more jobs than graduates, a degree virtually guarantees you a job. 'But you can begin with an institute of technology certificate course, and progress through a diploma to a degree, instead of taking a straight four-year degree. This decision may be influenced by the number of points you get in the Leaving Cert or may be affected by where you live. Either route will get you a job.'

Employers have a slight preference for courses with company placement included such as degree programmes in UL, DCU, WIT, NUI Galway and UCC. Maynooth's new degree will also include a work placement.

### FACT FILE

*Cut-off points for ab-initio degree courses 1997:*
UCC – computer studies/science 410; business information systems 470*
DCU – computer applications 410; céim in airgeadas, ríomhaireacht agus fiontraíocht 415
CIT – computer applications 370; software development and computer networking 410
WIT – applied computing 345
UCD – science 410*
NUI Galway – computing studies 350; information technology 445
UL – computer systems 385; language/computing 455; applied maths/computing 380; computer engineering 430; information technology 380*
TCD – computers/German 445; computers/French 480; computer/Irish 430; computer science 450*; management science and information systems 460; engineering 415
NUI Maynooth – science 340

New courses include computer science in Limerick IT, computer science in NUI Dublin (previously offered through science only); business information systems development in DIT (previously a diploma); computer science (previously offered through science only) in NUI Maynooth; BA (mod) in information and communications technology in TCD; electronic and computer engineering in NUI Galway (* means random selection applied; not all students at this points level were offered a place).

Cert/diploma courses: A tremendous variety of computing programmes are offered by the institutes of technology. In some cases these are combined with a language.

### Add-on degrees:
Athlone IT – software engineering
Carlow IT – software engineering
Dundalk IT – commercial computing
Galway Mayo IT – software development
Letterkenny IT – applied computing
Limerick IT – information systems
Sligo IT – computing
Tallaght IT – computing (information technology)
Tralee IT – BSc in computing
WIT – commercial software development

### Sample starting salaries:
Graduates of degree programmes £14,000 to £16,000 annually.

### Computer technicians in great demand
Computer technicians service and repair computers. There is a huge shortage of these people, according to Seamus Gallen of the National Software Directorate. The main reason is that

three large American companies – Intel, IBM and Hewlett Packard – have set up plants here.

'These companies pay good money – often more than £15,000 a year starting out. All you need is a certificate. So, at the age of 19, after two years in an institute of technology you could be in a good job,' adds Gallen. Many of the companies taking on technicians will pay college fees so that people can continue their studies to degree level on a part-time basis.

For more than 10 courses in 1997, you would have needed 200 points or less while four colleges were offering places to all qualified applicants. This means that five Leaving Cert passes would have been enough to get a place. In fact, many courses had difficulty filling their places. 'The courses may have off-putting names – electrical, electronic or mechanical engineering,' says Gallen. 'It's not rocket science. It's something almost anyone can do.' Whatever about software, these courses are way down most girls' wish list. The National Council for Educational Awards has recently produced a pack aimed at attracting women into engineering – your guidance counsellor will have a copy.

The points needed for a college place do not refer to the quality of a course or career prospects. They simply indicate supply and demand. Geography often has a lot to do with points levels. Students who do well in their certificates and diplomas can progress, via add-on qualifications, to degree level and beyond. So, students should not dismiss these qualifications out of hand.

## CHOOSING A COURSE

There is now a bewildering array of computing courses on offer. Some are hardware-orientated, others emphasise business and some combine business or a language with computing studies.

One course is offered through Irish. Many courses are direct-entry so students begin to specialise immediately. Others are offered through common-entry programmes such as arts, science and engineering.

Courses span all levels from certificates to diplomas to degrees. The best route into the industry is via a degree (but, of course, you can work your way from certificate to diploma to degree). As there are more jobs than graduates, a degree virtually guarantees a job.

Employers have a slight preference for courses which include work placements. Another option is to do a primary degree in any discipline followed by a one-year post-graduate course.

### COMMON-ENTRY PROGRAMMES:

These programmes allow students to sample several subjects and then specialise later. Students who are unsure of what they might specialise in find this approach very useful.

Unfortunately many students are unaware of the possibilities afforded by these degrees. They read 'science' or 'engineering' in the CAO handbook and don't realise that computing is one of the specialist courses on offer.

For instance, TCD's common-entry engineering degree allows students to follow a common programme for the first two years before deciding on one of five areas – electronic engineering, computer engineering, electronic and computer engineering, mechanical and manufacturing engineering and civil engineering.

UCC and NUI Maynooth also offer computing options through their common-entry science programmes. In addition, both colleges introduced direct-entry programmes in 1997.

Information technology may also be offered as a subject in arts. For instance, students in NUI Galway can take

## Software engineer

Information Technology through to the final year within an arts degree. When it became available in 1997, there was a huge response with 132 students taking IT. Dr Gerry Lyons, of the college's IT centre, expects that IT will become established as a second-level subject and it may be that people with arts degrees with IT will teach it.

### COMPUTING WITH OTHER DISCIPLINES:
Combining the study of computing with other disciplines, such as a language, maths or business studies is an increasingly popular and successful option.

For instance, UCC's four-year business information systems course came to fruition in 1997 when the first graduates left the campus. Course director Ciaran Murphy says all graduates have found work. Most had more than one job offer, with the record standing at seven. The programme is evenly divided between business and information systems.

A key aspect of the programme is the work placement, he says, with a large number of students going to the US to gain experience in the workplace there. There are 90 first-year places in 1998. The cut-off points were a high 470* (random selection applied) in 1997.

Dublin Institute of Technology also offers a business information systems degree which has developed from a diploma. Students who begin their studies this year will be awarded a DIT degree.

### DIRECT-ENTRY PROGRAMMES:
There is a huge number of direct-entry programmes available. Students should read through the college prospectuses carefully to see what each programme offers. The following are just four samples from the large array on offer:

# Career choice

## Computer science and software

This year, NUI Maynooth is introducing a degree in computer science and software with 80 first-year places. The four-year programme will include a six-month industrial placement. The core curriculum is supplemented by areas such as signal processing, business organisation and organisational behaviour. Professor David Vernon says that computer programmers don't work in isolation in front of a screen – they must understand the decision-making processes.

The department of computer science has produced a high-quality CD ROM which it is sending to schools in a bid to attract students.

## Information and communications technology

TCD introduced this degree in 1997, when it took in 82 students. This year, there are first-year places for 120 students.

Course director David Algeo says the course differs from TCD's other computer offerings in that it focuses on networks. 'The best-known example of networking at present is probably the Internet. Companies such as banks and airlines have large computer networks. Students will look at applications which run on networks and how these are built,' he explains.

Students take French or German for two years, with the focus on conversational skills. Hardware comprises less than 10 per cent of the course so there is proportionately more software, says Algeo.

## Airgeadas, ríomhaireacht agus fiontraíocht

DCU's four-year BSc in airgeadas, ríomhaireacht agus fiontraíocht offers students an opportunity to study finance, computing, enterprise and a European language – through Irish. An enthusiasm rather than a fluency in Irish is required.

Of the 65 students enrolled in the course (January 1998), 37 came from all-Irish schools in Dublin; eight from all-Irish schools in Cork; 14 came from English-medium schools and six came from Gaeltacht schools. While there are no graduates from the course yet, the college anticipates good employment prospects. There has been no difficulty securing industrial placements for them.

### INFORMATION TECHNOLOGY AT NUI GALWAY
NUI Galway's information technology degree is now in its third year. The intake doubled from 25 to 53 in 1997 but points remained high at 445. Next year, there will be up to 70 places available. The first graduates will leave NUI Galway next year.

### LIMERICK INSTITUTE OF TECHNOLOGY
The college has introduced a new degree course this year – LC024. This course focuses on object-orientated techniques and should equip students with a thorough understanding of software engineering practices.

### CERTIFICATES AND DIPLOMAS
All of the institutes of technology offer computing certificates and diplomas. New courses are being introduced in response to the needs of industry.

For instance, Letterkenny IT has introduced a new national certificate in electronics and computer engineering while Athlone IT has brought in a three-year ab-initio diploma in computing.

## Add-on degrees

Students who opt for the certificate/diploma route may wish to continue their studies to degree. The majority of the institutes of technology provide add-on courses to degree level.

Athlone IT – software engineering; Carlow IT – software engineering; Dundalk IT – commercial computing; Letterkenny IT – applied computing; Limerick IT – information systems; Sligo IT – computing; Tallaght IT – computing (information technology); Tralee IT – BSc in computing; WIT – commercial software development.

## Post-graduate conversion courses

Students who do not take computing in their primary degree can choose from a variety of conversion courses. These increasingly popular courses are usually one year in duration and allow students to develop additional skills.

There were an additional 450 post-graduate places created under the Government Skills Shortages scheme.

Guide to careers in computing: the National Software Directorate has produced a comprehensive guide to courses to careers in computing in Ireland. This has been circulated to guidance counsellors and should prove invaluable to students interested in computing.

# ACCOUNTANT

*Every day is its own adventure*

Martha Holmes talks to Catherine Foley about her work as a management accountant.

# Career choice

Yes, just as you'd expect, she was always good at maths. Yes, she is very organised and tidy as she sits at a large desk in an uncluttered office on the first floor of a grey building.

Martha Holmes is a management accountant at the Guinness Ireland Group Offices on James' Street, Dublin. In this environment there are no tantalising smells of hops or yeast to distract a visiting reporter. You don't hear the clanging of barrels as they are loaded onto lorries.

Here, in the administrative offices, there is a calm and carpeted hush about the place. There's a meeting going on in a board room on the first floor. Along the corridor, there are only closed doors and the low hum of people hard at work.

'The accountant's role is integral to the operation of any business,' says Holmes. 'You work hand in hand with other parts of the business. Being a management accountant does not mean that you're number crunching or punching in debits and credits all day long. We've become much more involved with information systems and systems have advanced so much that it has taken a lot of the drudgery out of the work. As a result we are becoming more and more involved in decision making. We are not the back-room boys or girls any more.'

The accountant is involved in the support part of the business, she continues. 'We help people in different parts of the company to make decisions in the day to day running of the business. We tell them how much it will cost and what the implications would be. It's a very exciting, fast-moving business.'

At the moment, Holmes is involved in a 'systems project' which will keep her busy for about two years. Her lips are sealed as to the day to day detail of her job. It's all hush-hush for the moment and she'd rather not say anymore, only that her days are 'hectic' and no one day is typical.

In general, however, she will say that to be an accountant 'you need to be organised, be a clear thinker, be logical, have good communications skills – and an aptitude for maths helps'.

Holmes' route to Guinness was relatively straightforward. After completing her education at St Louis' High School in Rathmines, Dublin, she went to TCD and studied economics and social studies. Although she was good at maths, she explains that she didn't study honours maths in the Leaving Cert. You have to be numerate and good with figures, she says, but economics is far more important.

'I chose economics and social studies because it was a broad-based course and I didn't have a clue what I wanted to do but by the end of my time there I began to specialise in the business side of things and I took the accountancy options.' She graduated with a degree in business in 1989.

She applied to Guinness to complete a three-year graduate programme, which is offered to a small number of graduates each year. She was accepted and was one of eight young graduates to start the programme for trainee accountants that year. During this three-year stint she was given experience in a range of areas, as well as being given time to study for the Chartered Institute of Management Accountants' exams.

For the first year, she worked in Guinness's London office. The next year she was sent to the United States to another section within the Guinness group, United Distillers in Stanford, Connecticut. Then, in her third year, she was based in the Guinness brewery itself in Park Royal, London.

Throughout the three years, the programme allows the graduates to 'do the work that is relevant to what you are doing in your studies. It's quite an organised scheme', she says. 'There were valuable lessons to be learned in each part of the business.'

After completing the programme, she returned to Guinness in Ireland. Since she came back to Dublin, she has worked in a number of different areas in a variety of roles.

Speaking about her newest assignment, which started in February, she is careful not to give too much detail. The work of a management accountant is classified but, for the moment, her new desk looks calm and organised. Perhaps aspiring accountants should take her message to heart – 'as the financial person, you just don't have a typical day.'

### CAREER FOCUS:

Job prospects for accountants are booming in tandem with the economy. Demand for part-qualified and fully-qualified accountants has never been stronger, according to Colleen Quinn, student development executive with the Institute of Certified Public Accountants in Ireland. Ben Lynch, education director of the Institute of Chartered Accountants, describes the scene as 'very buoyant'.

Part-qualified accountants can earn between £8,000 and £13,000 a year, Quinn estimates, while those going into industry may fare somewhat better with annual incomes ranging between £10,000 and £23,000.

Accountancy bodies report an increasing percentage of third-level graduates entering the profession. Quinn says that about 40 students each year would come in with a Leaving Cert as their sole background. But Tony White, divisional director of the Chartered Institute of Management Accountants, says that, although the numbers coming in directly from the Leaving Cert are dropping, he does not see accountancy becoming an all-graduate profession. 'There is always scope for people to come through the accountancy technician route or the certificate and diploma route,' he says.

## Accountant

A variety of third-level courses are on offer through the CAO, from certificates to diplomas to degree. Exemptions from the exams of the various professional bodies vary, so check this when deciding on a course.

It is not necessary to take a pure accountancy course to qualify as an accountant, although this is usually the quickest route. The advantage of a general business or commerce degree is that it allows students time to make up their minds and see which specialism would suit best . . . marketing, accountancy, finance or economics. Of course, if you're sure that you want to be an accountant, the obvious route is via the course with the maximum exemptions. All of the professional bodies require a minimum of three years professional experience as well as passing their exams.

White says that there is a problem with the picture that most people have in their minds when it comes to accountancy as a career. They see accountants as self-employed – with a brass plate outside the door. In fact, only about one-quarter of accountants are working in practice. The remainder are salaried.

'If you have a company with a turnover of more than £1 million you need at least one full-time accountant to manage the finances.' He also makes the point that people who qualify as accountants don't stay as accountants forever – they become financial managers and, in many cases, general managers.

### THE WAY IN:

To qualify as a professional accountant, you must fulfil educational and training requirements laid down by professional accountancy bodies. The four main bodies have their own sets of exams, generally organised in four stages. Exemptions from the various exams are given for approved third-level qualifications. The training requirement takes the form of a number of years' work experience in an approved environment.

The exams have the reputation of being very difficult. However, Ben Lynch of the ICA, says that they would expect most of their 2,500 students to qualify.

He attributes this to the quality of students – and points out that 78 per cent of the 1997 graduate intake had honours degrees.

Colleen Quinn, of CPA, says that the exams are very different from college exams, requiring a different set of skills. Students must be able to think on their feet, she says, and their practical experience is very relevant. There is a 50 to 60 per cent pass rate in the final CPA exam, she says.

### FACT FILE

Vacant places: Last year, 43 courses available through the CAO did not fill all of their places and had to advertise vacancies. These included accounting and management studies in Carlow IT (205 points), the Institute of Accounting Technicians course in Letterkenny IT (all qualified applicants were offered a place), chartered accountancy in Sligo IT (360 points) and WIT (AQA) as well as a number of business courses at certificate/diploma level.

Professional bodies (members of the Consultative Committee of Accountancy Bodies in Ireland):
ICA – Institute of Chartered Accountants in Ireland, 87-89, Pembroke Road, Ballsbridge, Dublin.
CIMA – Chartered Institute of Management Accountants, 44, Upper Mount Street, Dublin 4
CPA – Institute of Certified Public Accountants in Ireland, 9, Ely Place, Dublin 2
ACCA – Association of Chartered Certified Accountants, 9, Leeson Park, Dublin 6.

# GRAPHIC DESIGN

*There isn't a crayon or a marker in sight*

Photographer: Liam Burke/Press 22

Sean Reynolds talks to Catherine Foley about his work as a graphic designer.

## Career choice

Green circles expand like pulsating hearts. For a second they stay static, then they all begin to bleed into each other and suddenly, like magic, they become rectangles. Sean Reynolds, a graphic designer, is like a magician. Using a mouse, he changes a screen full of colours and shapes with the press of a button. He sits in front of his Apple Macintosh. There isn't a crayon or a marker, a rubber or a ruler in sight. Everything is done on the computer, he explains.

There is a creative element but his job today is also about understanding the technical limitations, being able to give clients a comprehensive costing list and knowing what the printer wants.

Having finished a degree course in art and design at Limerick IT, he and a friend set up their own graphic design business. 'In the early days, we started off doing small stuff – fliers, we designed logos, business cards, stationery,' he recalls. 'Initially, we were trying to get work, so anyone we knew, we told them. Then we started to get contracts and built it from there.'

Reynolds remembers the early days as being slow. 'In the line of printing, we did anything we could get our hands on. Our first colour job was a brochure for an equestrian centre. It would be fairly simple now but then it was our first. It went well. We put a lot of work into it and it was quite different.'

Their biggest challenge was learning about the printing process and understanding what a printer needs. Also they had to learn how to get their designs from the screen to paper.

Gradually they learned about the technical aspects of layout, size, colour and make-up. 'All of that was very new and there was a fair learning curve and there still is,' says Reynolds.

The first step was to sit down together with a pad and pencil to work out a concept for their design. 'Everything is put down on paper,' he says. 'The computer is only a tool. Essentially you are trying to come up with a creative idea. People imagine us as drawing pictures but it's really as much technical as it is creative. You get your ideas, you come up with a concept.'

When the copy comes from a client, it is typeset. 'Then you lay it out,' he continues, 'and you get photographs which have to be scanned onto the document. Then whatever creative work, you have you apply that. There are a lot of different stages and potentially any small thing can go wrong. So many things have to be checked. 'When the job is finished we give the disc to a printer and we would check it. He burns in onto a plate and then it's printed.'

Sean Reynolds comes from a farm in Co. Leitrim. He always wanted to study art. 'In primary school I loved it. Even in essays I'd have to draw a little picture. It was just a natural thing. It was almost a hobby, something to relax the mind.'

He went to Moyne Community School in Co. Longford mainly 'because they had a very well equipped art department'. His teacher, Anita Kelly, 'encouraged me and anybody else who had any talent.'

When he left second-level in 1988, 'I had made up my mind that I wanted to be an art teacher'. In the first year of the three-year diploma course at Limerick IT there were about 120 art and design students. Initially the course concentrated on developing the drawing skills of the students. 'We were trained to see something as it really was,' he says. 'We learned about colour and about shapes. It was a very hard year, with an awful lot of practical work.

'It's very difficult for people to change, to learn to look at things in a different way. You tend to draw things that are in your mind rather than what's in front of you.' After first year, 'there's a decision to be made about which road you want to go'. Some students choose fine art, others decide to study graphic design. 'For many people, there are livings to be made,' he explains. 'Fine art is a much longer road. Design students, while staying within the creative area, will at some stage be working for someone else but for those in fine art, it's much more a self-progression type of thing.'

For those who proceed through the course, 'it's about perseverance in what you're doing and trying to understand what you want to achieve in a project. Graphics is about communication – you're trying to get a message across in a creative way. There's a lot of concept solving in any project.'

An important aspect of college work is meeting deadlines, says Reynolds. 'Miss a deadline,' he cautions, 'and you were in trouble straight away.'

Having completed a diploma in art and design, Reynolds was among the first group to carry on and do the degree course. He graduated with an honours degree in 1992.

Today he does work for a wide range of companies, creating material for use in engineering, education and tourism. The Reynolds Boyce Graphic Design Consultancy has designed annual reports, exhibition posters and literature.

'A typical graphic designer is somebody who needs to be visually-minded, someone who sees a lot of things happen around them and someone who is good with colour. It also helps if you have reasonable English as well.'

CAREER FOCUS: GRAPHIC DESIGN

Getting a place on an art and design course is no mean feat. It entails a good deal more work than the average college application. Colleges use a variety of assessment procedures, from drawing tests to projects to portfolios to interviews to Leaving Cert points. Many operate a combination of these.

## Graphic design

All third-level courses, other than first-year core, the common first year in the National College of Art and Design, are offered through the CAO. For instance, DIT Mountjoy Square requires students to first submit a portfolio – if it reaches the required standard, students are called for interview. Six hundred points are allotted to the interview and portfolio and these are added to the Leaving Cert score.

Dr Dermot McGuinne, head of the department of visual communications, design and fine art, explains about 1,000 portfolios are received each year and, on average, about 700 people are called to interview.

'It's not seen as a severe screening process,' he says. 'If there is any kind of potential or merit in the portfolio, students will be called to interview.'

The college is looking for evidence of creative observational drawing ability, he adds. 'This can be best shown through a casual sketchbook rather than expensively finished pieces. Sometimes students think that they have to put a lot of money into presentation.' About 20 pieces of work showing a willingness to experiment with different media is fine.

The interview is informal and will usually include a discussion of the portfolio to establish that the student is the real author of the works. After all that, if you secure a place, you will spend four years in DIT Mountjoy Square. The course comprises 80 per cent practical work and 20 per cent theory. This is the norm for NCEA-approved art and design courses.

In first and second year in DIT Mountjoy Square, students are introduced to a broad range of design subjects such as composition, colour, typography and computer applications. In third year, they can choose to specialise in graphic design, illustration, photography or multimedia.

Job prospects for graduates of DIT's four-year course are good, according to McGuinne. The course was an advanced diploma and is now offered as a degree in the 1998 CAO handbook. He notes that job prospects are probably not enhanced by the degree status as employers tend to look at students' portfolios, but it should prove a popular move with students who are always eager to get a degree.

In addition to the two ab-initio degrees on offer at DIT and the National College of Art and Design, there are a variety of certificate and diploma courses on offer.

For instance, Waterford Institute of Technology offers a three-year diploma in design communications. Course leader Joy Rooney describes first year, which provides a general introduction to basic design principles and practices, as 'very hard work'. In second year, students have the opportunity to work with industry on various projects as well as learning more advanced skills.

Third year is more specialised, says Rooney, with the emphasis on typography and photography. Students also work on a personal project which allows them to explore their own area of interest in more detail. Most graduates of the diploma will go to study for a degree in Ireland or abroad, says Rooney. Her advice to second-level students is to visit the college you are interested in and find out about the course.

'It's remarkable the number of students we get who have no idea what graphic design is,' she says. 'They have a vague idea that it's some form of commercial art.'

Job opportunities in graphic design have widened with multimedia opportunities, website design, CD-ROM publishing and computer games as well as the more traditional job opportunities. With job prospects widening from the two-dimensional to the three-dimensional, graphic design is more commonly referred to as visual communications.

## Graphic design

### TWO ROUTES IN BRITAIN AND THE NORTH

Applications for art and design courses in Britain and Northern Ireland must be made through UCAS, the British central applications body. There are two application routes – route A and route B. Both routes are of equal status – the division is a historical legacy.

Students applying through route A must have their application in by 15 December. Applicants may list up to six choices in section 3 of the application form in UCAS handbook order. If you are applying through route B, the application dates were between 1 January 1998, and 24 March 1998. Up to four choices may be made and, again, these should be listed in section 3 in the order in which courses appear in the UCAS handbook.

Just to further confuse you, you may apply through both routes. A total of six colleges/courses may be selected but with a maximum of four in route B. Your British and Northern Ireland counterparts will have completed A levels and a year's art foundation course. Thus, they will be older and may have more developed portfolios. The advantage of going via route B is that it will allow you more time to build up your portfolio.

### FACT FILE

Full-time third level courses:
Ab-initio degrees:
DIT: design – visual communication
NCAD: design – visual communications

### CERT/DIPLOMAS:

Three-year courses:
WIT: Design (communications)
Athlone IT: Design (communications)

Letterkenny IT: Design (graphics)
Dún Laoghaire IT: Design (communication)
Limerick IT: art and design

### Two-year certificates:
DIT: design (display/presentation/visual media)

### Applying for art and design – CAO dates
Most of these courses fall into the CAO's restricted application category. This means that you must apply before 1 February. No late applications will be accepted. Entry to first-year core at the National College of Art and Design is not through the CAO. You must apply to the college directly.

### PLC courses
The proliferation of portfolio preparation courses at Post Leaving Cert level is one indication of the intense competition for places on third-level art and design courses. Most third-level colleges require a student to submit a portfolio of work; however, many students do not get the opportunity to put together a portfolio at second level. Hence the PLCs. In addition, a number of PLC colleges offer a variety of art and design courses which are complete in themselves. Check with your local Vocational Education Committee or PLC college for details. The more popular courses fill early so it would be wise to make enquiries.

# SPORT SCIENCE

*Using sport and exercise to study science*

The treadmill is being pounded by the feet of the Irish amateur heavyweight boxing champion, while the exercise bikes whir. This is not a training session but a laboratory. The physiology lab is used by science students and post-graduate researchers as a tool to study performance and ways of improving it. The off-putting contraption in the corner is used to lower an athlete into a pool and, using Archimede's Principle, to measure body weight with incredible accuracy.

Meanwhile, two second-year students, Rachel Brophy and Brian Nolan, are using a computer to work on their project. They had clamped a volunteer's leg into a fixed position and, using a mild electric current, looked at the muscle twitching to study voluntary contractions.

Further along, in the biomechanics lab, a post-graduate student talks us through her project – to over-simplify: she used high-speed film to record horses jumping over a fence, digitised the images and analysed the horses' jumping ability in a bid to find out what distinguishes good jumpers.

Upstairs in the biochemistry lab, frozen muscle biopsies are being cut on a cryostat into ultra-thin slices for staining and examination under a microscope. Meanwhile, reaction times and anticipation times are studied in another lab and the swimming pool and the diving pool are also available for experimental work.

Sports and exercise science is coming of age in Limerick. In 1993, the college introduced a four-year degree in sports science and exercise, the only such undergraduate programme in the Republic.

Professor Phil Jakeman explains that what they have is 'a young and exciting degree which uses the vehicle of sport and exercise in order to study science . . . there are three major strands – physiology, psychology and biomechanics.'

## Sport science

The multi-disciplinary approach is necessary, he explains, as performers are integrated organisms and the various approaches make up a composite picture of how an athlete works or fails. 'It's a tremendous challenge,' he adds.

It's not just about athletes. Increased health consciousness brings sport and exercise into the prevention of conditions such as osteoporosis.

The course director, Dr PJ Smyth, says that of the 24 students who graduated in 1996, the programme's first graduates, the majority have gone on to further study. A number have remained in UL on post-graduate programmes specialising further in biochemistry, sports psychology and biomedical engineering. Others have gone further afield to study areas such as sports nutrition and the physiology of exercise, says Smyth.

There are 35 first-year places on the degree and the cut-off points for 1997 were high at 480. Minimum entry requirements are grade C3 in two higher-level Leaving Cert subjects and grade D3 in four ordinary or higher-level subjects, including maths, Irish or another language and English.

There are also specific science subject requirements. A high level of sports performance is not required but 'it's essential that students should have a deep involvement in and commitment to sport and exercise'.

The first year of the course lays a foundation in basic maths, physics, human anatomy, physiology and psychology while the major core disciplines of exercise physiology, biomechanics and psychology are introduced. These core areas are carried right through the four years, with lab experience as an integral part of their study. Scientific principles and procedures are applied to sport and exercise science in field as well as lab settings.

# Career choice

Students have the opportunity in first and second year to take part in selected modes of training. This allows them to prepare for coaching awards and certification, if they wish, says Smyth. During the spring and summer of third year, students do a six-to-eight month work placement. In the final year, each student undertakes a major project.

Graduates of the programme may find work as a sport science or exercise science adviser, possibly with national sports agencies. Both Smyth and Jakeman point to the National Sports Strategy as a blueprint for future development and job opportunities. Graduates may also find work in the corporate sector as consultants on fitness programmes, or they could enter into leisure, recreation and tourism-based activities.

Other possible careers include college and university training or research and marketing with sports and exercise manufacturing firms. The most popular option so far has been to enter the post-graduate research arena.

# AGRICULTURAL SCIENCE AT UCD

*There's no sag in Ag*

## Career choice

More students are from non-farm backgrounds, more students are female. You don't need to own a pair of wellies and a tractor to apply. UCD's agriculture faculty is attracting increasing numbers of urban students in recent years. More than half of the students are now from non-farm backgrounds and 40 per cent are women. One-fifth of the students attended second-level schools in the Dublin area.

And there's more to agriculture than meets the eye. The faculty of agriculture in UCD offers nine specialisms under the umbrella of its bachelor of agricultural science programme. Students take a common first year and then go on to specialise in animal and crop production, animal science, agribusiness and rural development, agricultural and environmental science, food science, engineering technology, commercial horticulture, landscape horticulture or forestry.

The youngest of these disciplines is environmental resource management. One of the unforeseen results of the maximisation of production, under the EU's Common Agricultural Policy, was the extensive pollution of water due to the increased use of fertilisers and silage-making, explains college lecturer Dr John Feehan. There was also a drastic reduction in natural habitat, particularly in northern Europe.

'It was realised that this was too much of a price to pay in terms of health, environment and rural landscape,' he says. 'It was also of increasing concern to the voting public not just to those who managed the land.' Taking more care of the countryside means bringing new skills into agriculture. A number of policies, legislation and incentives are in place at present to persuade farmers to adopt more environmentally friendly strategies.

Students who want to specialise in environmental resource management must first take two years of a common core course in agriculture. 'This is a very important consideration,' says Feehan. 'It would be too easy to bring in ecologists who have no idea of the pressures behind rural resource management. It's also very important to realise that we are at the beginning of something.' Concern about the environment and the extent to which programmes and resources are channelled into this can only increase, he believes.

Students who specialise in the more traditional discipline of animal science will be involved in areas such as meat production, milk production, animal breeding and genetics. Professor Maurice Boland stresses that this is not a practical farming programme. Quite a lot of science is involved.

Animal husbandry includes the various components affecting beef, dairy and pig production, according to Boland. Animal welfare and behaviour are important, particularly with changes in EU regulations regarding animal housing, etc.

In third year, students finish classes at Christmas and they spend from Easter to the summer gaining professional work experience in areas such as farming, dairy processing and the food industry. Students from urban backgrounds do remarkably well in the course but they may have to work harder when it comes to the practical elements, comments Boland.

Many students will undertake post-graduate studies; some will find work in Teagasc managing Rural Environmental Programmes (REPs) while others will find work in animal production or food processing industries.

Students not attracted by the idea of animal production may find the leafy avenue of horticulture more to their taste. Commercial horticulture students are trained to manage operations both nationally and internationally, says Dr Owen Doyle.

This involves the production, storage and marketing of food crops such as mushrooms, potatoes and apples. They may also be involved with non-food crops such as cut flowers, trees and shrubs. Doyle encourages students to go abroad on their six-month work placement between third year and fourth year.

Second-level students may have the image of agriculture graduates driving tractors and ploughing fields but the reality is that most of them will find work as managers, says Doyle. As to job prospects, there were more jobs than graduates in 1997 and the situation was similar for graduates of the landscape horticulture programme. Students who specialise in landscape horticulture are trained for management, design, construction and maintenance.

Horticulture graduates have a portfolio of transferable skills and they may end up in non-horticulture areas, adds Doyle.

In addition to its nine undergraduate specialisms, the faculty offers a wide range of post-graduate options including equine studies, humanitarian assistance, landscape architecture and plant protection.

The good news for second-level students interested in studying agriculture at UCD is that 20 extra places were created in 1997. The cut-off points were 380* (random selection applied).